Lean Six Sigma Business Transformation For Dummies

by Roger Burghall, Vince Grant and John Morgan

Lean Six Sigma Business Transformation For Dummies®

Published by: **John Wiley & Sons, Ltd.,** The Atrium, Southern Gate, Chichester, www.wiley.com

This edition first published 2014

Registered office

John Wiley & Sons Ltd, The Atrium, Southern Gate, Chichester, West Sussex, PO19 8SQ, United Kingdom

For details of our global editorial offices, for customer services and for information about how to apply for permission to reuse the copyright material in this book please see our website at www.wiley.com.

For general information on our other products and services, please contact our Customer Care Department within the U.S. at 877-762-2974, outside the U.S. at (001) 317-572-3993, or fax 317-572-4002. For technical support, please visit www.wiley.com/techsupport.

A catalogue record for this book is available from the British Library.

ISBN 978-1-118-84486-1 (pbk), ISBN 978-1-118-84487-8 (ebk), ISBN 978-1-118-84488-5 (ebk)

Printed in Great Britain by TJ International, Padstow, Cornwall

10 9 8 7 6 5 4 3 2

Contents at a Glance

Table of Contents

Introduction

This book builds on *Lean Six Sigma For Dummies* (Wiley), which we wrote to make the topic easy to understand and apply. It's important to understand and apply it because we feel that Lean Six Sigma can help organisations of all shapes and sizes, both private and public, improve their performance. We also feel that Lean Six Sigma can help organisations in their transformation journeys, enabling them to deploy their strategy more effectively.

Readers of this book need to have at least some knowledge of Lean Six Sigma. If this isn't the case, we recommend you have a copy *of Lean Six Sigma For Dummies* (Wiley) to hand, as we make a number of references to that book which will help explain some of the terms and techniques we refer to in this book. Referring to another book so often isn't the usual *For Dummies* practice, but in this instance we wanted to avoid repeating everything about Lean Six Sigma and making this book twice as long.

We also stress that an organisation can deploy Lean Six Sigma without going through a business transformation. Likewise, an organisation can go through a transformation without using Lean Six Sigma. Our focus in this book is to demonstrate how Lean Six Sigma can help an organisation deploy its strategy and successfully undertake transformation.

Lean Six Sigma provides a rigorous and structured approach to both help manage and improve performance, and to support the transformation of an organisation. It helps you use the right tools, in the right place, and in the right way, not just in improvement but also in your day-to-day management of activities.

As often as not, an organisation's strategy fails because it hasn't been effectively deployed rather than because the strategy itself was ill-conceived. Lean Six Sigma and the DRIVE model (Define, Review, Improve, Verify and Establish) can provide a way forward that will keep deployment on track and ensure key milestones are met.

Lean Six Sigma really is about getting key principles and concepts into the DNA and lifeblood of your organisation so that it becomes a natural part of how you do things.

About This Book

The potential of Lean Six Sigma is still nowhere near as well harnessed as it could be. We feel that this is especially the case when it comes to helping organisations successfully deploy their strategies and transform their operations and culture.

It seems that many organisations lose sight of their strategic goals and ambitions and find it hard to focus appropriately on what needs to be done. Everyone's too busy, but it's important to recognise the difference between business and busyness – to know what's important.

We wrote this book with the aim of helping individuals and organisations identify a road map that can help them drive their organisations to their intended destinations. In particular, we wanted to draw out the role of the leaders and managers and introduce our DRIVE model and capability maturity road map as a route to success. We refer to these throughout the book, along with a collection of concepts, tools and techniques to help you on your transformation journey.

Foolish Assumptions

In Lean Six Sigma, avoiding the tendency for people – and managers in particular – to jump to conclusions and make assumptions about things is crucial. Lean Six Sigma really is about managing by fact. Despite that, we've made some assumptions about why you may have bought this book:

- You're contemplating a full deployment of Lean Six Sigma in your business or organisation, and you need to understand what you're getting yourself into.
- Your organisation is looking to transform in some way, and you're interested in knowing how Lean Six Sigma can help in the improvement of performance and the deployment of policy and strategy.
- Your organisation has already implemented either Lean or Six Sigma and you're intrigued by how it might help you achieve more.
- You're a student in business, operations or industrial engineering, for example, and you realise that Lean Six Sigma and its link to the deployment of strategy could help shape your future.

We also assume that you realise that Lean Six Sigma demands a rigorous and structured approach to understanding how your work gets done and how well it gets done, and how to go about improving your processes.

Icons Used In This Book

Throughout the book, you'll see small symbols called *icons* in the margins; these highlight special types of information. We use these to help you better understand and apply the material. Look out for the following icons:

This icon pops up alongside examples that show you how to apply an idea to your business.

Bear these important points in mind as you get to grips with Lean Six Sigma.

Information that isn't necessary for implementing your transformation but which you may find interesting.

Keep your eyes on the target to find tips and tricks we share to help you make the most of Lean Six Sigma.

We share true stories of how different companies have implemented Lean Six Sigma to improve their processes. We also share true stories of when things go wrong so that you learn from others' mistakes.

This icon highlights potential pitfalls to avoid.

Beyond the Book

Find out more about Lean Six Sigma Business Transformation by checking out the bonus content available to you at `www.dummies.com`.

You can locate the book's e-cheat sheet at `www.dummies.com/cheatsheet/lssbusinesstransformation`, where you'll find handy hints and tips.

Be sure to visit the book's extras page at `www.dummies.com/extras/lssbusinesstransformation` for further Lean Six Sigma business transformation-related information and articles.

Where to Go From Here

We hope you'll want to go for a drive! Grab the steering wheel and map and transform your organisation. But do remember it takes time, preparation and planning. And a lot of commitment.

Please also remember that, with a *For Dummies* book, you can begin wherever you like. Each part and, indeed, each chapter, is self-contained, which means you can start with whichever parts or chapters interest you most.

That said, if you're new to the topic, starting at the beginning makes sense. Either way, there's lots of cross-referencing throughout the book to help you see how things fit together and how to put them in the right context.

Part I

Getting Started with Lean Six Sigma

getting started with

Lean Six Sigma

For Dummies can help you get started with lots of subjects. Visit www.dummies.com to learn more and do more with *For Dummies*.

In this part . . .

- Find out more about Lean Six Sigma and 'transformation' and why it's needed.
- Learn about transformation and the link to Strategy deployment.
- Get to know the DRIVE Model and how to apply it.

Chapter 1

Introducing Lean Six Sigma

In This Chapter

- Understanding what transformation means
- Breaking down the PDCA cycle
- Choosing between DMAIC or DMADV

As well as an overview of the broad content of this book, this chapter provides an introduction to what we mean by transforming an organisation and why your organisation may need it. We take a brief look at the DRIVE and Plan, Do, Check, Act models that provide the framework for deploying the strategy that leads to transformation. The chapter also provides a reminder of the key principles of Lean Six Sigma and the DMAIC and DMADV methods used to improve existing processes or design and create new ones.

Defining Transformation

The *Oxford English Dictionary* describes transformation as 'a marked change in form, nature or appearance'. And in the context of business transformation that definition is a pretty accurate fit.

You may need to address organisational problems such as high error rates in dealing with customer orders, which in turn lead to increased complaints and ultimately loss of market share. But a burning platform situation may not exist at all. The organisation may be targeting growth in some way, perhaps through an entirely new market or product range, for example. It might even be seeking to change its identity and with it the perceptions of the marketplace.

One way or another, though, your organisation is seeking a marked change, be it in performance, appearance or both. And almost certainly, the change is likely to require a change of thinking and behaviour on the part of the people in the organisation, especially the leaders and managers.

Whatever the rationale that's driving the need for transformation, a crystal clear link to the organisation's strategy and its deployment is essential. The Plan–Do–Check–Act (PDCA) cycle comes into play here in terms of the planning for and support of the transformation and the deployment of strategy.

A business transformation takes time to achieve and requires the organisation to utilise an effective implementation methodology – the DRIVE model (Define, Review, Improve, Verify and Establish) – and to create a capability maturity roadmap to support the changes. The capability maturity roadmap provides a phased approach to deploying Lean Six Sigma capability in the organisation. Chapter 3 covers the DRIVE model and the capability maturity roadmap in more detail.

This book focuses on Lean Six Sigma as the vehicle to support and drive the changes needed in thinking and behaviour, and that also provides a framework for the improvement projects that emerge through the journey ahead. We provide only a relatively brief summary of the ins and outs of Lean Six Sigma, however, as it is described in detail in *Lean Six Sigma For Dummies* (Wiley).

Before we look at Lean Six Sigma in a little more detail, however, we need to take a look at the PDCA cycle.

Introducing the Plan–Do–Check–Act Cycle

The Plan–Do–Check–Act (PDCA) cycle, as illustrated in Figure 1-1, provides a foundation for strategy deployment.

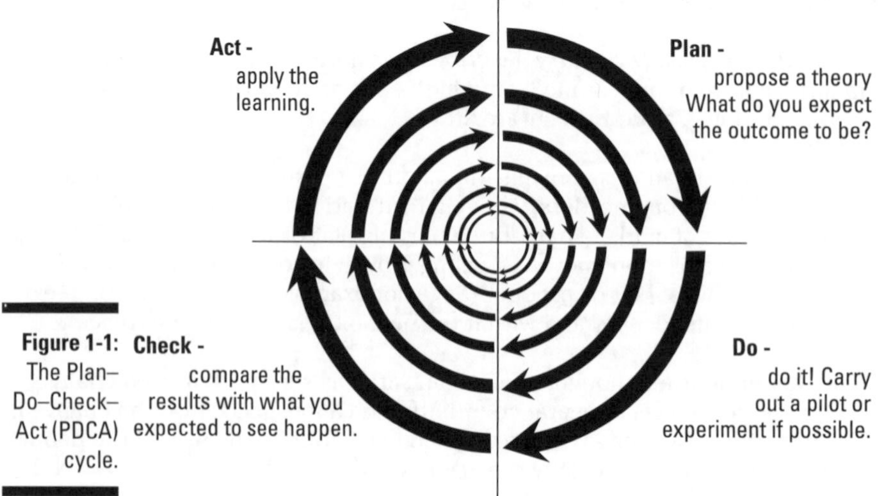

Figure 1-1: The Plan–Do–Check–Act (PDCA) cycle.

Although not overtly referred to in the Lean Six Sigma methodology, the PDCA cycle is very much at the heart of the DMAIC improvement method described in Chapter 2. The PDCA cycle breaks down as follows:

- **Plan:** This element refers to your theory or hypothesis. If you do this, you expect that to happen.
- **Do:** Here you put your theory to the test. Ideally, you undertake pilot activities or tests.
- **Check:** Here you look to see whether the outcomes of your actions in the Do phase are producing the results your Plan led you to expect. To do that properly, you need to ensure you gather the right data and also that you're viewing things from the correct perspective, something you will have determined in the Plan phase. Lean Six Sigma helps you get the measures right, but you need to recognise the importance of going to see actual results in the workplace – the 'gemba', as the Japanese call it.
- **Act:** Depending on your findings in the Check phase, you may need to make adjustments to the theory you developed in the Plan phase and then run through another PDCA cycle. If things have gone according to plan, however, you can act to put your theory formally in place, or run a larger test depending on the scale of the pilot.

We return to the PDCA cycle throughout the book.

Showing the Way with Lean Six Sigma

To apply the Lean Six Sigma approach successfully, you need to recognise the need for different thinking. To paraphrase Albert Einstein:

> *'The significant problems we face cannot be solved at the same level of thinking we were at when we created them.'*

You want to change outcomes but you also need to realise that they are themselves the outcomes from your systems. Not the computer systems, but the way in which people work together and interact. And these systems are the product of how people think and behave. So, if you want to transform and change the outcomes you have to change your systems, and to do that, you have to change your thinking.

You need to adopt thinking that focuses on improving value for the customer by improving and smoothing the process flow and eliminating waste. Since the establishment of Henry Ford's first production line, lean thinking has evolved over many years and in the hands of many people and organisations, but much of the development has been led by Toyota through the creation of the Toyota Production System. Toyota was able to build on Ford's production ideas to move from 'high volume, low variety' to 'high variety, low volume'.

Six Sigma thinking complements the lean approach through a systematic and robust approach to improvement that is based on management by fact. In particular, it looks to get the right data, in order to understand and reduce the variation in performance being experienced in the organisation's products, services and processes.

Identifying the key principles of Lean Six Sigma

Lean is not about cutting things to the bone. Rather, it's about providing value for your customers. Taiichi Ohno, the architect of the Toyota Production System, sums up the approach in a nutshell:

> *'All we are doing is looking at a time line from the moment the customer gives us an order to the point when we collect the cash. And we are reducing that time line by removing the non-value-added wastes.'*

And value is what customers are looking for. They want the right products and services, at the right place, at the right time and at the right quality. Value is what the customer is willing to pay for.

Explaining Lean thinking

We're sure you're aware of the half-full, half-empty glass analogy applied to whether someone looks on the positive or negative side. A Lean practitioner might well respond by saying 'it's the wrong sized glass!' Either way, you first need to understand the customer and their perception of value. You have to know how the value stream operates and enable it to flow, perhaps by removing waste and non-value-added activities.

The value stream and the process are one and the same; they're simply different terms. Essentially, you're talking about 'how the work gets done'.

Lean thinking also means looking for ways of smoothing and levelling the way the work flows through the process and, where possible, working at the customer's pace – in other words, it's a pull rather than a push process. And, of course, in the pursuit of perfection, you're always looking to improve things through the concept of continuous improvement.

Linking up with Six Sigma thinking

Six Sigma thinking is very similar to Lean thinking. Six Sigma also focuses on the customer. A key principle of Six Sigma is understanding customer requirements and trying to meet them. If you don't understand those requirements, how can you expect to provide the customer with value?

Again, as with Lean thinking, to understand your processes you need to understand how the work gets done. Data comes into play more so with Six Sigma thinking than with Lean thinking. If you're to manage by fact, you need to have the right measures in place and the data presented in the most appropriate way.

An appreciation and understanding of the variation in your process results enables you to more effectively interpret your data and helps you know when, and when not, to take action.

Six Sigma thinking also means equipping the people in the process so that they're fully involved and engaged in the drive for improvement.

Accessing the best of both worlds

Similarity and synergy exist between Lean thinking and Six Sigma and combining the two approaches creates a 'magnificent seven' of Lean Six Sigma key principles:

1. **Focus on the customer.**
2. **Identify and understand how the work gets done – the value stream.**
3. **Manage, improve and smooth the process flow.**
4. **Remove non-value-adding steps and waste.**
5. **Manage by fact and reduce variation.**
6. **Involve and equip the people in the process.**
7. **Undertake improvement activity in a systematic way.**

In Lean Six Sigma the key focus is on the customer. You need to understand their perception of value and their critical-to-quality customer requirements – the CTQs. The CTQs provide the basis for your measurement set; you can measure how well you're performing in relation to them. Focusing on the customer, and the concept of value-adding, is especially important because, in our experience, when we start work with new clients, typically only 10 to 15 per cent of process steps add value and often represent only 1 per cent of total process time. Naturally, many organisations have discovered that their continuous improvement efforts have significantly improved process performance; unfortunately, plenty still exist that have yet to realise the benefits of Lean Six Sigma.

Lean Six Sigma provides a set of criteria to help you determine whether or not a process step is value-adding:

- The customer has to care about or be interested in the step. If they knew you were conducting this step, would they be prepared to pay for it?
- The step must either change the product or service in some way or be an essential prerequisite.
- The step must be actioned 'right first time'.

A value-adding step meets all three criteria. Non-value-adding steps must be removed. Obviously, some steps may not meet these criteria but are nonetheless essential for regulatory, fiscal or health and safety reasons, for example. By identifying and understanding how the work gets done – the value stream – you highlight the non-value-adding steps and waste. In doing so, you ensure that the process is focused on meeting the CTQs and adding value. Understanding, managing and improving the value stream is key to eliminating non-value-adding steps as it sets out all of the actions, both value creating and non-value creating, that bring a product or service concept to launch or process a customer order.

Ensuring the senior team's understanding of the organisation's high level value streams provides a foundation for the prioritisation of value-adding steps in the various processes. 'Order to Cash' is a good example and is illustrated in Figure 1-2. Can you identify process steps that can be removed or reduced in some way? How can you close the gap, speed up the process and smooth the flow?

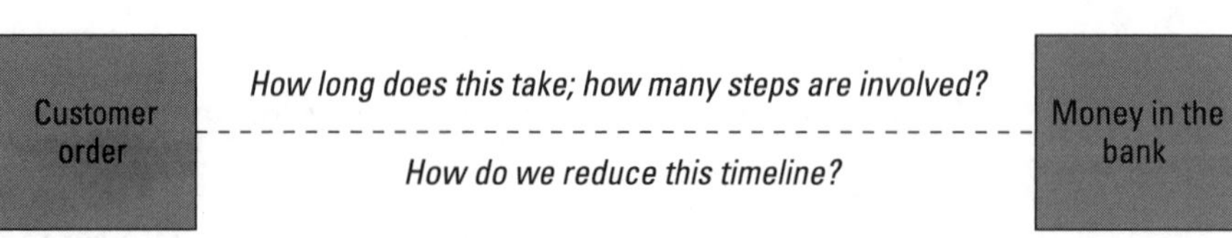

Figure 1-2: Looking at 'Order to Cash': Lean Six Sigma thinking in a nutshell.

Managing, improving, and smoothing the process flow provides another example of different thinking. If possible, use single piece flows, moving away from batches or at least reducing batch sizes. Either way, identify the non-value-adding steps in processes and try to remove them; at the very least, look to ensure that they don't delay value-adding steps. The concept of pull, not push, links to understanding the process and improving flow.

Pushing not pulling can be an essential element in avoiding bottlenecks. Overproduction, or pushing things through too early, is a waste. One way to improve flow and performance is to identify, remove and prevent waste or, as the Japanese call it, 'muda'.

Managing by fact, using accurate data, helps you avoid jumping to conclusions and solutions. You need the facts! And that means measuring the right things in the right way. Data collection is a process and needs to be managed accordingly. Using control charts enables you to interpret the data correctly and understand the process variation. You'll then know when, and when not, to take action and will be able to accurately describe the state of your process. You can find out more about control charts in *Lean Six Sigma For Dummies* (Wiley) and also in *SPC in the Office* by Mal Owen and John Morgan (Greenfield Publishing).

Involving and equipping the people in the process is vital. The 'soft stuff' mustn't be overlooked. In simple terms, the soft stuff refers to how you work with the people involved in the process, and the key stakeholders who can so easily make or break the improvements you plan. A *key stakeholder* is anyone who controls critical resources, who can block the change initiative by direct or indirect means, who must approve certain aspects of the change strategy, who shapes the thinking of other critical parties, or who owns a key work process impacted by the change initiative. And it's about their acceptance of what you're trying to do. You may well have developed an ideal solution, but its effectiveness is dependent on how well you've gained acceptance from the people in the organisation. Chapters 2 and 3 cover the soft stuff in more detail.

Lean Six Sigma provides two frameworks for improvement. The action you take in improving or designing your processes needs to be undertaken in a systematic way. DMAIC provides the framework to improve existing processes and DMADV covers the design of new products, services and processes.

Improving Existing Processes with DMAIC

The DMAIC cycle is a systematic approach to solving problems and improving existing processes. DMAIC stands for Define, Measure, Analyse, Improve and Control, and these phases are illustrated in Figure 1-3.

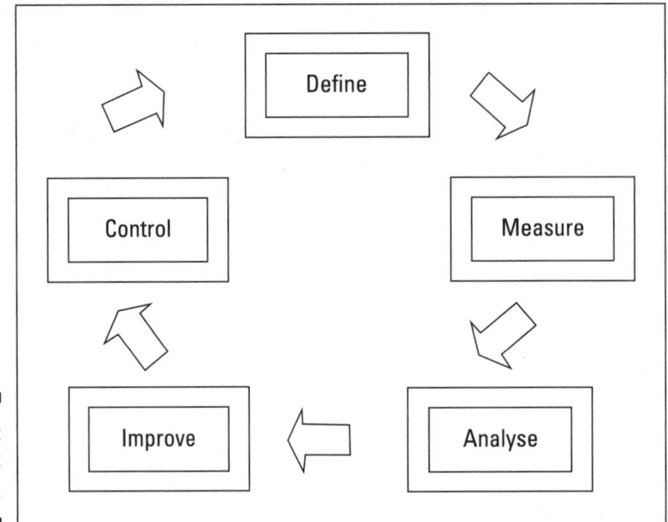

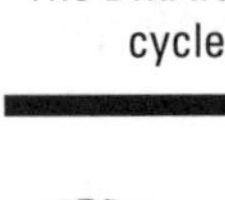

Figure 1-3: The DMAIC cycle.

The DMAIC cycle isn't necessarily linear. You could well find yourself moving back and forth, especially to the Measure and Define phases, as you find more information or suspect a particular root cause but need more evidence.

Isolating the problem

When you start any new improvement project, an essential ingredient for success is ensuring that you and your team have a clear understanding of why the project is being undertaken and what it's trying to achieve. With a DMAIC project, you start with a problem that needs to be solved.

Before you can solve a problem, however, you need to clearly define it, which isn't always as straightforward as it might sound. You might not have all the information you need to write a clear problem statement, for example. The Measure phase helps you understand things more clearly and, where necessary, you can update the problem statement and the improvement charter in the light of your new-found knowledge. See *Lean Six Sigma For Dummies* (Wiley) for more about problem statements and improvement charters.

Working out what's happening

In simple terms, the Measure phase is about understanding how the work gets done and how well it gets done. To understand the current situation, you need to know what the process looks like and how it's performing. You need to understand what's meant to happen, and why. You also need to recognise how your process links to your customer.

Naturally, being aware of current performance is essential – this becomes your baseline – but it will also be helpful to know what's happened in the past.

Ensure that you measure what's important to the customer, and remember to measure what the customer sees. Gathering this information helps focus your improvement efforts and prevents you going off in the wrong direction.

Understanding why it's happening

In the Measure phase you discovered what's really happening in your process. Now, in the Analyse phase, you need to identify why it's happening, and determine the root cause. You need to manage by fact, though, so you must verify and validate your ideas about possible suspects. Jumping to conclusions is all too easy. The usual suspects may well be innocent bystanders.

You can find the root cause using one of two approaches: either through an assessment of the process and how it flows or through analysis of the data. Often, you need to use both. Clearly, the extent of analysis required will vary depending on the scope and nature of the problem you're tackling and, indeed, what your Measure activities have identified.

Coming up with an idea

The Improve phase breaks into three distinct parts. You need to come up with your possible solutions, select the most appropriate and make sure that they'll work. This phase of DMAIC is where most people want to start!

Now you've identified the root cause of the problem, you can begin to generate improvement ideas to help solve it. Your ideas will need to be reviewed and prioritised and perhaps even tested on a small scale before selecting the most appropriate. Sometimes, the improvement solution is very straightforward – or at least it might seem to be. Your value-adding analysis may have identified several steps that can be removed from the process, for example.

The chosen solution may need to be developed in more detail, but will almost certainly need to be properly piloted – the PDCA cycle comes into play here (see the 'Introducing the Plan–Do–Check–Act Cycle' section earlier in this chapter).

Making sure it's really sorted

After all your hard work, you need to implement the solution in a way that ensures that you make the gain you expected and maintain it! If you're to continue your efforts in reducing variation and cutting out waste, the changes being made to the process need to be consistently deployed and followed.

A control plan is vital and is another stage in really getting to grips with working on the process. Getting the right measures in place is an essential element of control and you need to be satisfied that the data collection plan has been effectively deployed. The Control phase helps the organisation move towards a situation where processes are genuinely managed. Data collection and the development of a data collection plan are covered in See more about data collection and control plans in *Lean Six Sigma For Dummies* (Wiley).

Designing New Processes with DMADV

DMADV stands for Define, Measure, Analyse, Design and Verify, and is a framework for designing new products, services or processes (see Figure 1-4). You can also use DMADV when an existing process is so badly broken that it's beyond repair.

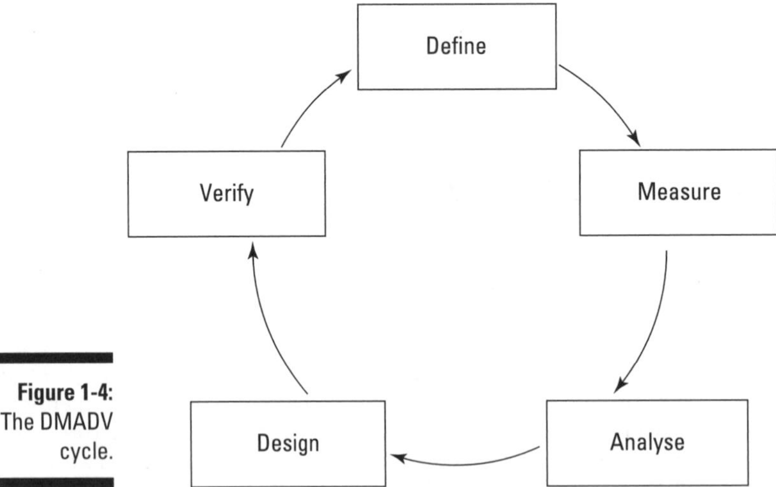

Figure 1-4: The DMADV cycle.

As with DMAIC, you may well find yourself moving back and forth through the phases – it's not necessarily linear.

The DMADV framework is focused on the customer and their CTQs. Where possible, you have to listen to and understand the voice of the customer, but you may also need to look beyond the voice of the customer in developing your designs.

As with DMAIC, managing by fact and not speculation ensures that new designs reflect customer CTQs and provide real value to customers in line with the principles of Lean Six Sigma. However be aware that sometimes customers may not realise what's possible, or what they want, as Steve Jobs recognised:

> *'A lot of times, people don't know what they want until you show it to them.'*

DMADV projects are often concerned with introducing radical change or transformation within an organisation.

Defining the design

The Define phase is concerned with scoping, organising and planning the journey for your design project. Understanding the purpose, rationale and business case is important, as well as knowing who you might need to help you, and how you'll go about managing things. Thus, understanding the boundaries of the project, including the processes, market(s), customers and stakeholders involved, is vital.

An essential ingredient for success is ensuring that you and your team have a clear understanding of why the project is being undertaken, and what it's trying to achieve. How does it link to your strategy, for example?

The Define phase is all about making sure that such understanding happens. You need to bring together the right people at the start, making sure that the relevant departments and functions are represented. All too often, this isn't the case and the definition and scope of the project suffers.

The first metre is often more important than the last mile!

Getting the measure of the design

The Measure phase is vital as it provides the framework around which your design can be built, and the basis for the design decisions needed in further phases. This phase focuses on defining and understanding customer needs, and understanding the different customer segments is essential. Design for Six Sigma (DfSS) projects using DMADV typically seek to optimise the design of products, services or processes across multiple customer requirements, so a detailed understanding of such requirements is essential.

The next step is to translate customer needs into measurable characteristics (CTQs), which become the overall requirements for the product, service or process. Your aim is to fully understand customer requirements, define the measures and set targets and specification limits for CTQs. If you're designing new products or services, you need to make sure that the design can be produced with existing processes; if not, you'll need to create new processes to accommodate the new design. Considering process capability at this phase, rather than after the design is complete, is a hallmark of DfSS. Six Sigma performance is dependent on the quality of the processes you maintain or create.

Conducting analysis

The Analyse phase involves developing the functional specification and high level designs. Analyse begins the process of moving from the 'what' to the 'how' – from what the customer needs to how you might achieve it. You begin by mapping the CTQs onto the internal functions and then look at alternative design concepts; as vacuum cleaner revolutionary James Dyson stated:

> *'Design means how something works, not how it looks – the design should evolve from the function.'*

For a service, analysis means identifying the key functions; for a more tangible product, it means identifying its key part characteristics. Typically, the sub-system characteristics are developed next, followed by the components (parts) of the sub-system.

Functions are what the product, service or process has to do in order to meet the CTQs identified and specified in the design process. In a service environment, functions are best thought of as key high level processes to be considered. So, for example, the product or service being designed could be a telephone ordering service, with a design goal of an order placement within five minutes. The functions involved could include 'answer the call', 'check requirements', 'check stock' and 'place order'.

You need to carry out an analysis of the functions to understand their performance capability and ensure that they're fit for purpose. The emphasis in a DfSS project is very much on alternative design concepts and the generation, analysis and assessment of a high-level design.

The second part of the Analyse phase involves analysing and selecting the best design concept and beginning to add more details to it. Each element of the design should be considered in turn, and high level design requirements specified for each.

You also need to consider how the different components fit together and interact with each other. This process usually involves creating several high level designs, assessing the suitability of each, and then selecting the best fit.

Developing the design

The Design phase is also in two parts. It begins by developing the 'how' thinking in more detail. The objective is to add increasing detail to the various elements of the high level design. The emphasis is on developing designs that will satisfy the CTQ requirements of the process outputs.

The design process is iterative – the high level design was established in the Analyse phase; now the design is specified at a detailed enough level to develop a pilot and test it. The detailed design activities are similar to those in the high level design phase but with a significantly lower level of granularity.

This step integrates all of the design elements into one overall design. Finally, the lowest-level specification limits, control points and measures are determined. These will form the basis of the control plan that needs to be in place following implementation.

Before implementation, however, you need to pilot the design. Enough detail should now be available to test and evaluate the capability of the design by preparing a pilot in the second part of the Design phase. The pilot must be effective and realistic.

Making sure the design will work

The design is piloted and assessed in the Verify phase and, subject to any adjustments that follow the pilot, implementation and deployment follow. As with DMAIC, the final step in the cycle is to assess the achievements made and lessons learned. The results are verified in relation to the original CTQs, specifications and targets. The project is closed only when the solution has been standardised and transitioned to operations and process management.

You need to ensure that no black holes exist in the handover to the process owner or operational manager. You must work closely with your team to achieve a well-planned and well-documented transition.

Recognising DMAIC and DMADV Transition Points

It's possible to start a project using the DMAIC method only to find yourself changing to DMADV at some point. Figure 1-5 illustrates the likely decision points in transitioning from one method to the other.

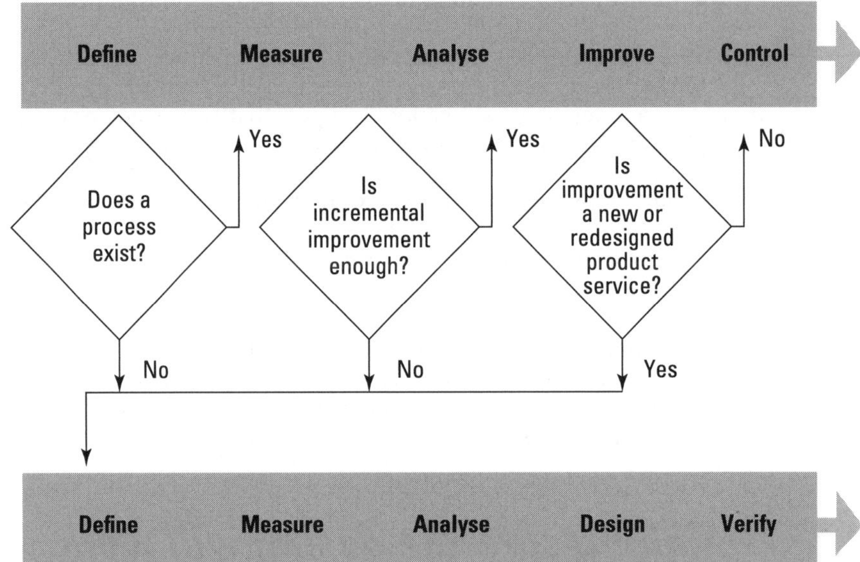

Figure 1-5: Choosing the right method.

Figure 1-5 highlights several decision points at which you might consider transitioning from DMAIC to DMADV. The decision is clear if you have no existing process – you have to design one and thus DMADV is the route to take. But you might find yourself starting a DMAIC project in the firm belief that you'll be able to remedy the problem you're tackling by improving a current process. As you gather information in the Measure phase, however, you may find yourself having second thoughts, and as you move into the Analyse phase you realise that incremental improvement really won't be sufficient.

You may also encounter occasions on which your conclusions in the Improve phase lead you to the recognition that the solution needs to be something new rather than an enhancement of the existing processes. Asking some searching questions might help you decide:

- Is a process already in place? Here we refer to a real process, not a series of cobbled together steps that try to get something done. If no process exists, switch to DMADV to create one.
- Is the process beyond repair? A process may be in place but it isn't really working, and trying to improve it resembles *Mission Impossible*. If so, start again using DMADV.
- Finally, is it a problem? Remember that DMAIC projects begin with a process problem. But, even if a problem does exist, it may still need to be solved using DMADV.

Bringing It All Together

This chapter has provided an overview of the Lean Six Sigma concepts, principles and methods, for both improvement and design projects. These projects are component parts of the transformation change that will not only enhance performance but also drive, and demand, a change in thinking and behaviour across your organisation.

Strategy deployment links your business strategy to a programme of projects to deliver that transformation and is covered in Chapter 8.

Chapter 2

Introducing Business Transformation

In This Chapter

- Establishing the organisation's True North and working out how to get there
- Doing the right things right
- Recognising what can go wrong along the way
- Communicating about the journey to your stakeholders

In this chapter we look at the importance of having a clearly communicated vision of where you want to be; one that engages the organisation and secures people's buy-in to the planned journey. To do this you need to establish and appropriately communicate your 'True North' and determine a route or road map to get you there.

The thing about maps, however, is that they're only really of use if you know where you are to begin with. Taking stock of the organisation's current performance and its capability to undertake the transformation journey is an essential early step. We introduce the DRIVE model as the overarching framework to successfully achieve the transformation, but throughout the chapter we highlight the importance of the soft stuff.

The transformation journey is unlikely to be easy, so wherever possible do seek to make things as simple as possible, but not too simple.

Determining Where You Are Now and Where You Need to Be

In many ways, the essence of this section is pretty much in line with a conversation between Alice and the Cheshire Cat in *Alice's Adventures in Wonderland* by Lewis Carroll:

> *'Would you tell me, please, which way I ought to go from here?'*
>
> *'That depends a good deal on where you want to get to,' said the Cat.*

'I don't much care where –' said Alice.

'Then it doesn't matter which way you go,' said the Cat.

'– so long as I get somewhere,' Alice added as an explanation.

'Oh, you're sure to do that,' said the Cat, 'if you only walk long enough.'

Before setting off on a 'transformation journey' you need to know where you are currently as an organisation. How effective are your products, services and supporting processes? And what do your customers and employees feel about things?

You may have a good idea of where you would like to be, but understanding the starting point and your current capabilities for setting off on a journey are vital. The approach we describe throughout this book provides the map, but a map is of little use without knowing where you're starting out from or, of course, where you're going!

Where are you now?

Where indeed? Before setting off on your transformation journey, answering that question is essential. And, as indicated above, you'll need to answer a number of other important questions too. In particular, you should ask questions that help you consider how good your organisation has been in the past and recently at executing its business strategy. Good questions lead to good data, which lead to good information, and finally to good decisions that will help you on your journey.

See if you can answer the following questions – and the answers really will count:

- **Customers:** How do your customers feel? What do perception surveys reveal? Is market share increasing or are you losing customers?
- **Employees:** How do your staff feel? Are they frustrated because they don't seem able to do things easily or feel that their roles are unclear? Do they feel empowered and involved in how the business is run? Maybe you're spending too much time dealing with unhappy customers and their complaints.
- **Processes:** How stable are the processes operating within your organisation? Do clearly defined ways of doing things exist – the one best way – or are lots of people doing their own thing and muddling through?
- **The organisation:** Depending on what you want the transformation to achieve, do you have a clear idea about whether the organisation has the right skills and expertise in place to be successful?

Obviously, you could ask many more questions. What's important, however, is asking the right questions. A particularly vital issue is finding out which members of the senior management team are likely to be supportive of the changes you have in mind. The 'Checking that everyone's on board' section, later in this chapter, covers stakeholder buy-in.

One of the key concepts of Lean Six Sigma is *managing by fact*. Managing by fact requires good data, and that data needs to be presented in an appropriate way. So, what does the data show? And is it the right data? Good data is different from the right data. Good data is representative, recorded using the appropriate measurement scale, timely, precise, and unbiased. The right data comes from measuring the right things.

But, as Albert Einstein once said,

> *'Not everything that can be counted counts; not everything that counts can be counted.'*

Our experience with organisations across the globe has shown us that many have data coming out of their ears – unfortunately, not necessarily the right data, and not always good. Often such data is merely that which can be obtained, rather than data that helps with understanding performance and taking appropriate decisions and actions. This requires that the user translates data into meaningful information, and then has a process for making decisions based on this information. Linking data with decisions is a principle for transformation efforts based on Lean Six Sigma.

Where are you going?

Unlike Alice, you need to be clear about where you're going – that is, your aim. Whether this means launching the organisation in new markets or enhancing performance in a bid to stop loss of customers, you need to articulate a clear objective and purpose.

Present your vision for the transformation as simply as possible: don't hide it within a voluminous management report. Use language that everyone can understand and present any data in a straightforward manner.

You may find techniques such as the 15-word flipchart and the elevator speech helpful in putting together a simple and easily understood vision. The 15-word technique involves people using sticky notes to draft their own vision statements in a maximum of 15 words. When these are put up on the flipchart, the team can highlight key phrases or words that need to be encompassed within the final statement, which can be as many words as you need.

This technique can also be helpful in drafting an elevator speech, which provides the basis for a brief 'sales pitch' of what you want to achieve. See Chapter 4 for more techniques to help with presenting your transformation vision.

How will you get there?

Transformation is likely to include more than Lean Six Sigma techniques and process improvements. Thus, although this book is about transformation using Lean Six Sigma, other approaches are also used, such as a focus on talent management and people development.

Successful transformation is achieved by following a maturity road map that sets out the stages of the journey ahead. Supported by Lean Six Sigma, the transformation process involves effective strategy deployment and needs the buy-in of people at all levels of the organisation. The importance of the people involved and their buy-in (often referred to as the 'soft stuff') cannot be overstated, but the route itself is unlikely to be soft – changing thinking and behaviours usually results in some bumpy ups and downs along the way. We look at the importance of the soft stuff in the 'Dealing with the soft stuff' section, later in this chapter, and in more detail still in Chapter 11.

Creating the right environment is a must. Essentially, the leaders must 'walk the talk'. As well as encouraging the application of Lean Six Sigma thinking, principles, tools and techniques, the leaders have to be seen to be using them themselves. Figure 2-1 highlights that lip service – 'Follow me, I'm right behind you' – simply doesn't work.

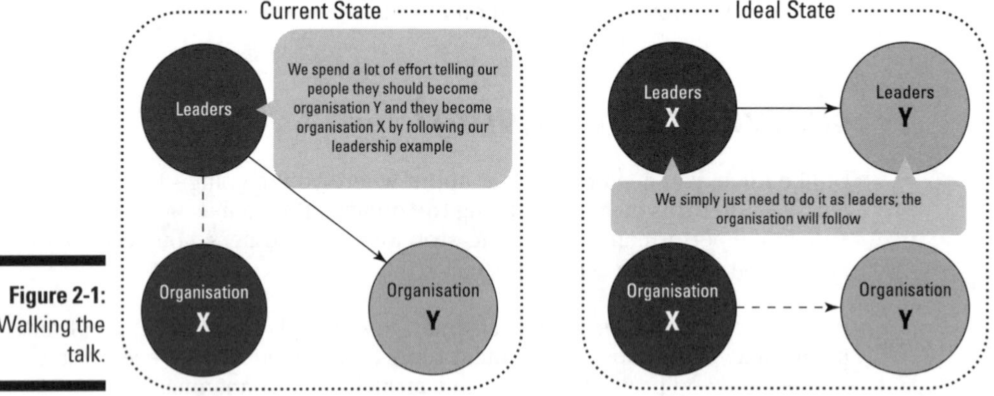

Figure 2-1: Walking the talk.

Leaders also need to provide the right training, coaching and support for people to ensure that the infrastructure necessary for success is in place. It might also be appropriate to review or introduce an appropriate recognition system that demonstrates appreciation for the efforts and achievements of people. A management sponsor, ideally the chief executive, must also be appointed, as well as someone to manage and co-ordinate the overall programme of activities.

You need to avoid duplication of effort by making certain that different improvement teams are not trying to improve the same thing. A transformation board or steering group that holds regular, focused meetings can help make sure that improvement activity in one area does not adversely impact on another. The transformation board needs to receive information from tollgate reviews (or other project reports) to do this. For large organisations, the entire steering group cannot be expected to attend every project tollgate review and an appropriate approach will need to be agreed. You'll probably want to create a programme management office to help co-ordinate things, something we refer to in Chapter 6. And if you want to find out more about tollgate reviews, check out *Lean Six Sigma For Dummies* (Wiley).

Without this co-ordination and an understanding of the processes and how they flow across the organisation, sub-optimisation can happen all too easily, and the journey can become confused by wrong turnings and cul-de-sacs.

Going for a drive

Successful transformation needs drive and energy; it won't happen without it. And transformation really is a journey. The DRIVE model (Define, Review, Improve, Verify and Establish), illustrated in Figure 2-2, provides the framework to help you travel from where you are to where you want to be.

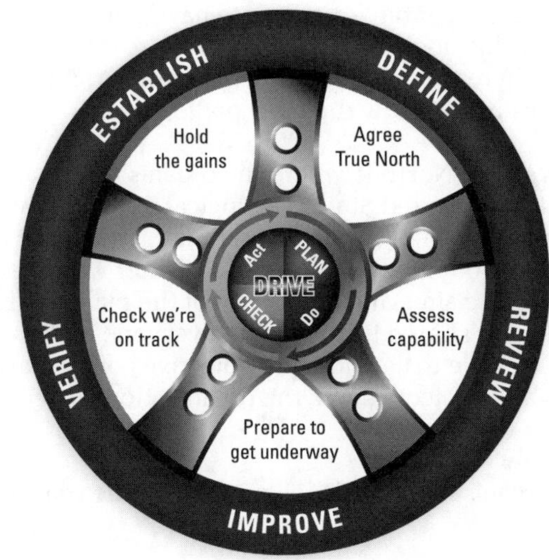

Figure 2-2: Steering in the right direction with the DRIVE model.

In the Define phase, you've recognised the need to transform and have agreed where you want the organisation to be – its 'True North'. The Review phase provides a reality check that assesses the organisation's capability in terms of achieving the change needed. The Improve phase has three elements: preparing for the journey, shaping and scoping what needs to be done, and implementing the agreed actions and projects.

In the Verify phase you're monitoring progress and performance against plan to ensure that you're on track. And in Establish, you ensure the gains made are held as you seek to embed the new ways of working into the organisation's DNA. We look at the DRIVE model in more detail in Chapter 3, and many of the subsequent chapters refer to the various elements of the model as the journey to True North unfolds.

Understanding the Key Principles of Business Transformation

The overall goal of transformation is to get the whole organisation moving in the same direction and doing the right things to increase capability and achieve strategic intent. The strategy needs to be broken down into actionable steps, but in a way that ensures the scope of the tactical actions are properly agreed and clearly link to the strategic thinking.

Identifying True North

Finding True North is essential for accurate navigation, hence the metaphor we use throughout this book. In life's journey we're often uncertain about where we stand, where we're going and what path is right for us. Knowing our True North enables us to follow the right path.

The organisation's True North is where the organisation wants to be. On maps published by the United States Geological Survey, True North is marked with a line terminating in a five-pointed star. And it may well be that 'five-star' performance is your organisation's goal. Either way, the strategic and potentially philosophic aims and objectives of the planned transformation need to be agreed and shared in a way that everyone understands. And everyone should be able to see how the objectives of the various transformation plan actions and projects move the organisation closer to its True North destination.

Everyone in the organisation needs to know where the transformation journey is taking them.

Following a clear strategic direction

The organisation needs to be aligned and to share a common focus and purpose.

Olympic rowers know only too well that unless the team is rowing in time and in the same direction they'll never achieve gold. Organisations are no different, though often a lack of common purpose is evident and, while everyone is working hard, they're not all focused on working on the right things. Getting everyone working well together in the quest for True North won't happen overnight. It will take time and effort and it demands clear direction from the top.

Planning the route

The organisation's strategy needs to be formulated and effectively deployed. Different approaches to strategy or policy deployment exist, including the application of the balanced scorecard (see Chapter 5), and what the Japanese refer to as Hoshin Kanri. The scorecard approach tends to look at the deployment of holistic strategy, whereas Hoshin Kanri is usually more tightly focused on specific strategic objectives. In the US, Hoshin Kanri tends to be focused on policy deployment.

Hoshin Kanri has several meanings, including 'shiny metal' or 'a compass'. The latter fits well with another interpretation: 'ship in a storm going in the right direction'. The image most often depicted in US literature on Hoshin Kanri is that of a ship's compass distributed to many ships, properly calibrated such that all ships through independent action arrive at the same destination, individually or as a group, as the requirements of the voyage may require. And, of course, this is what you're trying to do with all the different teams and departments in your organisation as you move towards your True North. Hoshin Kanri is a method devised to capture and cement strategic goals as well as flashes of insight about the future, and develop the means to make them a reality. Hoshin Kanri makes it possible to get away from the status quo and introduce a major performance improvement, the transformation, by analysing current problems, determining the actions needed and deploying appropriate strategies. It cascades down from top management and through the management hierarchy. Each level of management is, in turn, involved with the level above it to make sure that its proposed strategy, plans and projects fit together appropriately and avoid any disconnects or duplications.

Actioning the deployment in this way ensures that everyone in the organisation is made aware of the overall vision and targets, and the way that these are translated into specific requirements for their own behaviour and activities. In the most successful organisations, all employees clearly understand how their roles and objectives link to the key goals.

Using Hoshin Kanri, top management vision is translated into a set of consistent, understandable and attainable actions to be applied at all levels and functions. This approach turns a vision into reality; it sets out the route to success and begins the process of lining up the arrows referred to in Figure 2-3. The route will almost certainly need a series of DMAIC and DMADV projects that will become the vehicles for moving the organisation forward (see Chapter 1).

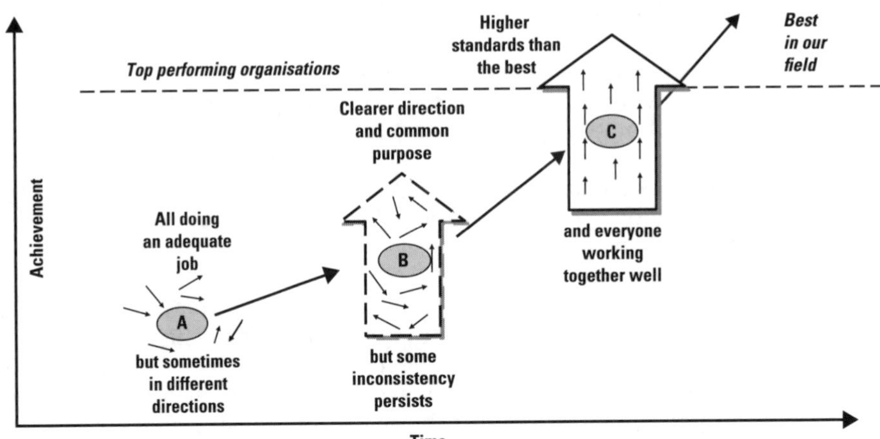

Figure 2-3: Lining up the arrows.

Hoshin Kanri was developed by Yoji Akao and uses Walter Shewhart's Plan–Do–Check–Act (PDCA) model (see Figure 1-1 in Chapter 1) to create goals, agree measurable milestones and link daily control activities to strategy.

The strategy or policy deployment approach provides an opportunity to continually improve performance by disseminating and deploying the vision, direction, targets and plans of the organisation to people at all job levels, ensuring their involvement and understanding. In organisations using Hoshin Kanri everybody is aware of management's vision for the transformation. Departments don't compete against each other, projects run to successful conclusions, and business is seen as a set of co-ordinated processes.

Whichever route you select to ensure deployment, it doesn't happen on its own and hard work, energy and commitment are crucial.

Keeping it simple

Organisations should always look to find ways of keeping things simple. Unfortunately, simplicity looks easy – but isn't. In fact, it's much easier to complicate than to simplify. Simple ideas enter the brain quicker and stay longer. In the words of the philosopher Bertrand Russell, simplicity is thus 'a painful necessity'.

Keeping things simple removes irrelevance and waste. With simplicity of thought it may be possible to change the world, but starting with your own organisation and its processes is a good first step!

Winston Churchill was a great believer in simplicity. He liked to quote a letter French mathematician and writer Blaise Pascal wrote to a friend. It began: 'I didn't have time to write a short letter, so I wrote a long one instead.' He knew that achieving simplicity is difficult, but also necessary. Churchill stressed this theme again when he said that to deliver a two-hour speech he needed 10 minutes of preparation, but to deliver a 10-minute speech he needed two hours of preparation.

The strategies should be clear and simple. Less is more, so present them on no more than a page. And keep that to a side of A4, too!

Keeping on track

On most journeys you usually encounter tempting diversions en route. You have to stay focused and ensure you're making progress and meeting targets. Developing a plan is usually pretty straightforward – it's achieving it that's a challenge. This applies both to the individual actions and improvement projects, as well as, of course, to the transformation plan overall.

You need to keep checking progress, which means having good data and holding regular tracking meetings. Consider again the PDCA cycle. You've developed your Plan and you're now doing the things that have been agreed. The Check phase involves looking to see whether what you thought would happen is happening. If it isn't, you need to Act in some way. It might be that your plan and theories need some adjustment.

The individual Lean Six Sigma projects, whether using DMAIC or DMADV, will have tollgate reviews built in to the process. A tollgate review checks that you've completed the current phase properly and reviews the team's various outputs from it. These reviews also identify issues relating to risk. New risks may surface; feared risks may be downgraded or eliminated. Risk assessment is important in both project reviews and transformation reviews. For more on tollgate reviews, see *Lean Six Sigma For Dummies* (Wiley).

The project team and the management sponsor or champion of the improvement activity should conduct the tollgate reviews. In effect, you're passing through a tollgate. Let's take a look at DMAIC by way of example. Chapter 1 provides an overview of the Define, Measure, Analyse, Improve and Control phases. Before moving from one phase to another, you need to step back, assess progress and ask some key questions, such as:

- How are things going?
- Are we on course?
- What have we learnt?
- What's gone well, and why?
- What conclusions can be drawn?

You need to make sure the project will deliver your planned benefits, so three benefit reviews' are built into the DMAIC framework. Before the project began, you've probably best guessed a business case that justifies starting the work. By the end of the Analyse phase, you'll know what's happening and why, and should be able to determine the benefits to both the organisation and your customers. These could be financial savings for the organisation, or enhanced service delivery to the customers, for example.

In the Improve phase, you select the most appropriate solution. Once you've carried out a pilot you should be able to confirm the benefits both for the organisation and the customer. The final review at the end of the project and following the implementation of the solution enables you to confirm the actual costs and benefits and whether any unexpected debits or credits have emerged. You should also know the answers to these questions:

- Do your customers recognise that an improvement has occurred? How do you know?
- Can lessons, ideas or best practices from this project be applied elsewhere in the organisation?

The DMAIC and DMADV projects are component parts of achieving the transformation. Taking time for these reviews and tollgates not only keeps you on track but also forms an important element in developing a culture that manages by fact. So, take the opportunity to review progress – it will help ensure your projects are successful and the desired benefits are actually delivered.

Other projects that don't fall into the DMAIC or DMADV methodologies may also be necessary for a transformation. These might include, for example, expanding the number of computer servers, or erecting a new building; neither would be DMAIC or DMADV projects. Rapid improvement events, referred to below, use the DMAIC framework and should also be included in any reviews.

Doing the right things

You need to ensure that the right improvement projects are selected and are appropriately focused and scoped. They should clearly link to the organisation's strategic aims and objectives so that everyone involved can see how successful implementation will help improve overall performance and move the organisation towards its desired state.

Understanding the top-level processes or value streams of the organisation and being able to pinpoint the areas for improvement activity should lead to the appropriate identification of improvement projects.

This process is further facilitated where you're able to genuinely manage by fact, using accurate data that measures the right things.

One of the key principles of Lean Six Sigma thinking is focusing on providing value for the customer – so ensure that you're measuring your performance in this area.

Doing things right

At a literal level, you're looking to avoid errors and defects by doing the work right. But the focus here is on using the right methods and approaches to do so. At a process level, 'one best way' of doing the work should exist. With process improvement projects, for example, it's important to distinguish between those problems that can be tackled as a 'Rapid Improvement' or 'Kaizen Events' and those that need to be approached in a more formal way using DMAIC over a period of perhaps three or four months.

Kaizen (pronounced Kai Zen) means change for the better. It's often associated with short, rapid, incremental improvement and forms a natural part of an organisation's approach to continuous improvement (see Chapter 12). These events usually have a narrowly scoped focus and address and solve a process problem in a series of workshops over a few days.

The DMAIC method will not be appropriate for some projects, such as purchasing a new computer system or developing a new factory site, and these need to be project managed, possibly using the PRINCE methodology. PRINCE (**PR**ojects **IN** **C**ontrolled **E**nvironments) is a recognised method for effective project management. It is used extensively in the public and private sectors, both in the UK and internationally. The Project Management Institute (PMI) in Philadelphia provides another internationally recognised method as an option.

Given the aim of transforming the organisation, it's highly likely a need will exist for design projects using the DMADV method.

Dealing with the soft stuff

The 'How will you get there?' section earlier in this chapter looked at the importance of creating the right environment for transformation. An appreciation of the 'soft stuff' is crucial here. Successful transformation isn't simply about setting a series of projects in motion.

So what exactly do we mean by the 'soft stuff'? In simple terms, it's about how well you work with the people involved in the transformation process and the stakeholders who are affected by it. You may well have developed an ideal solution or approach, but its effectiveness will depend on its acceptance.

The effectiveness of an improvement project or, indeed, the deployment of the strategy overall hinges on two broad factors: quality and acceptance. George Eckes, CEO of a Colorado-based consulting group and a former psychologist, came up with a formula to help express the importance of the 'soft stuff': $E = Q \times A$.

E = Effectiveness: E represents the effectiveness of the implementation, which depends on the quality of the solution and its level of acceptance.

Q = Quality of the solution: An ideal solution may have been identified, but its effectiveness is dependent on its acceptance.

A = Acceptance of the solution: The level of acceptance of the solution is key because it affects the overall success of the implementation throughout the organisation.

The A part of the equation is much more important than the Q. Try to get the two parts balanced. So, for example, with Q and A both at 60%, the E is 36%, whereas with Q at 80% and A at 40%, E is only 32%. Getting the A score to at least as high as the Q should be the aim, as these example numbers show.

Clearly, communication will be vital throughout. You need to develop a communication plan as part of your overall deployment plan to ensure you get the right messages to the right people at the right time and in an appropriate medium. Try to think about the different audiences both as teams and individuals.

Looking Out for the Pitfalls

Transforming an organisation is unlikely to be without its challenges. Unfortunately, it's all too easy for things to go wrong, not only when you're en route but even before you've set off on the journey. Understanding who's on your side and who isn't is vital – you'll probably encounter some people who say the right words but don't walk the talk.

Because some people will be tempted to try to do things faster than is practicable, look to agree actions in bite-sized chunks. You may find a technique such as Multi-Generation-Planning (MGP) useful here.

The MGP technique provides the basis for a series of projects for your products, services and processes, perhaps over several years. It is based around the concept of a 'step–stretch–leap' strategy. It's described in more detail in the 'Taking on too much too soon' section later in this chapter.

Checking that everyone's on board

Not everyone will like the destination or the route. Hopefully, those people can be won round, but that might not be the case. Carrying out a stakeholder analysis – see Figure 2-4 – is an important step both before and after you announce the planned destination of your journey.

The stakeholder analysis will be based on your perceptions, of course, but you need to feel you have the right people on board for the journey ahead, especially when it comes to the senior management team.

Stakeholder Matrix

Names	Strongly against	Moderately against	Neutral	Moderately supportive	Strongly supportive	Hot/cold spots

Figure 2-4: Stakeholder analysis.

No matter what issue you're addressing, some people will be very much for it, some completely against, some in-between, and some indifferent. And that's pretty much life so don't be surprised when you find this picture applying to your transformation objectives or to the changes emerging from the DMAIC and DMADV projects that your teams eventually develop. And if you can't see that picture, then you better find out what the situation looks like, both on the surface and beneath it.

Stakeholder analysis helps you develop a detailed sense of who the key stakeholders are, how they currently feel about the change initiative, and the level of support they need to exhibit for the change initiative to have a good chance of success. It also helps determine ways to influence relationships and develop strategies that will be effective for each key stakeholder.

First, you need to identify the stakeholders.

Consider these questions:

- Who are the stakeholders?
- Where do they currently stand on the issues associated with the change initiative?
- Are they supportive?
- How supportive?
- Are they against?
- And how much against?
- Are they broadly neutral?

Given their status or influence on your project, where do you need these stakeholders to be? It may be both desirable and possible to move some stakeholders to a higher level of support. How will you do that? Can you identify their hot and cold buttons? How can you present the vision and its supporting projects in a more appealing and effective way for them? Sometimes it may be entirely appropriate for stakeholders to adopt a neutral position. And every now and then, it might be appropriate to scale down someone's support.

Figure 2-4 provides a framework for your stakeholder analysis, enabling you to capture and present your perceptions. You begin by mapping your perceptions of each stakeholder's current position. List each stakeholder along the left side of the chart and then consider where you feel each one is at the moment. In assessing each individual, examine both objective evidence and subjective opinion. A key stakeholder is anyone who controls or influences critical resources, who can block the change initiative by direct or indirect means, who must approve certain aspects of the change strategy, who shapes the thinking of other critical parties or who owns a key work process impacted by the change initiative.

Once you've identified whether each stakeholder is against, neutral or supportive, you need to decide where each stakeholder needs to be for the change initiative to be successful. Remember, some stakeholders may need only to be shifted to neutral to stop them being an active blocker.

While it might be nice, it probably won't be necessary for everyone to be strongly supportive of the change initiative.

The next step is to develop an effective strategy for influencing the stakeholders in order to increase, or at least maintain, their level of support. The hot and cold buttons come into play at this point. Sometimes it will be a simple matter of presenting information in the right way for a particular person. Some will prefer lots of detail; others will want only a high-level summary. Some will want facts and figures; others will prefer pictures.

Whatever the approach, you need to give careful thought to which person will have most impact on a particular stakeholder, the nature of the message that needs to be delivered, and how and when the influence process should begin.

In determining ways in which to move particular stakeholders, remember that help may be available from those who are supporters of the initiative. A strongly supportive key stakeholder might also be a thought leader for others on your list. Consider how you can enlist their support in shaping the thinking of other, less supportive, stakeholders.

Considering what can go wrong

Just about anything and everything can go wrong! But it can all go right, too. For some people, changing their thinking and behaviour may be too difficult. What's more, attempting to action all the tasks needed may seem beyond you. You're probably going to be faced with trying to keep the existing work running at the same time as taking on the planning, scheduling and actioning of a whole series of projects.

The soft stuff can be forgotten about, deliberately or otherwise, and you may well have some staff trying to block progress and derail the change process. You may face a whole host of other potential problems, including lack of the right skills and expertise, insufficient resources and poor communication. As with any project or programme, carrying out a risk analysis will help you to identify the potential problems and prevent at least some of them from occurring. You can also use a risk analysis to develop contingency plans for when something does go wrong.

In terms of things that can go wrong with processes, we recommend using Failure Modes and Effects Analysis (FMEA). FMEA looks to identify what might go wrong (the 'failure modes') and assess the impact if it does ('the effect'). It also considers how often the failure mode is likely to occur, and how likely you are to detect the failure before its effect is realised.

For each of these, you assign a value, usually on a scale of 1 to 10, to reflect the risk. To determine priorities for action, you need to calculate an RPN – a risk priority number. This value is simply the result of multiplying your ratings for the severity of the risk, the frequency of occurrence and the likelihood of detection. And, of course, you need to find ways to reduce the RPN. FMEA is described in more detail in *Lean Six Sigma For Dummies* (Wiley).

Taking on too much too soon

Taking on too much too soon is tempting but potentially hazardous. Change is best carried out in bite-size chunks. Anything else can overwhelm you. Resist the temptation to try to do everything in one go.

With a transformation programme, you know where you want to be but recognise that getting there will take some time and effort. And, of course, transformation is likely to be achieved in a series of projects rather than in one hit. The MGP provides the basis for a series of projects for your products, services and processes, perhaps over several years, based on the concept of a 'step–stretch–leap' strategy (as illustrated in Figure 2-5). Each 'generation' looks to focus on a different aspect of meeting market and customer requirements, with the longer-term aim of securing market leadership. Imagine that service delivery is the issue that needs to be dealt with; the typical three-part strategy would then be along these lines.

In the first generation of a product or service, and in the management and improvement of the supporting processes, you're looking to take remedial action and close the gaps in order to prevent the defection of customers to competitors. Doing so may include identifying and closing gaps in the market itself. The second generation looks to build on the success of this first strategy by enhancing your processes further, and perhaps developing products and services that target new markets, the customers of competitors, or attempting to win back lost customers. Finally, in the third generation, you try to achieve market leadership through breakthroughs. These might be in technical expertise, productivity, exceptional service or possibly a combination of all three.

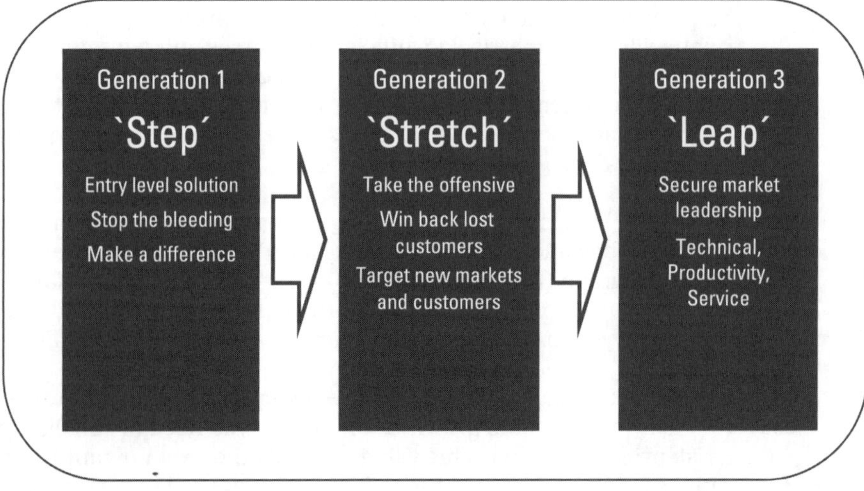

Figure 2-5: Step, stretch and leap towards transformation.

Developing an MGP helps you to present a vision of what you're trying to achieve, but does so in a way that highlights the phases and rationale behind what you're doing. And, of course, you can incorporate the feedback and learning from one generation into the future generations of the product or process. Doing so should help you manage risks and contain costs more effectively, and lead to a smoother and perhaps faster transition to the longer-term desired state.

Accentuating the positive with negative brainstorming

Negative brainstorming identifies what you don't want to achieve. So, for example, you might ask a team, 'How can we ensure our strategy deployment plan fails?' or 'How can we make certain the transformation journey never leaves the station?' Potentially, the ideas will come thick and fast. Some may be a little silly, but that's okay – a little fun will be no bad thing. Using sticky notes and creating an Affinity Diagram by sorting the notes into common themes and agreeing descriptive headers for each group is the best way to carry out a negative brainstorming exercise. Chapter 4 provides more detail about creating an Affinity Diagram.

Next comes the interesting part. You can do one of two things – or indeed both. First, you can identify those things that are already happening, which can be a salutary experience. Second, you can turn the statements, ideas and actions on the sticky notes into positives, providing a whole series of the things you need to do to achieve what you really want – a successful transformation and strategy deployment.

Negative brainstorming can work well in helping to identify some of the potential failure modes we referred to in the earlier section describing FMEA, 'Considering what can go wrong'.

Creating the Vision

Engaging people and maintaining that engagement means you will need to have effective and ongoing communication in place. That communication must be appropriate for the different levels of staff within the organisation. Naturally, people will need to know what the organisation is seeking to do, just where True North is, and how the journey there is progressing.

Going backwards – more or less

Visions paint a picture that appeals to hearts and minds and helps answer the question, 'Why change?' In developing the desired state from the perspective of your customers, the business and your employees, you are effectively developing a future vision that you're working towards.

A vision should provide a clear statement about the outcomes of the change effort, and in doing so, help identify at least some of the elements that need to be changed. A vision secures commitment and support by helping people understand what it is that has to be done – and why.

Depending on the aims of the transformation, the vision will look at things in terms of the performance of your products and services, and the processes that support them, for example, or perhaps at the new image the organisation is creating. But you also need to consider some of the softer issues of behaviour, too.

Backwards visioning provides a helpful framework for developing influencing strategies and can be linked with your stakeholder analysis (see the 'Checking that everyone's on board' section earlier in this chapter) and the development of your elevator speech (see the 'Where are you going?' section earlier in this chapter). It seeks to create a picture of the future that is expressed in behavioural terms. Improvement teams, for example, need to imagine that their change has been successfully completed. If that were the case, what would they expect to see, both internally and externally, in terms of things such as:

- Behaviours?
- Measures?
- Rewards?
- Recognition?

On a larger scale, what will the transformed organisation look and feel like?

In determining perceptions of these issues, you begin to understand the actions that need to be taken as part of your progress towards the desired state. These will include the activities and behaviours that you need to reduce and remove and those you need to introduce and increase. Progress can really be seen in terms of 'more or less?'

Locating True North

The vision and the supporting communications need to clearly show exactly what is meant by the organisation's True North – what it is, where it is, and why you want to be there. You should allow no scope for misconceptions or confusion.

We touched on communication in the 'Dealing with the soft stuff' section earlier in this chapter. It's essential that your approach to communications is appropriate and relevant to the different groups of people within the organisation. In particular, recognise that the communication plan should be tailored to the specific stakeholder groups in terms of format and frequency.

To develop a communication plan, you have to consider some basic questions, such as:

- Why do you want to communicate?
- Who is your audience?
- What message do you want to communicate?
- How do you want to communicate it?

Keeping people focused on arriving at True North means that communication will need to be an ongoing activity. Clearly, as you make progress on the journey, the purpose, audience, message, and formats may change, but the need to keep everyone appropriately informed is vital.

Remember to celebrate as you reach landmarks en route.

Answering what's in it for me?

People at all levels in the organisation will want to know the answer to this question, and addressing it in the creation of the stakeholder analysis, the vision and the communications plan is vital.

Ideally, your communication incorporates what the desired answer should be to this question. Get that right and they won't need to ask the question. The answer they're looking for will be plain for them to see.

Spreading the word

You need to keep the transformation aims on the agenda and on everyone's radar. Visual management comes in here. *Visual management* takes many forms in the workplace and outside of it, too – traffic signs being an obvious example! In the workplace you could use a variety of displays, charts, signs, labels, colour-coded markings, and so on. This helps everyone see what's going on, understand the process and check that everything's being done correctly.

Displays and controls could include data or information for people in a specific area, keeping them informed on overall performance or focused on specific quality issues. Visual controls could also cover safety, production throughput, material flow or quality metrics, for example.

Visual management is an essential element in engaging people, securing their buy-in and helping them to communicate performance and progress generally and, in this case, in terms of the transformation journey. Visual management is described in more detail in *Lean Six Sigma For Dummies* (Wiley).

Chapter 3

Learning to DRIVE

In This Chapter

- Taking a look at the DRIVE model
- Shaping the plan and getting the measure of things
- Building skills and capability
- Considering the soft stuff

This chapter begins with more detail about the DRIVE model and the route to an organisation's True North. The transformation journey takes time. Leaders will need a genuine understanding of the organisation's customers, effective teamwork and appropriate communication, as well as managers who clearly understand their role in managing and improving process performance and equipping their staff with the skills they need.

Importantly, transformation will also involve an understanding and appreciation of the 'elements of change' – the importance of the 'soft stuff'. Without it, success is unlikely.

Introducing DRIVE

We provide an overview of the DRIVE model in Chapter 2; it's a systematic approach to ensuring a successful transformation journey to True North. Chapter 2 also defines what we mean by True North, explaining its use as a metaphor for where the organisation needs to be.

In this section, we describe the five DRIVE phases – Define, Review, Improve, Verify and Establish – which are illustrated in Figure 3-1.

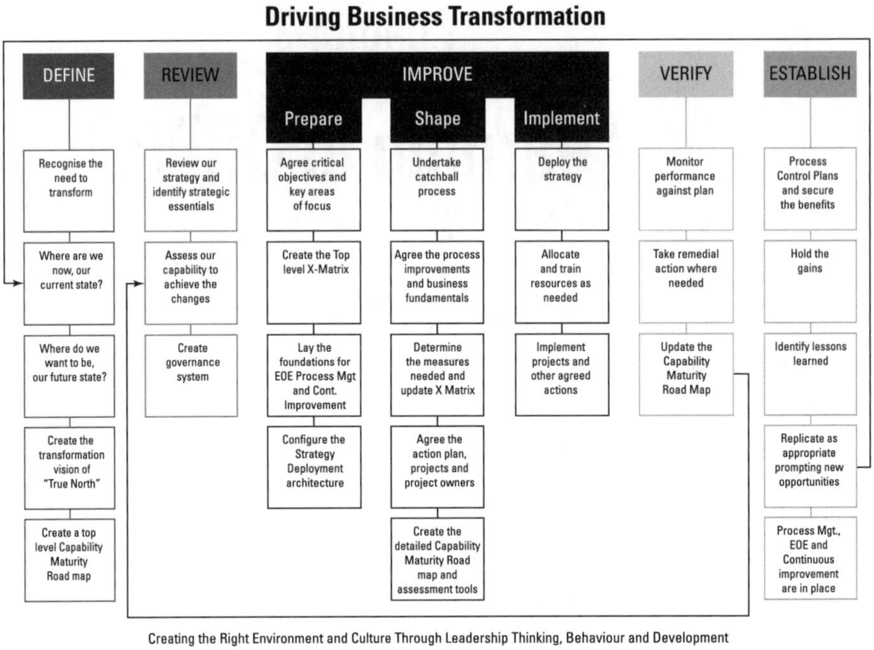

Figure 3-1: The DRIVE model.

Define

In the Define phase, you recognise the need to transform and describe your current state – where you are right now, warts and all. It's possible that the picture you uncover may prompt the need for transformation; now you need to ensure that you really understand what's happening currently. This will help you provide at least an outline vision of where you want to be – the future state you want to achieve.

You need to make the vision really clear by identifying True North, as we describe in Chapter 2, and create a maturity road map that will help identify the stages of your journey. We provide an overview of capability models in the 'Taking a Mature Approach' section of this chapter, but Chapter 14 provides more detail, introducing a capability road map that links to the DRIVE model. Not only will this map plot your route, it will also help you assess progress and make clear that the journey may well take some time.

Review

In this stage, you focus in on your strategy and identify the strategic essentials you need to achieve. Strategic essentials are the vital few essential general statements of direction for the organisation in the medium to long term.

In part, this phase is also a bit of a reality check. Given where you are right now, you need to consider whether the proposed journey is feasible or is possibly too ambitious. This is a serious question and you need to be honest in your assessment and reply.

Assessing your capability to achieve the necessary changes means confirming the gaps that need closing and at least some of the actions that will be needed along the way to close those gaps and progress towards True North. In light of this knowledge, you may have to go back a stage, to Define, and scale down your aims, or you can progress to the Improve phase knowing exactly what needs to be done, perhaps augmenting your resources by bringing in new and experienced people or developing appropriate and timely training plans, for example.

Before moving on, however, an appropriate governance system must be established to ensure that everyone is clear about what needs to be done and who is responsible for what. As well as appointing people to select and review the projects and actions necessary for the transformation process, someone must also be in charge of the normal day-to-day running of the business.

Improve

The Improve phase is divided into three distinct parts. The first two parts make sure that you don't start your journey in an unplanned rush. Everyone needs to be clear on the direction they're going in and their ultimate destination. They must understand their own role and those of everyone else.

Prepare

You've already identified the strategic essentials in the Review phase. Now you need to break these down into critical objectives and agree the key areas of focus. This process is described in Chapter 8, but essentially you need to specify what the strategic essentials actually mean.

You're aiming to establish a 'from this to that' picture that everyone can visualise and relate to. One way of doing so is to create a first draft of the X Matrix, which shows how the various actions and projects fit together. The X Matrix is a key document in the transformation process and is described in detail in Chapter 8.

In developing the critical objectives and focus areas you're beginning to pull together the elements needed to lay the foundations for everyday operational excellence (EOE) that will result from better managed processes and a culture of continuous improvement (CI). See Chapter 12 for more information on everyday operational excellence and how to achieve it.

The strategic essentials, critical objectives and focus areas define what the organisation will work on and this information needs to be cascaded across and down the organisation. Chapter 8 shows how the strategy deployment architecture can be structured and tasks appropriately allocated across the organisation. How this is done will depend on the nature of the focus areas and the structure of the organisation. Everyone in the organisation must work together in the journey to True North.

Shape

The Shape phase translates critical objectives and focus areas into specific projects and action plans. The catchball process comes into play here. *Catchball* is a metaphor describing how the leadership team 'throws' their strategic essentials, critical objectives and key focus areas down to the next level of management to assess what it means for them and their direct reports. These managers will determine what they believe each of their teams and reports must do to be able to achieve the various objectives, before sending the 'ball' back to the leadership team for their verification and agreement. The 'circle of catchers' increases as managers throw their ideas back and forth from one level of the organisation to another as the detailed action plans, projects and supporting measures are shaped and finally agreed. The catchball process is simple, but not necessarily easy. It involves listening to the people responsible for the actions and results and accepting that their input may well lead to amending plans or timescales. Actioned properly, catchball is a great way to secure buy-in and increase the understanding of what's needed on the journey to True North. The catchball process is described in more detail in Chapter 8.

Now that the improvement projects, action plans, and those responsible for them have been identified, measures can be agreed upon and the X Matrix updated.

Implement

Now that everyone is clear on who's doing what, it's time to get on with it and make it happen! In the Review phase, the organisation assesses its capability to achieve the changes. So, in practice, the Implement phase might well begin with the allocation of people to project teams, and the training and up-skilling of staff to enable them to successfully complete the agreed actions.

Verify

As with any series of action plans or projects, progress and performance against plan need to be monitored. The DMAIC process, which we describe in Chapter 1, has tollgate reviews at the end of each phase, for example, and benefit reviews after the Analyse, Improve and Control phases.

Scheduled review meetings must be set up with the project champions or sponsors. In light of these, remedial action may need to be taken or plans and timescales adjusted.

Establish

The Establish phase has parallels with the Control phase in DMAIC. You're looking to secure and hold the gains, identify the lessons learned, and look for opportunities to replicate the success elsewhere in the organisation.

Step by step, you're enhancing the organisation's capability as you develop and evolve a culture of continuous improvement, building on the foundations of everyday operational excellence and managed processes. The DNA of the organisation is improving step by step.

Creating the Framework

Almost regardless of the extent to which Lean Six Sigma plays a part in the transformation, a framework is needed to ensure effective co-ordination and monitoring of the plans and progress. In Chapter 8, we introduce the X Matrix as the key format for providing a visual picture of your strategy deployment and transformation activities. It's a one-page document that captures decisions and provides a framework for monitoring and updating progress against plan.

But for success in achieving your transformation, you need the right people in place to carry out that monitoring and to lead and champion the various projects and activities involved.

Building the team

Naturally, the leadership team has to be in complete support of the approach you're taking and the destination you're aiming for. But so, too, do the people in the wider organisation. Almost certainly, you'll need their support and involvement as project team members, for example as subject matter experts providing input or as the people on the ground who are going to keep the day-to-day work ticking over.

In terms of the leadership team, you need some, or possibly all of them, to form a steering committee or transformation board. Ideally, the chief executive will take the role of transformation director, but he'll need to appoint someone else to act as the transformation programme director or co-ordinator. This person needs to hold a senior role in the organisation, must be a good communicator and have experience in programme management.

As the governance system is created and projects are agreed, members of the leadership or management teams should take on the role of project sponsor or champion. At the project level, every improvement initiative deserves a champion who's prepared to devote the time and support needed to help the project team overcome any roadblocks on their journey.

The project champion is involved in selecting the project and the team members for it. As the project progresses, the project champion stays involved by providing strategic direction to the team and taking an active involvement in project reviews, for example. You can find more detail about the role of the project champion in *Lean Six Sigma For Dummies* (Wiley).

Creating a small programme management office staffed with people seconded from the organisation is sensible. These people should be well known and respected throughout the organisation. They need to have project management experience and, ideally, expertise in Lean Six Sigma, to at least Green Belt level. The different 'belts' (Yellow, Green and Black) represent the depth of Lean Six Sigma training, knowledge and experience, and are described in Chapter 12.

Developing the plan

Chapter 8 takes you through the strategy deployment process, which enables you to shape and refine your plans, develop the work streams, and agree the specific owners and timeframes for projects and activities at different levels within the organisation. You can develop the fine details of your plans in several ways, but we think the most effective way is to use Affinity, Interrelationship and Tree diagrams, as shown in Figure 3-2.

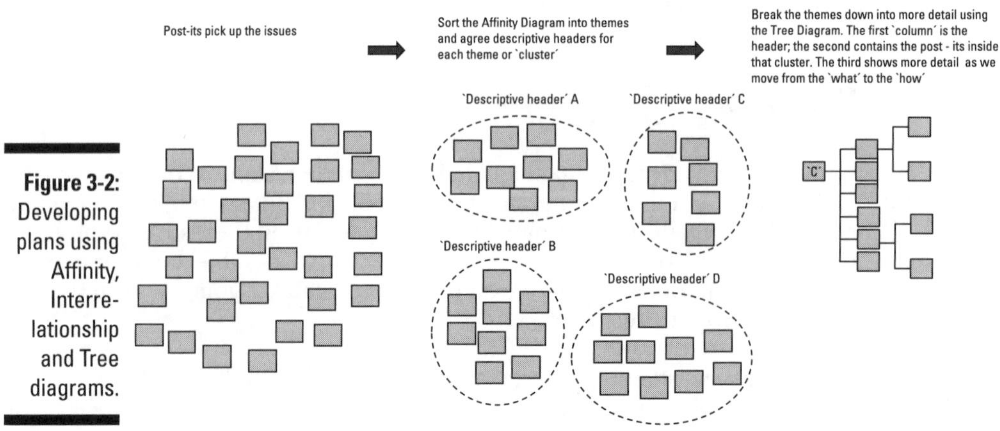

Figure 3-2: Developing plans using Affinity, Interrelationship and Tree diagrams.

The interrelationship diagram would have considered the relationship between the 'themes' and identified the driver of the project. Along with the affinity diagram, it's covered in more detail in Chapter 4 of this book.

Communicating effectively

Keeping everyone appropriately informed is often easier said than done, especially in a transformation programme that affects and involves the entire organisation. As with any presentation, stage show, film or television programme, knowing your audience is critical. Tailoring the messages and media appropriately, especially to the key stakeholders, is likely to be an essential activity.

In so many organisations, we've heard managers claim that 'all the information is on the intranet, so everyone knows what's happening.' In our experience, this is rarely the case. Not everyone uses the organisation's intranet or, even if they do, the style and content of the information isn't necessarily appropriate to all levels of staff.

Some while ago, one of the authors was working with the US Army and was surprised to discover that its rule book is available in two forms: as a comic and as a more formal document. This is a great example of understanding the different segments of the 'audience' – many of the soldiers read comics and so it makes sense to provide important information in that format as it's appropriate for them.

Visual management, the use of activity boards to display information, and daily team meetings will go some way to ensuring effective communication, but need to be supplemented by, for example, a transformation-specific magazine or news sheet. For more on visual management, see Chapters 2 and 12 of this book and *Lean Six Sigma For Dummies* (Wiley).

Ensuring clear ownership

Clear ownership must be established for all work streams, plans and emerging projects. Even communication must be one specific person's responsibility.

A responsibility matrix, as shown in Figure 3-3, can help you establish and communicate ownership for at least some areas of activity. In Figure 3-3 you can see how the matrix has been linked to the actions identified in a tree diagram.

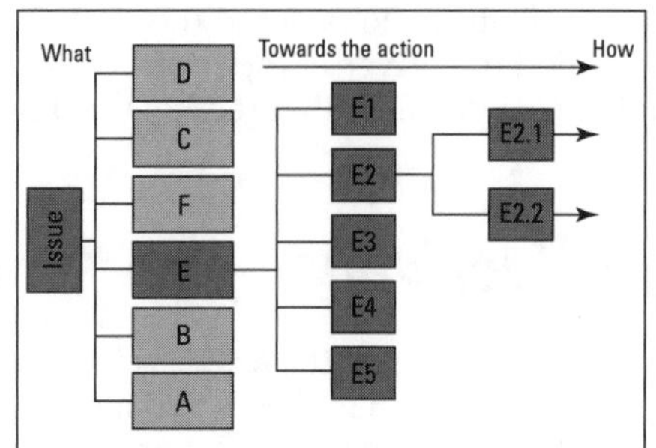

Improvement Team Members

Project tasks from tree diagram	Ann	Brian	Clare	Phil	Jo
Design Questionnaire	△	◉	△	○	△
Issue Questionnaire	◉	○	△	△	△
Analyse Questionnaire	○	△	◉	△	△
Present Results	△	△	○	△	◉

◉ Primary responsibility ○ Secondary responsibility △ Keep informed

Link the tree diagram to a matrix diagram identifying who is responsible

Figure 3-3: Taking responsibility.

Another very effective option is the RACI (responsible, accountable, consulted, informed) matrix, shown in Figure 3-4.

RACI	Who	What
Accountable		
Responsible		
Consulted		
Informed		

RACI. CARI, ARCI - whichever sequence you prefer!

Figure 3-4: Feeling a little RACI?

As you can see in Figure 3-4, it doesn't really matter which sequence you use in the matrix; the important thing is to identify the 'who' and the 'what'.

Whichever of these matrices you use, they tend to be more appropriate to the project and activity levels. Providing the overarching picture will be the X Matrix.

Getting the measure

One of the key Lean Six Sigma principles is the need to manage by fact. You need good data, as defined in Chapter 2, but, of course, you need to be measuring the right things. And you need to present the data appropriately to ensure it's interpreted correctly and the right actions are taken when needed. At a process level, you need to be measuring the inputs and in-process activities that affect your performance against the customer requirements, Presenting this type of data in control charts is the most effective way of understanding the 'voice of the process'.

The need for a sound data collection process and the use of control charts is covered in some detail in *Lean Six Sigma For Dummies* (Wiley), and the need for a balance of input, in-process and output measures, the Xs and Ys, is covered briefly in Chapter 12 of this book.

Taking a Mature Approach

Transforming an organisation takes time. Potentially a lot of time! Having a road map to keep you on track and assess the progress that you're making on your journey can be really helpful. Maturity models are one way of helping you do just that.

Using maturity models

Chapter 14 focuses on the capability maturity journey and introduces a road map that links to the DRIVE model. It is specific to transformation. Lots of different maturity models are available on the Internet, however, covering all sorts of things, including progress against the criteria of the Baldrige or EFQM Models, for example.

They provide a helpful framework for you to assess progress and gain a clear sense of the next stages in your journey. They might be relatively simple in their design or go into some detail, so you need to decide which is appropriate for you and your plans. The design will be influenced by a number of factors, such as whether the transformation is organisation wide or for a particular division or business unit; or if it requires cultural change or focuses on developing new markets or product lines.

To give you a flavour of their format, the model illustrated in Figure 3-5 may be useful. It is a relatively simple and self-explanatory example that serves to highlight that changing attitudes and behaviour takes time, and a culture of continuous improvement and everyday operational excellence will not become the norm overnight.

In developing a maturity model for your organisation, bear in mind that each team will itself need to go through a maturity process.

Teams go through four stages as they develop, as shown in Figure 3-6. In the *Forming* stage, team members may be highly dependent on the team leader for guidance and direction. There may be little agreement on team aims other than those set by the leader. The individual roles and responsibilities are likely to be unclear or not fully agreed upon, and the team members may test the leader and other team members to help them understand parameters.

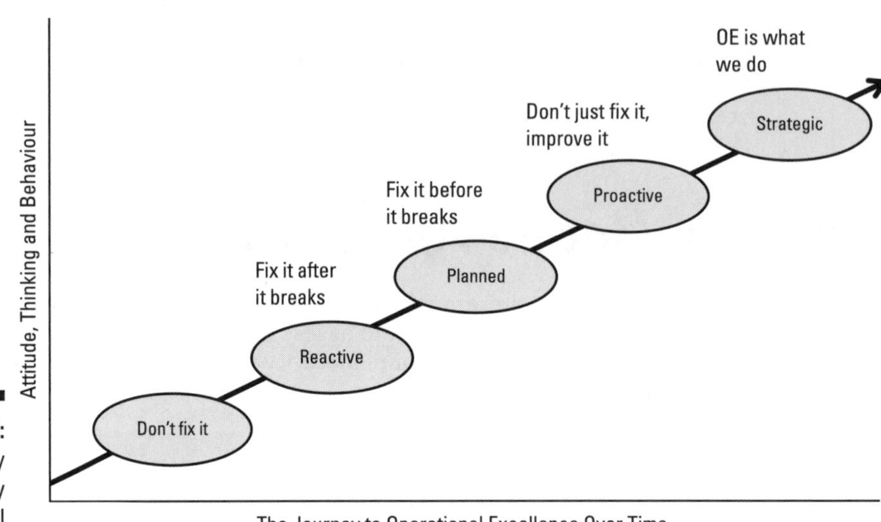

Figure 3-5: The journey to everyday operational excellence.

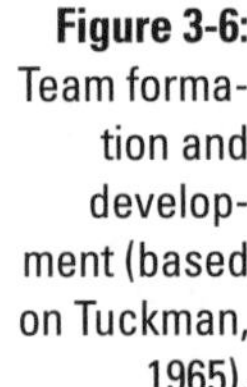

Figure 3-6: Team formation and development (based on Tuckman, 1965).

As the team moves to the *Storming* stage, the members are likely to be vying for position as they attempt to establish themselves in relation to other team members and also the leader, who may receive challenges from them.

Clarity of purpose increases during this stage, but plenty of uncertainties persist. Cliques and factions may form and power struggles occur. The team needs to be focused on its goals to avoid becoming distracted by relationships and emotional issues.

Compromises may be required to enable progress. Beware if this is the case because there may be implications for plans and timescales.

The *Norming* stage sees the development of more positive behaviour. Agreement and consensus are generally the norm among team members, who respond well to facilitation by the team leader. Roles and responsibilities are clear and agreed. The team may engage in fun and social activities. The team discusses and develops its processes and working style. General respect for the leader is evident and some of the leader's activities are shared by the team.

In the *Performing* stage things are motoring! The team is more strategically aware; the members know why the team is doing what it's doing and how it fits into the bigger picture. They understand the organisation's vision and have one of their own as they seek to ensure that they meet their goals. The Improvement Charter will have helped here, by the way. The charter is referred to in *Lean Six Sigma For Dummies* (Wiley).

Disagreements still occur, of course, but now they're resolved in a positive manner within the team, and necessary changes to processes and structure are made by the team as a whole. The team is able to work towards achieving its goals, and also to attend to relationship, style and process issues along the way. Team members look after each other.

The steering committee must know what the team and its members will do once a project is completed and ensure that effective and timely communication is in place to help avoid potential frustrations and upset.

Figure 3-7 provides a simple checklist to help teams review and discuss their ongoing relationships and become a more capable unit. GRIP can be used by the project team at any stage in the project to review how the team is working together. It's a simple assessment process, best carried out separately by individuals on the team. You can then share your results. Look for areas of commonality and difference in views or areas of strength and weakness and agree improvement actions that will address any issues and improve team performance.

	Low				High
Goals Are we clear on the goals?	1	2	3	4	5
Roles Are our roles agreed and understood?	1	2	3	4	5
Interpersonal How well are we working as a team?	1	2	3	4	5
Processes How confident are we in our plan and approach?	1	2	3	4	5
	Low				High

Figure 3-7: Getting a GRIP.

Assessing capability

Various methods exist for assessing the overall performance and capabilities of your organisation. In identifying the need for transformation, your organisation may well have analysed its financial, customer and process performance results using the balanced scorecard, which also covers issues surrounding learning and growth. It might also have undertaken a self-assessment against the criteria of the Baldrige or EFQM models, and thus determined its capability against those criteria too. These models provide a framework for achieving business excellence and provide a set of benchmarks against which organisations can compare themselves. Chapter 5 explains these models and the balanced scorecard in more detail.

The X Matrix, action plan and tracking chart (described in full in Chapter 8) can be used to monitor progress against plan and to some extent, therefore, the evolving capability of the organisation.

In terms of process capability, control charts enable you to assess the state of the process, both by broad description and through the use of the Cp and Cpk measures. These capability indices compare process performance and variation to the critical to quality requirements (CTQs) and provide both a theoretical and actual measure to demonstrate the relationship. They tell you precisely how capable the process is in terms of meeting customer requirements. It's likely that these measures will have been analysed in both the Define and Review phases of the DRIVE model.

Deploying the Strategy

As part of the Define phase of the DRIVE model, the CEO and leadership team agree their vision for the organisation and update the strategic plan as appropriate. Together with senior management, the longer-term strategic essentials, critical objectives and short-term focus areas can then be determined.

The organisation breaks the focus areas down into short-term process improvements or design projects and ensures consensus and alignment through the 'catchball' process described earlier in this chapter. In order to achieve the business transformation, breakthrough improvements will probably be required that necessitate the introduction of new ways of working. Other projects may well be needed that don't follow the DMAIC or DMADV frameworks, for example purchasing specific equipment. Ownership of the various activities is agreed, and teams identified to establish the detailed action plans, targets and metrics to track progress. That progress is managed through monthly and annual reviews and corrective actions, sometimes referred to as counter measures.

Leading the way

The leadership team and management generally are responsible for leading the way through the change process. The leaders need to see their role as 'working *on* the organisation' with their focus on developing and delivering the strategy. Through their behaviour and actions, they need to demonstrate their commitment to the journey and the destination. Managers need to be 'working *on* the processes', which we cover in more detail in Chapter 12. Their role is to work with the people in the process to find ways to continuously improve performance and meet the customers' requirements.

Everything the leadership and management team does must demonstrate belief in and adherence to the transformation process.

Keeping it focused

It's so easy to get diverted. Everyone in the organisation, but especially the leaders and managers, needs to be very focused on how they spend their time. The main thing is to keep the main thing the main thing!

Reviewing how you're spending your time is sensible. The XY Grid in Figure 3-8 highlights four broad areas where people spend their time according to the dimensions of importance and urgency. All too often the focus slips – so where are you spending most of your time? Hopefully, not in the 'urgent but not important' quadrant! You need to maintain focus on the actions that lead to True North.

urgency \ importance	Low	High
High	Urgent but not important	Both urgent and important
Low	Neither important nor urgent	Important but not urgent

Finding the time...

Figure 3-8: Where does all the time go?

Your organisation should focus on preventing problems, error proofing the processes, planning, preserving and enhancing relationships with customers and suppliers, both internal and external, and on accomplishing the transformation plan. Research in Japan suggests that managers in highly successful organisations spend 65 to 80 per cent of their time in the 'important but not urgent' quadrant.

Focusing on the Customer

A particularly vital relationship is, of course, with your customers, both internal and external. In focusing on your customers, you're looking to provide value for them and to meet their *critical to quality requirements*, or their CTQs.

The CTQs are vital elements in Lean Six Sigma, providing you with the basis to assess how well you're performing in meeting your customers' requirements.

Always bear in mind that different types of customer may well have different requirements and CTQs. Their priorities will not be the same and you must thus tailor your product or service accordingly.

Knowing your customers – past, present and future

Ideally, the organisation will already have grouped your customers into segments. This helps you to identify your customers' different requirements. By segmenting them, you can develop the right products and services for each group, and create specific measures to help you to understand your performance in meeting their differing requirements, something that will have been undertaken in the Define and Review phases of DRIVE.

To help you segment your customers, list some categories that describe both your current customers and the people or organisations that you consider to be potential customers. You can look at past customers in this way, too.

When you're carrying out this exercise, consider how the proposed transformation activities and goals will impact on all of your customers.

Valuing your customers

Customers are looking for value. Amongst other things, this means customers want the right products and services, at the right time, the right price, of the right quality, and delivered to the right place.

Identifying what they want

Truly focusing on customers, as opposed to simply saying that you're doing so, requires real investment in understanding your customers' needs. Knowing who your customers are, how they're segmented, and which ones are your priority is a vital prerequisite to any research and data gathering. Identifying the wrong customers, or not being aware of the different segments, can mean you collect information on requirements or customers that aren't related to the process or service you're designing.

Your customers may be both internal and external. Thinking in terms of processes helps you identify where you need to focus, and highlights who your internal customers are.

Lean Six Sigma For Dummies (Wiley) provides some detail about segmenting and researching your customers and explains how to develop the CTQs. The same book also introduces the House of Quality, or Quality Function Deployment (QFD), as a technique to help you in the design of new products, services or processes. Fundamental to the design will be a clear understanding of the customers and their requirements and perceptions.

Recognising how you're doing

If you've established the CTQs correctly, they'll be measurable and you can determine the relevant output measures (the Ys) needed to assess your performance in meeting them. You can also look at customer survey results. All of this data will be presented at the appropriate level in the organisation's visual management charts (see the 'Communicating effectively' section earlier in this chapter), and on the balanced scorecard (see Chapter 5).

Building Links and Strengthening the Supply Chain

Performance in relation to CTQs, as monitored by the Y measures, will be dependent on the important X measures that assess the performance of the inputs to the process and the in-process variables and activities. In this section, we look at the inputs from your suppliers, be they internal or external.

Getting the measure of suppliers

You need to identify how your suppliers are affecting and influencing your performance. Some typical aspects to look at concern time, accuracy and completeness, as well as the overall quality of their inputs – are they meeting your requirements?

Ideally, you'll have established your CTQs with them – you are their customer and they should be looking to meet your requirements. So, are you receiving things on time or is delivery somewhat variable, be it too early or too late? When you receive their inputs, are they complete or are items or information missing? Take a long, hard look at the number of defects or errors in an average order.

Your customers aren't interested in the performance of your suppliers and won't be impressed if you blame poor service elsewhere.

Making the right links

Working with your suppliers to agree requirements and establish measures that you can both measure and discuss is an effective means of developing relationships with them. In turn, this two-way communication enables you to drive the concept of continuous improvement into the suppliers' organisations. You'll soon see whether you're working with the right suppliers.

A supply chain is only as strong as its weakest link.

Joining up the thinking

If you've made the right links then, almost certainly, you'll find opportunities for joint improvement projects, some of which may well help speed up the transformation process.

The process becomes even more powerful if you're able to involve both your customers and suppliers in the improvement activities you need to undertake.

Recognising the Importance of the Soft Stuff

In Chapter 2 we touch on the importance of the soft stuff and introduce a formula for expressing its importance: $E = Q \times A$. Briefly, E = Effectiveness, Q = Quality of the solution and A = Acceptance of the solution. The 'soft stuff' is the hard stuff; it's about how well you work with the people involved in the transformation process and the stakeholders who are affected by it. You may well have developed an ideal solution or approach, but its effectiveness will depend on its acceptance.

So many organisations and their leadership and management teams seem to ignore the 'A' part of the formula and then seem surprised and frustrated that the outcomes aren't what they'd expected.

As true today as it ever was, the quotation below sums up the challenges that await the leaders of change, whether of an improvement project or a full-scale transformation programme:

> *'It must be remembered there is nothing more difficult to plan, more doubtful of success nor more dangerous to manage than the creation of a new system. For the initiator has the enmity of all who profit by the preservation of the old institution and merely lukewarm defenders in those who would gain by the new ones.' – Nicolo Machiavelli*

Understanding the soft stuff and being fully aware of the E = Q × A formula are vital ingredients in optimising your chances of success. In Chapter 11, we go into more detail about managing change and look at some of the work of change guru, John Kotter. For the moment though, we're going to look at our 'elements of change' model, which is based around Kotter's ideas. This model can be used as a simple but effective tool to assess how well you're doing in relation to the change management elements of individual projects and also of the overall transformation programme. Figure 3-9 includes at least some of the key questions you'll need to address in working through the elements, but you're certain to have your own organisation-specific questions to add to these.

Figure 3-9: The elements of change.

Deploying the strategy and transforming the organisation is likely to demand some different thinking as well as some different and enhanced skills and expertise. You need to conduct a skills analysis to identify the current situation in your organisation and locate any shortfalls. Following that, you need to decide whether the shortfalls can be addressed through training or if you need to recruit new staff with these skills. Both training of existing staff and recruitment of new people may be necessary, but carry out the analysis and see. Another option is to bring in consultants or recruit some suitably qualified interim resources.

Make sure you thoroughly investigate the skills and potential already to hand. We've worked in organisations where existing staff held Lean Six Sigma qualifications that were unknown to management and thus unused.

Defining the need

Ideally, you'll already be fully aware of the skills and potential of the people working in the organisation. If not, you'll need to conduct a review, taking account of current and new or enhanced products, services and supporting processes. New or enhanced services or processes, for example, may call for different skills and behaviours.

Making sure that your process or value stream maps really do show how the work gets done, or will be done, will help you identify the skills needed to operate them. Clearly defined and presented user guides should be in place, which will be especially important in ensuring standard work. The details laid out in the user guides are often referred to as standard operating procedures (SOPs), which everyone adheres to.

Now you can introduce training and coaching where you believe it's necessary and begin to assess which members of staff are capable of actioning the various activities. You might find you need to recruit from outside the organisation.

Analysing the gaps

Identifying the skills gaps in your organisation is likely to involve some observation and monitoring of output. If you're going to transform the organisation, then the resulting assessments and remedial plans should form part of your visual management system, as shown in Figure 3-10.

Skills Matrix for Andy's Team

Name / Process	A	B	C	D	E
Ann	◉	△	○	◉	◉
Brian	◉	○	○	○	△
Clare	◉	◉	○	○	○
Sue	◉	△	△	△	◉
Jo	◉	○	○	◉	○
Jim	○	◉	◉	◉	○
Alan	◉	△	△	△	△

All the staff will have started out as 'untrained'

△ Untrained in the process
○ Training received but not yet accredited
◉ Can constantly meet set quality and productivity standards

Figure 3-10: Using a skills and accreditation matrix to assess employees.

The skills and accreditation matrix will prompt questions such as:

- Who is capable of what?
- Who has been updated with changes?
- Who needs more training?
- How can the organisation be flexible to meet changing demands?

So, very simply, you need to consider how effectively the people in the team can action the different processes and the individual steps within them.

Consider using a traffic light-style code, with green indicating that the team member is fully trained and capable of the work; amber highlighting that some coaching or focused additional training is needed; and red demonstrating that the individual has yet to be shown this task and is thus untrained, for example.

You can determine your own code, of course, but either way, the next step is to create the training or coaching plan.

Creating the training plan

Figure 3-11 shows the evolving picture following the introduction of a new or improved process. As with the skills and accreditation matrix, the training plan – ideally complete with schedule – should also form part of your visual management system and be available for everyone to see. Naturally, it should include appropriate monitoring, so that the skills and accreditation matrix is updated in a timely way to reflect the progress being made by people as they increase their skills and competence levels.

Going outside

You may need to consider either bringing in people with specific experience from outside your organisation to fulfil particular roles or using a specialist training organisation.

Be clear about what you're looking for, both in terms of skills and culture. The potential recruit must share and display your organisation's values. In addition, if you're new to Lean Six Sigma and want to recruit Black Belts, for example, make sure they know their stuff! Check out their project experience and always seek references and testimonials.

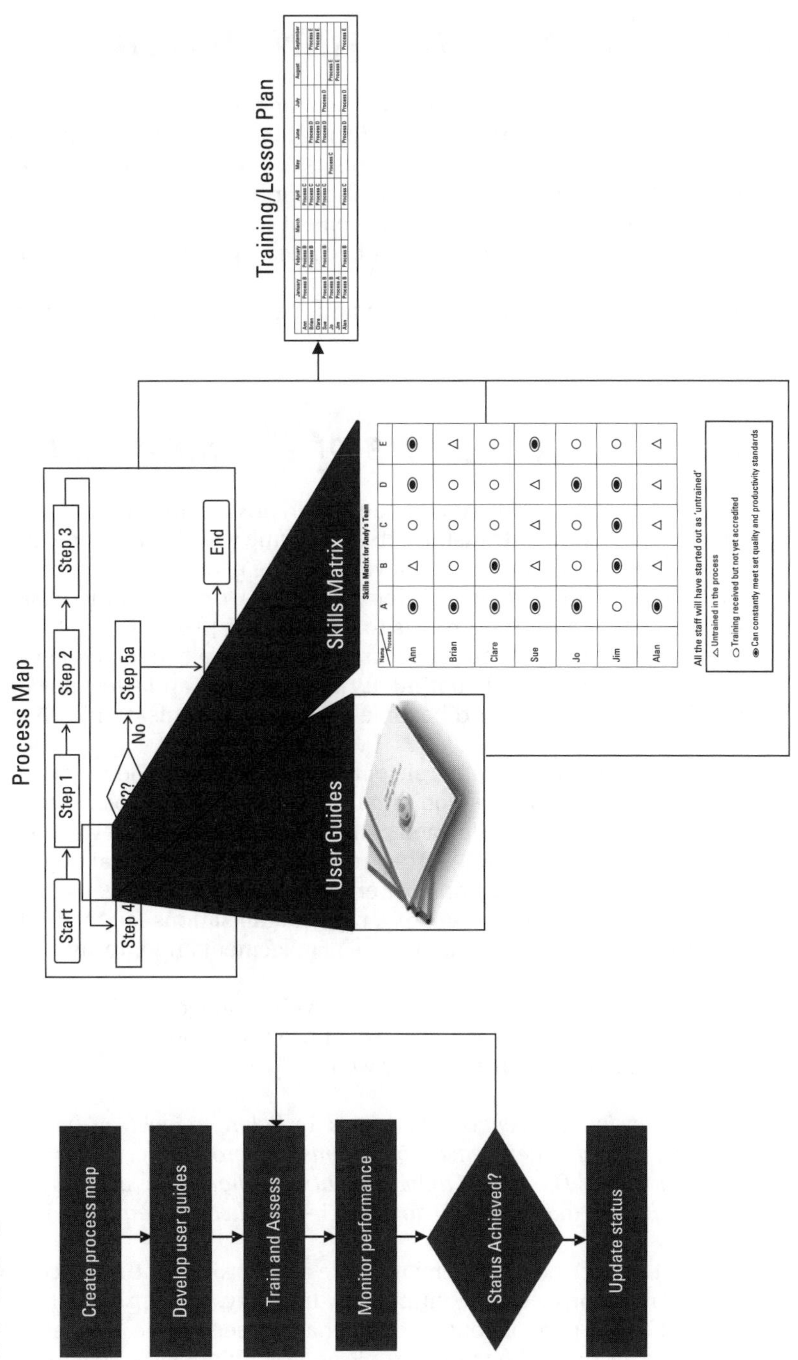

Figure 3-11: Developing the skills.

Enabling Continuous Improvement

On top of the very specific improvement and design projects that form part of the organisation's journey to transformation, it's essential that an ongoing culture of continuous improvement emerges. A cadre of trained Black, Green and Yellow Belts will provide the foundation for this cultural change, but the example set by the leadership and management teams is the determining factor in whether continuous improvement becomes a part of the organisation's DNA.

The roles of the project champion and the manager in everyday operations are pivotal.

Looking at the role of the manager

One of the vital ingredients for success in any organisation, but especially one that's looking to transform itself in some way, is clarifying individual people's roles. Of particular relevance is the need for leaders to recognise that they should be focusing their efforts on working on the business, and for managers to realise their role is to work on the process. What's more, they need to be working on the process with the people involved in the process in order for a culture of continuous improvement and everyday operational excellence to develop and become part of the organisation's DNA.

This section focuses on the role of the manager. In all too many organisations the majority of managers don't really understand their role. Often the manager is someone who has performed extremely well in their previous role and has been promoted as a result. If they're lucky, they receive training in a variety of topics, including, for example, interview techniques, budget setting, appraisals and report writing. Unfortunately, many organisations fail to see the need to also train their managers in process management and improvement activity.

As a result, the processes aren't effectively managed and the people in the process are often seen as the cause of process problems. The following quotation sums up the position very well:

> *'Eighty-five per cent of the reasons for failure to meet customer expectations are related to deficiencies in systems and process . . . rather than the employee. The role of management is to change the process rather than badgering individuals to do better.' – W. Edwards Deming*

We like to describe management's role as 'working on the process with the people in the process to continuously find ways of improving the process.' For that to happen, of course, the manager needs to be clear about their role and to be aware of the various tools and techniques that can be used to help improve process performance. Visual management and the daily team meeting all come into play here.

Assembling the toolkit

Lean Six Sigma pulls together a vast array of improvement tools ranging from the very simple to more sophisticated statistical analysis techniques. In the quest for everyday operational excellence, managers need to understand which tools to use to manage their processes.

The tools don't need to be as comprehensive as those in the toolkit used by Green and Black Belts. The managers don't necessarily need to be able to use the tools; they simply need to know which ones give results that they can use. The Belts can get the data and apply the tools; the manager needs to know how to act on the results. This knowledge should enable managers to not only improve their everyday performance but also take on board at least some of the common language of Lean Six Sigma. Knowledge of the relevant terms will help them more easily provide the information needed by Green and Black Belt projects that link to their processes.

For managers to own and manage their processes, the following need to be in place:

- **A clear customer-focused objective, together with prioritised customer requirements.** Measureable CTQs have been identified and the Y measures put in place.
- **Appropriate process maps.** This will involve at least a SIPOC diagram and a deployment flowchart or value stream map. These 'pictures' of the process can be found in *Lean Six Sigma For Dummies* (Wiley).
- **A balance of input, in-process and output measures.** The vital few Xs and Ys are being measured and the correlation between these variables is understood and managed.
- **Statistical control or an improvement plan is in place to establish such control.** Control charts are part of your visual management system and the variation in the process is understood, enabling appropriate decision-making. Where special causes are present, improvement activity is underway to prevent their recurrence.
- **The process meets the CTQs, or an improvement plan is in place to do so.** Performance in meeting the CTQs is monitored through the Y measures and understood, and improvement activity is underway where the CTQs are not being met.
- **The process has been error-proofed.** Taking action to avoid or reduce the impact of errors or problems is important. We think of this as causing something not to happen, and Failure Modes and Effects Analysis (FMEA; refer to Chapter 2) and error-proofing ensure prevention has been built in where possible. The identification of new prevention or error-proofing opportunities forms part of the daily team meeting.

- **A control plan is in place.** The control plan helps to ensure that the process is carried out consistently. It also identifies key points in the process where measurement data is needed; additionally highlighting what action is required depending on the results. Ensuring you have the right ongoing measures in place is extremely important.

Feeling able and being able

Owning and managing processes is a crucial element in changing the way that people think and behave, which is an essential ingredient in the transformation of an organisation. But there's more, of course!

The people in the process need to feel empowered; they need to be an integral part of the journey the organisation is undertaking. Empowerment means 'to enable'. And that's what the manager has to do as part of their role.

Our approach to empowerment centres on four vital elements for employees:

- **They need to feel a sense of their own competence:** They're learning from experience and gaining new skills and abilities as their potential is developed.
- **They need to feel part of a team:** They're contributing to the team's performance.
- **They can see how their activities link to the goals of the organisation:** They understand that they're an integral part of a larger effort.
- **They enjoy the work and have fun:** Something we should all do!

With these ingredients in place, an organisation significantly increases its chances of being successful.

A direct and very strong correlation exists between employee and customer satisfaction. Research shows the correlation coefficient to be in the order of 70–80 per cent. With an engaged staff on board, the transformation journey has a greater chance of heading in the right direction and reaching its goal.

Part II

Scoping the LSS Transformation Journey

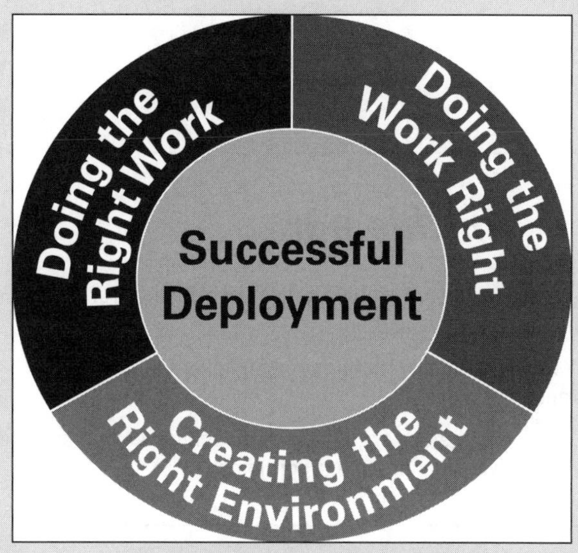

For some online extras about lean six sigma business transformation, head online and visit www.dummies.com/extras/lssbusinesstransformation.

In this part . . .

- Identify the longer-term objectives of business transformation and how to achieve them.
- Create a Capability Maturity road map for your transformation.
- Get wise to the system, actions and techniques that are needed to effectively manage the programme.

Chapter 4

Defining Your Transformation Objectives

In This Chapter

- Understanding the need for transformation
- Identifying your breakthrough objectives
- Putting together a Transformation Charter

In transforming an organisation, you're looking to achieve something specific and substantial. This transformation can mean switching focus from one market sector to another, entering an entirely new market, streamlining the organisation, or performing at a previously unprecedented level.

Throughout this book we focus on business transformation through Lean Six Sigma. Whilst this focus doesn't preclude any of the above types of transformation, it does tend to focus effort on transforming business *performance* in some meaningful way. The best starting point is to have one clear corporate objective (or at most a couple) that is fundamental to sustained future success. That objective has to be established with and agreed among key stakeholders; it also has to be set out in an unambiguous way to communicate the key points to everyone involved in the transformation process. The *Transformation Charter* is an appropriate way to communicate this information (see the later section 'Creating a Transformation Charter' for more details). This chapter looks at how to develop and define the key transformation objectives.

Identifying Your Need

You've identified that you need to make a substantial change in your organisation. Very often (but not always) the desire for business transformation stems from the need to address a 'burning platform' (that is, urgent) issue, examples of which include:

- Unacceptable levels of customer churn – with the associated high cost of acquiring new customers to replace those leaving

- Systemically low efficiency or reducing profit margins
- Interventions by industry regulators

You don't have to be facing a problem of crisis proportions to make the need for a transformation surface, however. Other reasons include:

- The need to create competitive advantage through sustained levels of efficiency or customer satisfaction
- Changes in technology enabling radically new and different business models
- New market opportunities (in new locations or market sectors, for example)

Maybe a combination of opportunities and problems is what's driving your need for a business transformation. Whatever your motivation for seeking a transformation, it needs to tie into the strategic objectives of your organisation.

Spotting longer-term corporate objectives

The overarching strategic objectives of your organisation may define your transformation objective. Although the corporate objectives are likely to be at too high a level to form transformation objectives themselves, they can help to identify where transformation is required.

Start by listing the core longer-term objectives that define the approach to business over the next few years. The trick is to keep these objectives simple, balanced, yet comprehensive – written in a way that does not prescribe how they are to be achieved.

Management guru Peter Drucker suggests that corporate objectives should cover eight key areas:

- **Market standing** – Market share, customer satisfaction, product range
- **Innovation** – New products, better processes, use of technology
- **Productivity** – Optimum use of resources, focus on core activities
- **Physical and financial resources** – Factories, business locations, finance, supplies
- **Profitability** – Level of profit, rates of return on investment
- **Management** – Management structure, promotion and development

- **Employees** – Organisational structure, employee relations
- **Public responsibility** – Compliance with laws, social and ethical behaviour

Hewlett-Packard provides a good example of corporate objectives:

- Customer loyalty

  We earn customer respect and loyalty by consistently providing the highest quality and value.

- Profit

  We achieve sufficient profit to finance growth, create value for our shareholders, and achieve our corporate objectives.

- Growth

  We recognize and seize opportunities for growth that build upon our strengths and competencies.

- Market leadership

  We lead in the marketplace by developing and delivering useful and innovative products, services and solutions.

- Commitment to employees

  We demonstrate our commitment to employees by promoting and rewarding based on performance and by creating a work environment that reflects our values.

- Leadership capability

  We develop leaders at all levels who achieve business results, exemplify our values and lead us to grow and win.

  Global citizenship

  We fulfil our responsibility to society by being an economic, intellectual and social asset to each country and community where we do business.

These are Hewlett-Packard's corporate objectives, not its transformation objectives. However, they may help identify where transformation may be appropriate. Think about your own organisation and answer these questions:

- Is the company delivering best-in-class levels of customer satisfaction? Are customers loyal to the business? Is customer churn a problem?
- Is the current profit level generated sufficient to meet the expectations of shareholders or to finance the desired future growth of the business?

- Is the current rate of growth adequate to sustain and grow market share?
- Are regulatory bodies constantly challenging the company's business standards and practices?

If your answers suggest that one or more corporate objectives are not being met, then you're potentially facing a burning platform issue that may demand business transformation.

While corporate objectives should be regularly reviewed and refined, they should remain consistent over several years. It may be appropriate to add, modify or remove one or two objectives in any given year, but, if effective, most will remain unaltered for several years at a time.

Corporate objectives are those that relate to the business as a whole. They're usually set by the Board or top management of the business and they provide the focus for setting more detailed objectives for the main activities of the business.

Factors that can influence these objectives include:

- Age of the organisation
- Size and legal status of the organisation
- Ownership (privately owned; stock exchange quoted)
- Views of owners and managers
- Market conditions
- Legislation
- State of the economy
- Competition
- Risk and attitude to risk
- Corporate culture
- Political factors
- Social attitudes

Working out corporate objectives

The devil is in the detail, and the next level of objectives needs to be SMARTer:

- **S**pecific – The objectives should state what is to be achieved.
- **M**easurable – The results should be capable of being reliably and consistently measured.

- Achievable – The proposed strategy may be stretching, but should nonetheless be capable of being realised.
- Realistic – Any objective should be relevant and meaningful to the organisation.
- Time-bound – A deadline should be set for the achievement of the objectives.

The business-level objectives should relate more specifically to the organisation's current and next financial year, rather than the longer term. Taking Hewlett-Packard's objectives from the preceding section, these could be developed along the following lines:

- ***Customer loyalty:*** to be recognised this year as number one in our industry sector in the survey of customer satisfaction.
- ***Profit:*** to achieve a 12 per cent increase in earnings per share before taxes (and dividends).
- ***Growth:*** to increase the organisation's turnover to £105m in the next financial year.
- ***Market leadership:*** to launch our next generation of online training products in the European marketplace by November of this year.
- ***Employees:*** to resolve the issues that emerged in last year's Employee Satisfaction Survey by raising the Employee Motivation Index into the first quartile amongst those in the survey reference group.

Some of these corporate objectives will be more challenging than others; some may be critical to the continued existence of the organisation, others may be more routine, continuing to develop success at its natural pace.

You now need to distinguish breakthrough objectives from operational day-to-day objectives. Breakthrough objectives are those that, when executed, will transform the business. They're distinguished from day-to-day objectives that, when executed well, simply deliver good but otherwise normal operational performance. Consider whether any of the corporate objectives you identify are addressing a burning platform issue like those listed in the 'Identifying Your Need' section earlier in this chapter.

Linking with breakthrough objectives

At this stage you should now have two lists of objectives:

- Potential breakthrough objectives – which should include any burning platform issues
- Day-to-day operational objectives

Hold the second set for now and concentrate on your first list. You now need to prioritise those objectives to identify the vital few. From these, you will in due course establish your breakthrough objective(s).

Focusing on the Vital Few Breakthrough Objectives

You'll probably identify several possible breakthrough objectives – after all, you've more than one corporate objective. Success in improving your profit margins can require dramatic improvement in your customer service, which in turn may require a major change in the way your company is organised, and so on. Your possible breakthrough objectives are likely to be interconnected so, to avoid being overwhelmed with detail, try to focus on just the few drivers of success.

To achieve this focus:

- Identify any objectives or details that are outside the scope of the planned transformation
- Group together overlapping or related objectives
- Understand any cause–effect relationships between the objectives (to confirm which are fundamental)

Once you've focused on these points, you can identify these fundamental objectives as the vital few breakthrough objectives. You can then select the particular objective (or objectives) for the proposed transformation.

Looking at who should be involved

In going through the transformation process, you need to involve a wide range of people:

- Senior executives with leadership responsibility.
- Individuals with relevant expertise or a particular interest in the outcome.

- Capable change managers to guide the process. Facilitators need to focus on keeping things on track rather than being responsible for the content. Good facilitators will involve everyone and bring out the best from the team whilst ensuring a good outcome.

A workshop or series of workshops is most appropriate. Senior management has to buy in to and own the outcome, so involving them directly in workshops is highly desirable. Doing some preparatory work with a group of people working for senior management first may, however, be a good idea.

The next sections look at this process step by step.

Step One: Scoping

In this step, the possible transformation objectives, activities and elements are brainstormed by the workshop group, and the outcomes are discussed and reviewed. The aim of the scoping workshop is to establish what is definitely going to be part of the transformation effort – and what is not.

Use Rudyard Kipling's honest serving-men below to focus your brainstorming session:

I keep six honest serving-men
(They taught me all I knew);
Their names are What and Why and When,
And How and Where and Who.

Your questions may cover:

- The customer and market segments
- The products and services
- The processes involved
- The people affected
- The computer systems involved
- The type and extent of the results in improvement that are expected

You can use a simple Lean Six Sigma tool to help identify what you will and won't include in your transformation process – the 'In Frame/Out of Frame' tool (see Figure 4-1).

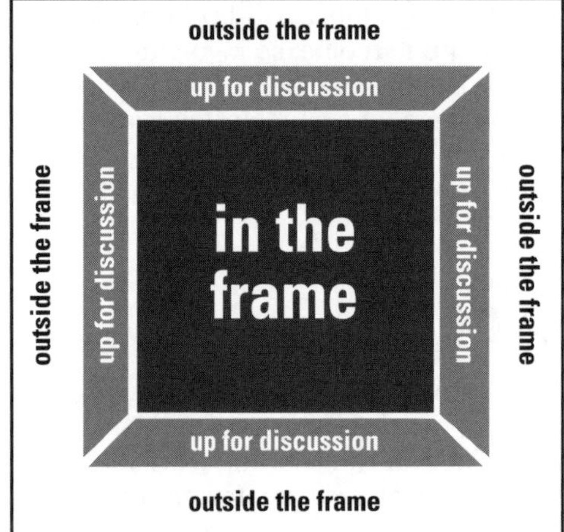

Figure 4-1: The In Frame/Out of Frame tool.

Using the In Frame/Out of Frame tool is a straightforward process. Follow these steps:

1. **Draw a picture frame, resembling the one shown in Figure 4-1, on a flipchart.**
2. **Brainstorm the various issues and write each one on a sticky note.**
3. **Stick the issues in what appear to be the most appropriate positions.**
4. **Review and discuss unresolved issues – essentially, those items that are on the 'frame'.**
5. **Make a decision on each of these issues that needs clarification and then reposition them individually either inside or outside the frame.**

The workshop team should now have a list of agreed-upon issues to address in the proposed transformation. The next step is to structure these issues and turn them into specific transformation objectives.

While no limit exists on the number of items you should have left in the frame, limiting them to a workable number makes sense. Before going on to Step Two, go through the sticky notes again and eliminate any duplication, combining any issues that significantly overlap.

Step Two: Grouping

Now that you've established what's in the frame, you need to review and structure that information. The Affinity Diagram (see Figure 4-2) is a useful Lean Six Sigma tool for doing so.

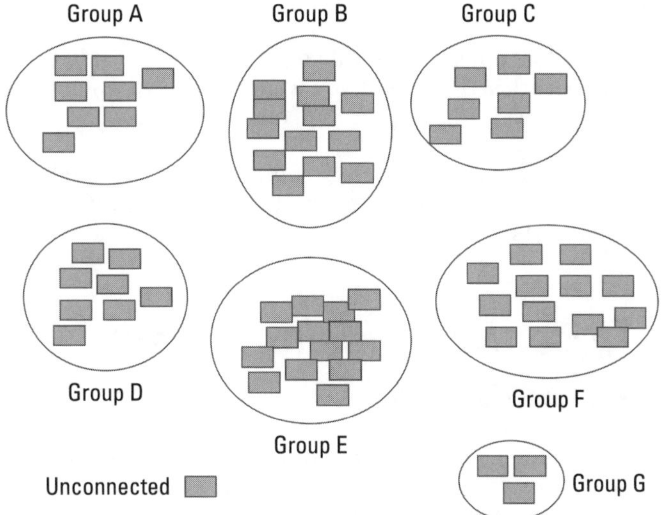

Figure 4-2: The Affinity Diagram.

Ask participants to read the sticky notes placed 'in the frame' in Step One and then to consider whether any other issues need to be added.

When all conceivable issues are written on sticky notes, remove them from the In Frame/Out of Frame diagram and stick them on the wall. Now ask everyone, simultaneously and in silence, to move the sticky notes around, putting them into what they perceive to be groups or clusters of similar ideas or themes.

Additional sticky notes can be written at any time. Also, an idea may appear more than once and in different clusters.

The facilitator will determine when it's appropriate to break the silence. Almost certainly particular sticky notes will need clarifying and the thoughts behind emerging clusters may need discussing. The facilitator will also determine when it's appropriate to move to the next activity in this step. Get the workshop participants to agree on a definition or description for each of the clusters and write them down on sticky notes of a different colour. These definitions or descriptions are termed 'headers'. Using the headers (together with the associated individual sticky notes), get participants to draft associated transformation objectives.

Write these transformation objectives on individual sticky notes (using suitable names for them) and repeat the Affinity Diagram process until you have a small number of groups of objectives.

Merge the individual objectives within each group into a single overarching objective that best describes what you want to achieve. Each of these grouped objectives could now be a breakthrough objective in itself.

You still need to decide which of these potential breakthrough objectives is (are) to become the vital breakthrough objective(s) on which to focus your improvement efforts. Two more steps will get you there.

Step Three: Recognising causal interrelationships

Now you have a small number of potential breakthrough objectives. These potential objectives are probably interrelated, and if you can identify how they're linked you can establish whether some are secondary to others – that is, they're causally linked – or whether in essence they're parallel objectives.

For example:

- **Causal linkage:** 'Improve efficiency by 20 per cent p.a.' and 'Reduce waste by 40 per cent' are causally connected; reducing waste will inevitably contribute to improving efficiency.
- **Parallel objectives:** 'Re-focus the company to become recognised primarily as a services company (rather than a hardware vendor)' and 'Establish the talent management required to support our re-aligned business' are both necessary for the sustained success of a company whose overarching strategic objective is to switch from being a hardware manufacturer to a professional services company in the IT industry. The first is a breakthrough objective with a marketing focus; the second is a breakthrough objective with a human resources focus.

The Interrelationship Diagram (see Figure 4-3) is a useful Lean Six Sigma tool for identifying causal relationships between your potential breakthrough objectives.

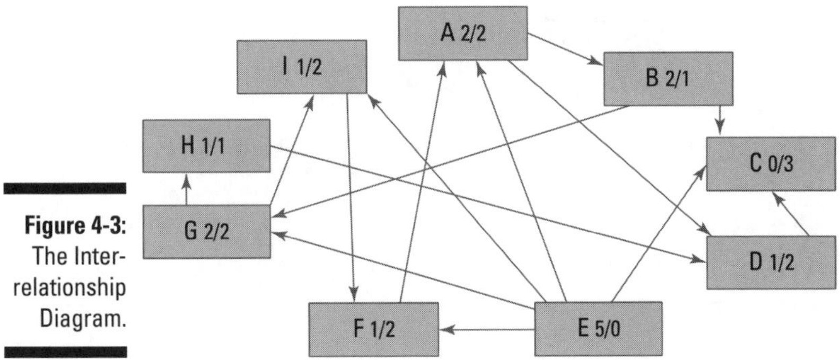

Figure 4-3: The Interrelationship Diagram.

Follow these steps:

1. **Write the headers for the individual potential breakthrough objectives on separate sticky notes and place them in a circle on a flipchart.**
2. **Look at the stickers in pairs to determine whether a relationship exists.** For example, if the objectives are labelled A, B, C, D and E, you start with A and look at AB, AC, AD and AE. Next you move on to B and look at BA, BC, BD, BE, and so on.
3. **Draw a line connecting two headers if you spot a relationship between them.**
4. **Determine which of the connected objectives logically drives the other.** Now turn the connecting line into an arrow by drawing an arrowhead on it that points towards the objective which is affected by the achievement of the other objective. Repeat this process for all of the objectives.
5. **Count the 'arrows out' and the 'arrows in' for each objective.** The objective with the most arrows leading from it is the one on which you need to focus. The other objectives are in essence subsidiary to the one you have selected. You should also be able to identify objectives that, although loosely related to others, are parallel rather than subsidiary.

Step Four: Selecting your transformation objective

You are now in a position to decide on the focus of your transformation efforts. You need to step back and look at the output pattern of your Interrelationship Diagram (see Figure 4-4).

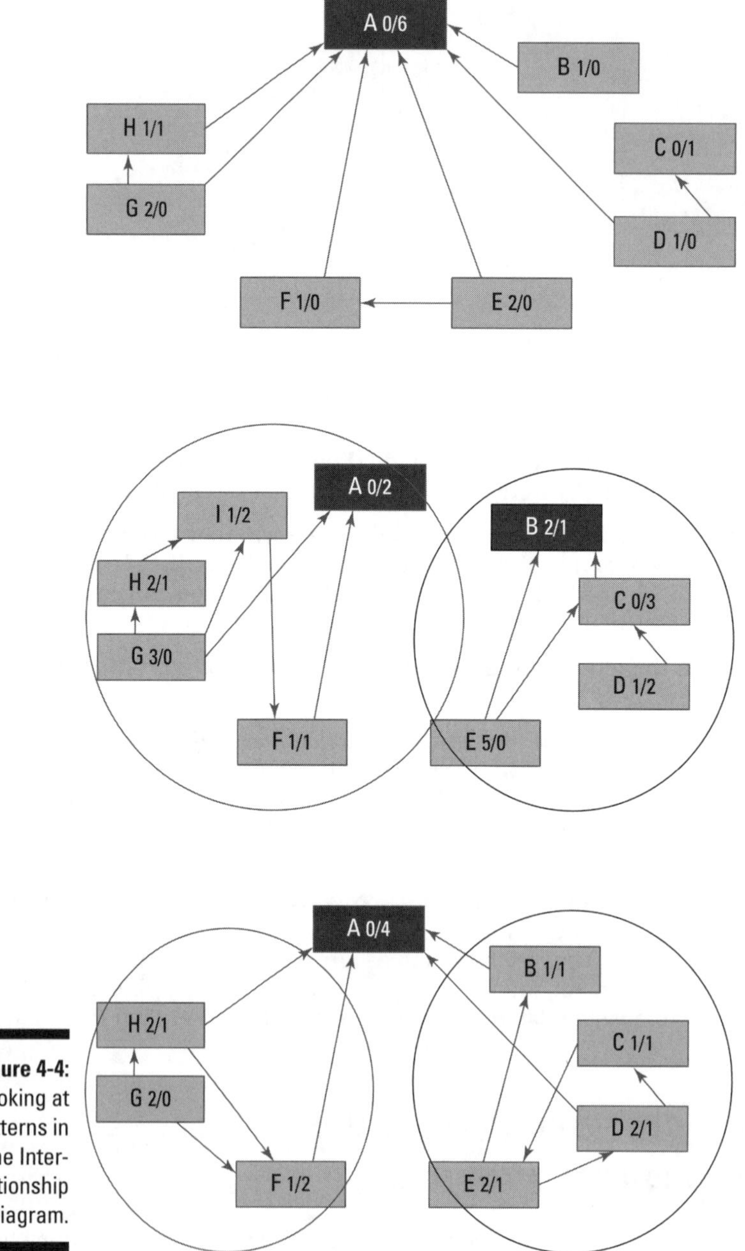

Figure 4-4: Looking at patterns in the Interrelationship Diagram.

- If you see one clear overarching objective to which all others are subsidiary – but without those others being particularly interlinked amongst themselves – select this one as your single transformation objective.
- If you see a pattern in which no single clear overarching objective is obvious but two or more clusters of interlinked objectives are evident, you may have more than one single focus for your transformation efforts.
- If you see a combination of these two patterns (one overarching objective and other objectives effectively split into distinct groups, interdependent within the groups but not between them), consider establishing separate workstreams for transformation but with each subsidiary to the overarching transformation objective.

Transformation workstreams

If you selected more than one single breakthrough objective that you need to address, it makes sense to establish parallel (but interconnected) workstreams. For the IT company introduced in Step Three, for example, its overall breakthrough objective might be: 'To transition from an engineering company focused primarily on hardware manufacturing to a marketing-focused professional IT services company'. The workstreams for these two breakthrough objectives could be:

- **Operational capability:** Developing the business processes required to cost-effectively run the new business.
- **Culture:** Shaping a new culture consistent with the marketing rather than engineering focus of the new organisation.
- **Talent management:** Locating the right people to work in the new company, and providing support for current employees who may not be able to make the transition.

If you've selected just one overarching breakthrough objective, then just a single transformation workstream may be necessary.

Limit the number of separate transformation workstreams to three at the most. You will be concentrating your strategy deployment efforts from the workstream level (see Chapter 9) so having more than three parallel breakthrough objectives at any one time is likely to prove unmanageable in practice.

Creating a Transformation Charter

You now have your proposed workstreams and their associated transformation objectives. Now you need to ensure that everyone sees those objectives in the same way. Having everybody singing from the same hymn sheet is important with any major project; for a key transformation programme it's absolutely vital. The *Transformation Charter* (sometimes also called an 'A3') is a very simple tool for making sure that everyone involved in the transformation understands it.

Ensuring it's a living document

The Transformation Charter is a living document; it changes and develops in line with the programme. Version control will therefore be important. The first draft of your Transformation Charter may be a little fuzzy on the details and subject to confirmation, quantification and refinement. This first draft must be prepared right at the start of the transformation process.

If you have more than one workstream, consider having a summary overall Transformation Charter, together with more detailed subsidiary charters for each workstream. It isn't necessary for the Transformation Charter to repeat details covered in the individual workstream charters; however, it will need to show how the workstreams are planned to collectively deliver the overall transformation objective, who is leading each workstream and, in due course, how they're progressing.

Breaking down the contents

Let's consider the contents of a Transformation Charter for an individual workstream.

Figure 4-5 shows an example Transformation Charter and illustrates the key elements. The Charter obviously starts with the transformation objective itself – known here as the Transformation Statement – and then builds on this to become the summary document communicating the purpose and plan for the transformation effort. The core contents of the Transformation Charter are:

- The name of the transformation programme
- The transformation vision
- The Transformation Statement
- Associated or collateral objectives
- Transformation outcome
- Business case

- Key people and their responsibilities
- Time plan

Let's look at each of these in turn.

Transformation Charter: Project Cloud.		**Version 1.1 April 2014**
Vision: By two years' time we will have become an organisation selling, servicing and supporting data management solutions rather than one manufacturing and supplying data management hardware. We will become mark eting-led rather than engineering-led.		
Key Objectives: 1. To regain a leading position in the IT industry 2. To become much more customer centric 3. To restore and enhance our profit margins and shareholder value		
Business Case: There has been a rapid and fundamental change in our market place with declining margins for our hardware products. This contrasts with increasing customer demand for tailored data management solutions which may not even require them to directly operate or own the supporting hardware. Unless we respond to these changes our profit margins will continue to erode and we risk losing our leading position in the data management market.		
Scope:		
In Scope Acme Data Management Corp.	**Out of Scope** All other parts of the Acme Group	
Work-streams:		
1. Business Processes To develop those core processes needed to support a professional solutions and support business, whilst improving those required to support the current manufacturing and sales operations during the transition	2. Organisational Culture To re-focus our culture on the customer and on service excellence rather than on engineering excellence - but without compromising product quality	3. Talent Management To recruit and develop the people and skills we will require in our future business – with a focus on the retraining and development of our existing staff to the fullest possible extent, and with a caring approach to those other individuals who may be out-placed
Key people and roles: • Executive Sponsor: John Carey • Transformation Programme Director: Martin Cole • Head of Programme Office: Angela Marshall • Work-stream Leaders: o Business Processes: Jean Hollande o Organisational Culture: Jan vandenBroek o Talent Management: Lucy Schmidt • Associated Continuous Improv ement Programme: Kim Reilly		
Key Milestones: April 2014: Acceptance of 9th MTP; Kick-off of Transformation programme July 2014: xxxxx Sept 2014: xxxxx December 2014: xxxxx July 2015: xxxxxx December 2015: xxxxxx July 2016: xxxxx March 2017: New Business fully operational.		

Figure 4-5: Example Transformation Charter.

Name of the transformation programme

This name may be a code name, for example 'Fit for the Future' or 'Programme Orange', or it may be more suggestive of the nature of the programme, for example 'Strategic Waste Reduction'.

If the existence of the programme is intended to be confidential for a period of time, then a code name is more appropriate than something descriptive. But once the programme is launched, a name that conveys its intent will be easier to communicate. In all cases, the programme name needs to fit the culture and style of the organisation.

Transformation vision

This is a clear statement about the desired outcome of the transformation effort. The statement needs to identify at least some of the elements that need to be changed. Visions secure commitment and support by helping people understand what needs to be done and why. Below are some example visions:

> 'Our company will remain customer focused but with a new marketing-led culture. Our primary products will be the added-value IT services we deliver and we will no longer be dependent on sales of hardware products for the majority of our revenue.'
>
> 'Waste will largely be a thing of the past. We will dominate our market through our ability to deliver products and services that are essentially defect and waste free and at a cost that no competitor can even approach, let alone match.'
>
> 'Number one in every customer satisfaction survey, everywhere, all the time.'
>
> 'Not a penny in regulatory fines. We will know that we are compliant in all we do, without bureaucracy.'
>
> 'By next year and every year thereafter we will have the best profit margin in the industry, without compromising in any way.'

Consider the different perspectives of the organisation, its customers and employees, and other relevant stakeholders. The vision should be inspiring to both them and, in particular, to everyone working on the transformation effort.

You will have the opportunity to further clarify the vision when you work on the transformation statement and the business case. The vision aims to appeal to hearts and minds rather than being factual and specific.

Transformation Statement

This is a brief description that answers the question, 'What is this programme seeking to achieve?' Examples are:

- Reducing waste by 80 per cent year on year over the next five years
- Delivering the best customer service over the next two years

Associated or collateral objectives

This is simply a statement describing any other objectives directly associated with the main transformation objective. To avoid waffle and reduce the possibility of misinterpretation, try to describe each objective in fewer than15 words (this also applies to the main transformation objective).

Transformation outcome

Your Transformation Charter needs to spell out the desired outcome of the transformation process; for example:

- By January 2015, Acme plc will be delivering not less than 22 per cent net margin.
- JC Smith Ltd will secure an average increase of 70 per cent based on all customer feedback during the next financial year.

Business case

This statement should answer the questions, 'Why is the organisation carrying out this transformation process?' and 'Why now?' Example responses are:

- Without a sustained world-class level of customer satisfaction we will not be able to gain the profit margins needed to finance our planned business growth.
- Our business strategy calls for cost leadership; to secure and retain this we need to reduce the waste in our business processes by 80 per cent year on year, every year, for the foreseeable future.

Try to make your business case statement succinct. This is a tougher goal than the 15 words demanded in the transformation statement because the 'why' questions demand both context and explanation; nevertheless, keeping it to 25 words or thereabouts should be your aim. If more than one reason for the transformation exists, then try to identify the most important ones and then describe the others as secondary or collateral reasons.

Key people and their responsibilities

Draw up a list of the individuals responsible for each of the key roles in the transformation programme. For example:

- **The transformation sponsor:** This is likely to be the chief executive or another member of the senior leadership team.
- **The programme director:** This will be a senior manager who may be seconded full- or part-time to manage the operational aspects of the transformation programme. For a Lean Six Sigma transformation, consider appointing a senior manager who is already an effective Lean Six Sigma practitioner or champion. In larger organisations, this person should be a Black Belt or Master Black Belt; that is, they are already responsible for leading the deployment of the current Lean Six Sigma programme in the company.
- **Key members of the programme management office:** You need to establish a small programme office staffed by individuals seconded from within the organisation. This office should include people with relevant project management experience and, ideally, expertise in Lean Six Sigma. Choose individuals who are well-respected and know how to get things done in your organisation.

Time plan

You need to create a detailed plan outlining the key phases of the transformation and the relevant milestones and deadlines. Consider using a Gantt Chart (see Figure 4-6) to help you structure this plan.

1. IT Industry: By two years' time we will have become an organisation selling, servicing and supporting data management solutions rather than one manufacturing and supplying data management hardware. We will become marketing-led rather than engineering-led.

2. Consumer Products Manufacturer: Over the period of our current three year MTP (medium term plan) we will increase our market share from 12% to 17% through the introduction and development of new third-party distribution channels to supplement our current direct ones.

3. Banking Group: We will restore the reputation of our organisation by putting our customers back at the core focus of all our activities. This is where they should always have been had we not forgotten that before the recent financial crisis.

Figure 4-6: An example Gantt Chart.

You may also want to use a multi-generation plan. You need to include milestones covering:

- The holding position based on current processes and capabilities of the organisation.
- The introduction of the new breakthrough capability in an initial pilot/'proof of concept 'phase.
- The completion of the full transformation throughout the organisation.

Chapter 5

Assessing Readiness for Transformation

In This Chapter

- Identifying your business strategy
- Considering your strategic plan
- Getting to grips with the capability maturity road map

This chapter discusses the importance of assessing whether your organisation is ready to undertake a major transformation and how to undertake that assessment. We consider various ways you can validate that your strategy is likely to be effective, robust and comprehensive – which will all be required for an effective transformation. These include using capability maturity models and we look at how these can be used not only for this purpose before starting on the transformation journey but also as that journey progresses.

Assuring an Appropriate Business Strategy

Having an appropriate business strategy is a prerequisite to an effective transformation programme. Our approach to successful Lean Six Sigma deployment involves:

- Doing the right work
- Doing the work right
- Creating the right environment

Figure 5-1 demonstrates these key considerations for effective deployment of Lean Six Sigma.

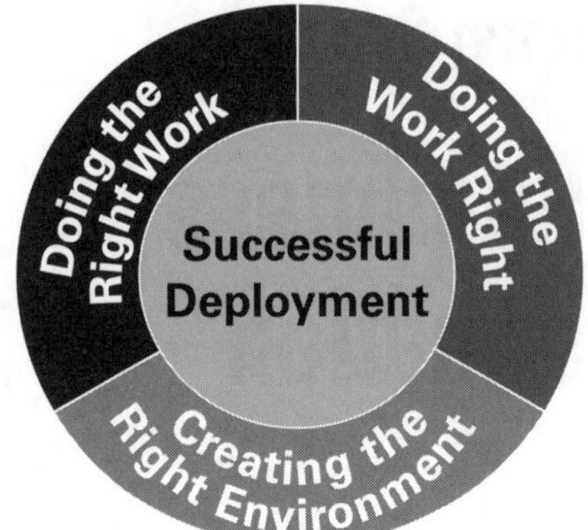

Figure 5-1: Effective deployment of Lean Six Sigma.

Applied to transformation these points can be read as:

- Having the right strategy
- Deploying the strategy right
- Creating the right environment

Figure 5-2 demonstrates effective deployment of transformation.

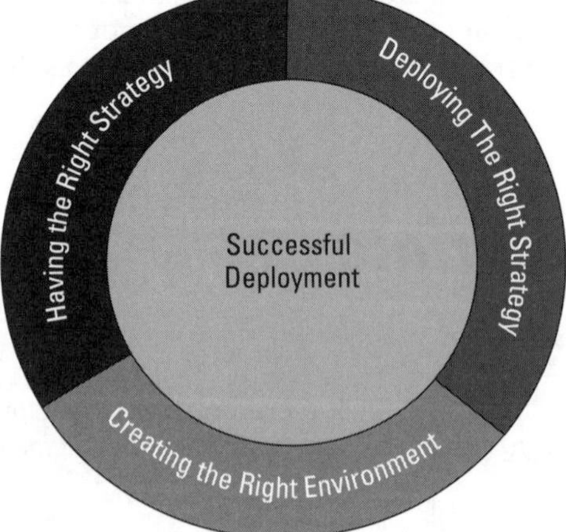

Figure 5-2: Effective deployment of transformation.

This book isn't focused on creating or developing strategy, as that should be a prerequisite of organisational transformation. However, covering the ways in which you can verify whether or not a given strategy is likely to be appropriate will be useful. While no guarantees exist that any given strategy will be successful, you can apply certain tests that will, at the very least, screen out inappropriate or incomplete strategies or those involving an unacceptable level of risk.

Identifying your strategy

The typical key components of a strategic plan include an understanding of an entity's vision, mission, values and strategies. In a commercial organisation a vision statement or a mission statement may encapsulate the vision and mission.

- *Vision* outlines what the organisation wants to be or how it wants the world in which it operates to be.
- *Mission* defines the fundamental purpose of the organisation, succinctly describing why it exists and what it does to achieve its vision.
- *Values* are beliefs that are shared among the stakeholders of an organisation.
- *Strategy* is the means by which the mission and vision are to be achieved.

An organisation's strategy describes *how* it intends to achieve its mission and vision and create value for its stakeholders (including shareholders for a commercial business), customers, and society at large. Its mission is the *what* it attends to achieve; its vision is *where* it wants to be.

For any strategy to be effective it must be appropriate, comprehensive, and well described and articulated; it should also be robust in relation to future external developments. You can reasonably test for each of these requirements and validate how well your strategy meets them.

For a strategy to be *appropriate*, it needs to take proper account of the external business and economic environment and have a real understanding of the competitive landscape. It must also realistically address the internal environment; that is, whether those in the organisation are capable of operating, growing, and developing together within the resource constraints that define and limit options. An effective strategy needs to be both realistic and stretching.

For a strategy to be *comprehensive*, it must be holistic and address all reasonable internal and external perspectives. It cannot take the form of just a financial plan for revenue and profit growth nor for products and services; nor can it simply focus on a core operational process value stream or on the organisation's employees. It has to cover all of these and more, including addressing the perspectives of key external stakeholders such as customers, suppliers and other business partners, competitors, and regulators – as well as the organisation's owners or shareholders. And all of these perspectives need to be joined up without gaps or undue overlaps.

Testing and validating your strategy

A *well described and articulated* strategy requires it to be effectively quantified and documented. It should be capable of being simply demonstrated, visually as well as in words, and the numbers need to be credible and to add up. A *robust* strategy should be capable of continuing to be deployed even if significant changes occur in the external and competitive environment. It should be able to address a range of foreseeable different scenarios.

Of course, some overlap exists between these requirements, so unsurprisingly the tools available to test and validate your strategy may well cover more than one of them. These tools include:

- **Strategy maps:** These enable you to visualise the strategy. They also show the cause-and-effect relationships amongst the components of an organisation's strategy.
- **Balanced scorecard:** This ensures that a holistic approach is taken from four perspectives: 'financial', 'customer', internal processes', and 'learning and growth'. The balanced scorecard also requires quantification because the outcomes of appropriate metrics and their associated targets link to strategic activities across it.
- **Scenario planning:** This tests that the strategy is robust in relation to a reasonable range of evolving circumstances.
- **Capability/maturity assessment and road map:** These test that the strategy is realistic and meaningful.
- **DRIVE model:** This overall methodology explicitly incorporates the testing and validation of strategy.

We cover each of these tools in more detail in the following sections and later in this chapter.

Strategy maps

You use *strategy maps* to ensure that your strategy is balanced; they allow you to see how operational plans and initiatives are linked and work toward achieving your strategic objectives. In the example shown in Figure 5-3, a 'swimlane' approach is taken to show how the various elements populate the four different scorecard perspectives (for example, ERP system in 'Learning and Growth', faster service in 'Customer').

Clearly all of the various elements must connect through to the desired strategic goal, otherwise any loose ends will demonstrate that the strategy is incomplete or not fully thought through. Likewise, each individual path must be logical and credible. Furthermore, the viewer can reasonably question whether further paths are necessary for the strategy to be realised.

This approach is highly visual and if a strategy cannot reasonably be pictured in this way, there's likely to be something wrong or incomplete about it. The strategy map doesn't guarantee that the strategy is appropriate, but it does provide a simple test for checking comprehensiveness and articulation; however, it does not test for quantification.

Figure 5-3: Example strategy map.

Draw a strategy map for all of your key strategies, making sure it's comprehensive and illustrates all relevant linkages.

The balanced scorecard

Still considering appropriateness and comprehensiveness, an effective strategy must cover all bases as they relate to stakeholders and competitors. You need to consider what the strategy will deliver to them – and how it will do so.

One way of checking that your organisation's strategy covers all bases is to view it through the perspective of a balanced scorecard, as illustrated in Figure 5-4. A *balanced scorecard* is a means of presenting a holistic set of performance measures for the organisation. In its most typical configuration it has four perspectives, or quadrants:

- **Financial:** It encourages the identification of a few relevant high-level financial measures. It should answer the question, 'How do we look to shareholders?'
- **Customer:** It encourages the identification of measures that answer the question, 'How do customers see us?'
- **Internal business processes:** It encourages the identification of measures that answer the question, 'What must we excel at?'
- **Learning and growth:** It encourages the identification of measures that answer the question, 'How can we continue to improve, create value, and innovate?'

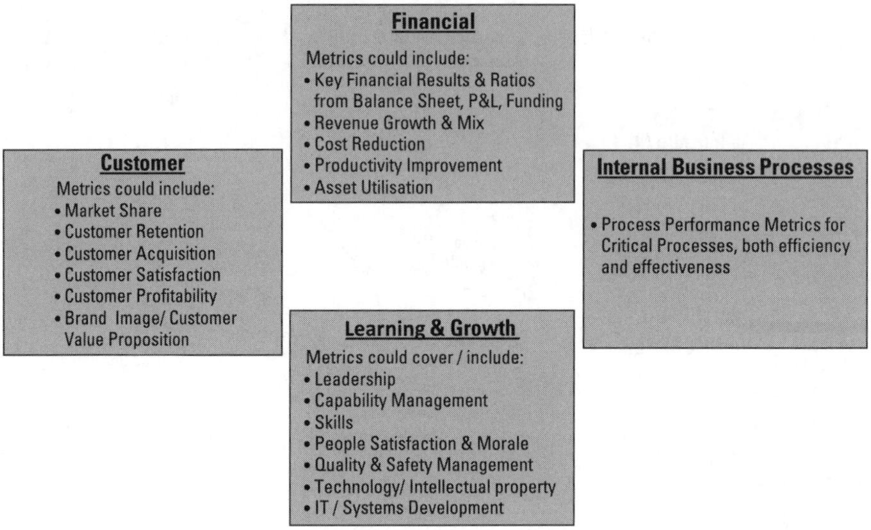

Figure 5-4: The balanced scorecard.

You can also impose a strategy map over the balanced scorecard quadrants to show how the individual metrics are interrelated and delivered using the strategy in question. Thus, from the *financial* perspective, you look at things through the eyes of the organisation's owners and investors. What has the strategy got to deliver to them in return for their investment? From the *customer* perspective, you look at the impact on other external stakeholders. Although nominally the customer quadrant, it can also encompass other stakeholders such as regulatory bodies. Accordingly it looks at the strategy from their perspectives and asks what value it will deliver to them. Competition is also considered in this quadrant because market share and account penetration are typical outcomes targeted and reported here.

The internal perspective is addressed in the *internal business processes* quadrant. As it is representative of core operational issues, process effectiveness and efficiency are reviewed. Reviewing these issues will also reveal how the organisation's processes are seen by employees and suppliers.

The *learning and growth* perspective essentially covers the impact of investment in the organisation's staff and systems. This can also include the impact of investment in Lean Six Sigma – showing the number of people trained and certified – as well as people development more generally. Investments in IT systems and technology are also reported in this quadrant.

Taken as a whole, these different quadrants should cover all the different perspectives, stakeholders, and bases. Most commercial organisations typically use this four-quadrant configuration. For public and voluntary sector organisations, the more complex range of stakeholders may require alternative configurations, with additional perspectives identified and separately shown – but the principle remains the same.

Wherever possible, develop and review a suitable balanced scorecard showing the core target metrics tying back to the organisation's strategy. Doing so will soon illustrate whether the strategy is holistic or purely one-dimensional.

If your strategy is holistic, the various metrics shown on the balanced scorecard should exhibit suitable cause-and-effect linkages, which can also be shown as strategy maps across the scorecard. If any loose ends exist, the various elements of your strategy won't all hang together.

To ensure a process of transformation rather than evolutionary change, the strategy must involve stretching goals and objectives. 'No pain, no gain' is certainly true here; the more stretching, the more challenging the strategy will be to resource, and the quicker the changes will need to happen.

Identify the constraints potentially bounding the strategy and consider the degree of challenge they pose. Unless innovative approaches are required to address these constraints, it's quite likely that the strategy is insufficiently stretching. In the opposite direction, you have to be realistic – it's clearly impossible to have more than a 100 per cent market share and you can't move faster than the speed of light!

Assess the constraints from a realistic perspective and consider whether any aspect of the strategy is indeed a step too far or too fast.

Scenario planning

You need to test the robustness of your strategy. The only certain thing you know about the future is that it will be different from what you forecast; what's uncertain, of course, is *how* different it will be. Thus, whatever strategy you've devised must not only be appropriate for the future scenario you forecast but also have a realistic chance of remaining appropriate for the actual future that will, in due course, occur.

The best way to test the robustness of your strategy is to consider a set of alternative scenarios that are likely to be within a reasonable range of what might actually occur.

Consider the possible main factors that proscribe your forecast of the future planning period. These could be economic (growth, unemployment, interest rates and so on), market related (assumptions regarding competitors' behaviour, performance and products), internal (relating to performance or efficiency savings) or others. Assess the likely range these factors could reasonably be expected to demonstrate and develop a suitable set of scenarios, the central one of which should be the most likely planned outcome, with a manageable number of alternative scenarios covering the range of values of the more relevant factors. Assess the extent to which the proposed strategy is likely to require modification and/or risk failure within these scenarios; the less the impact, the more robust the strategy.

Working With Your Strategic Plan

The strategy has to be more than just a high level outline with target outcomes. It needs to be turned into a detailed plan. Not everything in that plan needs to require a breakthrough for the organisation to undertake a transformation, but obviously some things will require it. The trick is to see the wood for the trees – to distinguish clearly those vital few objectives and measures for which breakthrough is required from the many others that don't, and plan for and manage these distinctly differently.

Looking at the components of the strategic plan

The typical key components of a strategic plan include an understanding of an entity's vision, mission, values and strategies.

Organisations sometimes summarise goals and objectives in a mission statement or a vision statement. Others begin with a vision and mission and use them to formulate goals and objectives.

The overall strategic plan is likely to contain key information such as:

- **A baseline statement:** Where the organisation is currently.
- **Assumptions:** Typically including key political, economic and business environmental information and market, regulatory and competitor developments.
- **Scenario details:** Although a single main set of assumptions will probably exist, alternative scenarios may also be included and their impact explored.
- **Subsidiary business plans:** These may include:
    - Financial plan
    - Marketing plan
    - Technology plan
    - Product plan
    - R&D plan
    - Operations plan
    - Admin plan
    - Plans for subsidiary divisions or semi-autonomous units

In the context of this book, the strategic plan may well separately identify the contributions required of any transformation programme from the remaining 'business as usual' development.

The strategic plan is likely to be outcome focused, leaving the details regarding how these outcomes will be achieved to the subsidiary operational plans that will be developed through the strategy deployment process. The individual and component strategies should be clearly visible and well-articulated in the strategic plan, together with how they interrelate, and contribute overall to the achievement of the vision and mission.

Reviewing the strategic plan

We discussed earlier in this chapter how to review an individual strategy. Thus in essence reviewing the strategic plan is the validation of the individual strategies taken as a whole.

If your transformation is to be successful, not only do you need to validate the associated strategy but also ensure that the strategy itself is appropriate within the context of the overall strategic plan. To make this clear, consider a specific example.

Acme Inc. provides a range of facilities management services to its corporate clients across the globe. The company is planning a transformation programme in one of its UK operations because contract renewal with the client involved is likely to require a progressive price reduction of more than 15 per cent over the next three years. The company's overall business plan calls for growth in both overall business and operating profits.

The UK operations strategy for this particular client calls for:

- A successful outcome from negotiations with the client regarding renewal of and extension to the contract in question.
- A transformation programme to progressively drive efficiency improvements, cost and waste reduction to cut operating costs by at least 15 per cent over the next three years.
- A service delivery enhancement programme to sustain or improve the quality of the services delivered under the new contract.

This is, of course, a perfect opportunity for transformation through Lean Six Sigma – addressing the aspects of both service delivery quality and cost.

Acme Inc.'s overall strategic plan includes corporation-wide strategies for the progressive application of common IT platforms across the group and the development of shared service operations spanning multiple clients. A clear potential interdependency exists between the local UK operations strategy and these two corporation-wide strategies. Common IT platforms may impose constraints on the process architectures that operating companies can adopt. Shared service operations can significantly lower unit costs overall but also impact the freedom of local operations to deliver services in line with local client requirements.

In this example a need exists to review the impact of both the local company's strategy and associated aspects in the wider corporate-level strategic plan.

Before embarking on your proposed transformation, ensure that the scope of your strategy review includes not only the directly associated local strategy but also any aspects of the wider corporate strategic plan that could impose constraints or otherwise interrelate with that local strategy.

Defining strategic essentials

The *strategic essentials* are the vital few statements of direction distilled from the strategic plan. They must:

- Be customer focused
- Have a measurable and verifiable end goal
- Summarise the core elements of the strategy
- Cover the medium to long term (three to five years or longer)

An example is: 'Be number 1 or 2 in our chosen markets.'

Associated with these strategic essentials are *critical objectives* – stretching goals containing or spanning multiple processes. These goals should be SMART, cover a period of two to five years, and at this stage in your planning you don't yet know how you'll achieve them.

SMART = Specific, Measureable, Achievable, Realistic and Time-bound!

An example of a critical objective linked to your strategic essential of 'being number 1 or 2 in our chosen markets' is: 'Capture an additional 30 per cent market share from a current base of 37 per cent within the next 5 years.'

From your multi-year plan to deliver the strategic essentials you need to develop a rolling short-term plan (one year), including *focus areas* that are able to be cascaded across and down the organisation; their targeted outcomes will be aligned to the critical objectives, focusing on the vital few.

An example focus area linked to the strategic essential and critical objective above is: 'Develop indirect sales channels from 15 per cent to at least 20 per cent by the end of this coming financial year.'

We cover the strategy deployment process in Chapter 9. For now, suffice it to say that the development and review of strategy are the responsibility of senior management. Senior management identifies and develops the longer-term strategic essentials and critical objectives together with the shorter-term focus areas. It typically does so through a facilitated workshop process. Subsequently the managers in the business as a whole break down the focus areas into aligned short-term processes and related improvements.

Checking Out the Capability Maturity Road Map

You can use a number of different approaches to assessing current capability maturity and mapping out its intended future development. These include using business excellence model frameworks such as those of the European Foundation for Quality Management (EFQM) or the Baldrige Award Framework, which are widely adopted in Europe and North America, respectively; see Figures 5-5 and 5-6.

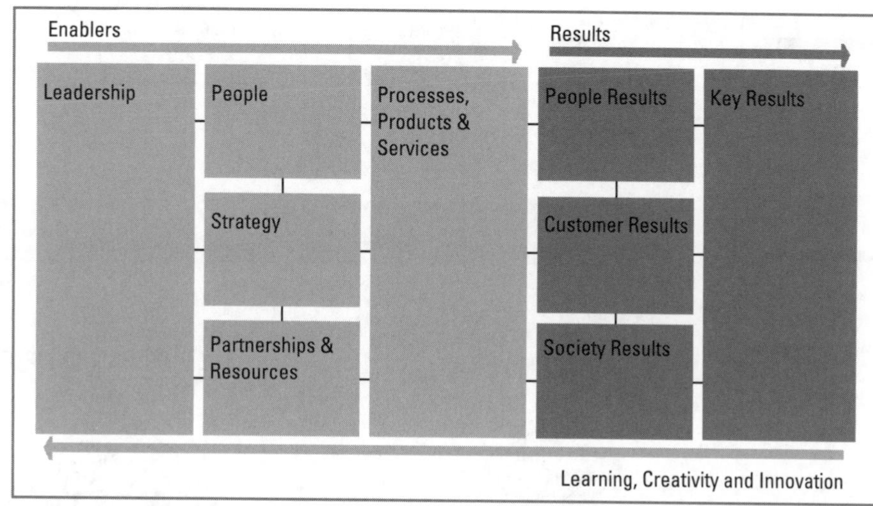

Figure 5-5: EFQM Excellence Model. © European Foundation for Quality Management.

These excellence models were originally developed to support national quality awards to stimulate the widespread development and adoption of world-class best business practices in Europe and the USA in order to increase their global competitiveness. Subsequently, these models become widely adopted as frameworks for organisations to self-assess their own management systems. Neither model is directly prescriptive, but each encourages organisations to carefully consider how they achieve effective leadership, as well as the results obtained from doing so. Developments stemming from such self-assessment approaches include specific capability maturity matrices indicating various levels of performance from the very basic to world class for each of the constituent criteria.

Another internationally recognised framework is the Shingo Prize Model, as illustrated in Figure 5-7.

Figure 5-6: Baldrige Excellence Model. © Baldrige Foundation.

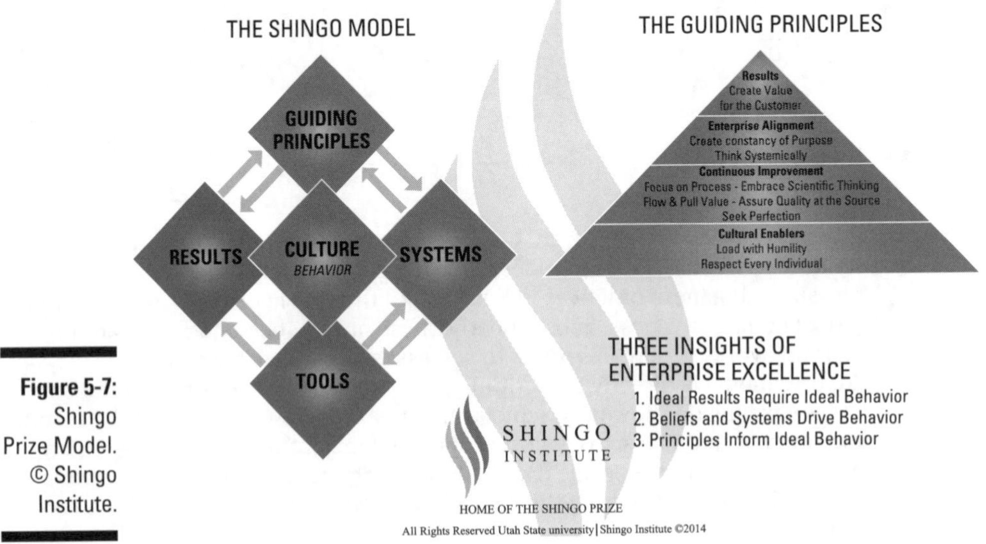

Figure 5-7: Shingo Prize Model. © Shingo Institute.

The Shingo Prize Model™ and Application Guidelines provide a framework for identifying and evaluating the standard for operational excellence. The Shingo Prize Model™ and Application Guidelines generally do not prescribe one single best method, system or route to attaining operational excellence. Principle-driven organisations are clearly viewed as the best paradigm for achieving operational excellence.

The guiding principles of the Shingo Model™ are:

- Respect every individual
- Lead with humility
- Seek perfection
- Assure quality at the source
- Flow and pull value
- Embrace scientific thinking
- Focus on process
- Think systemically
- Create constancy of purpose
- Create value for the customer

In a similar vein to the EFQM and Baldrige models, the Shingo Prize Model™ can be used to develop a capability maturity matrix.

You can also consider custom developing a capability maturity framework building on all of the models above but adapted to the specific requirements of your own organisation's transformation. We've developed such a framework – DRIVE – which aligns with the DRIVE transformation methodology described in Chapter 3. Figure 5-8 illustrates Elements of the DRIVE model and Figure 5-9 the resulting capability maturity model.

- Strategy
  - Business Vision and goal oriented
- Culture
  - Leaders and People Leadership and Ethics
- People
  - People Development, Education and Training, Empowerment and Involvement, Reward and Recognition, Environmental, Health and Safety System awareness
- Partnerships and the Supply Chain
  - Managing and leveraging end to end value streams, collaborating with suppliers and partners for strategic gain
- Enabling Resources and Asset Management
  - Identifying and exploiting the resources needed to deliver the strategic goals including: Finance, IT, Knowledge, Information, Technology. Asset Management including Buildings & Equipment, TPM, Security, Safety
- Processes
  - Operations – Everyday Operational Excellence and Continuous Improvement
- Customer Centricity
  - Customer focus and relationship management, Product and Service development and delivery
- Metrics and Business Results

Figure 5-8: Elements of the DRIVE model. © Catalyst Consulting Ltd.

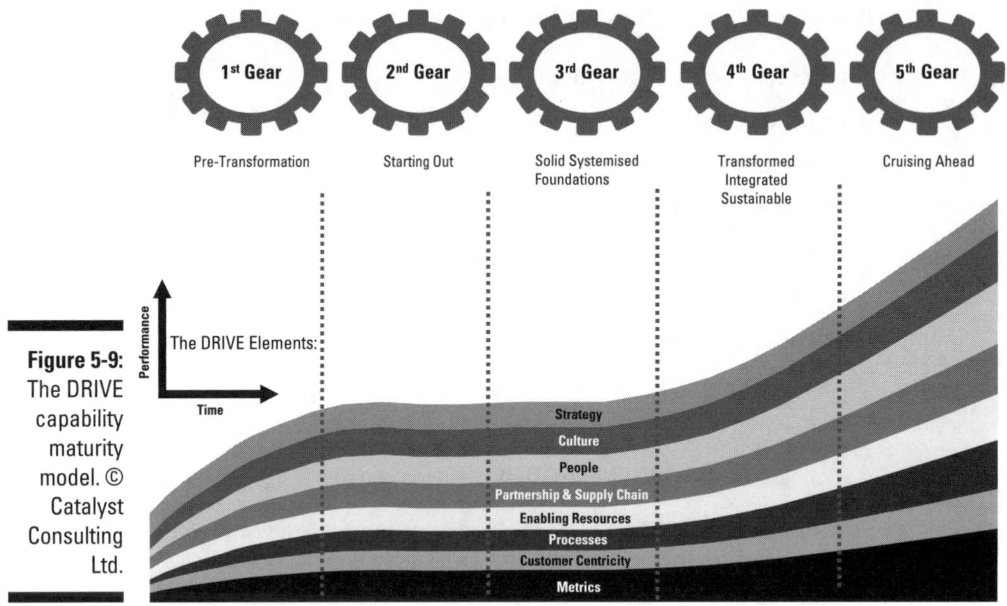

Figure 5-9: The DRIVE capability maturity model. © Catalyst Consulting Ltd.

Recognising that every organisation is different

Every organisation believes itself to be different and many organisations require proof that Lean Six Sigma can work in their own organisation, rather than evidence from other companies. However, in our experience many similarities exist between different organisations; indeed, the similarities may arguably be bigger than the supposed differences in many cases. Such similarities enable the establishment of specific characteristics likely to be present in organisations at different levels of capability maturity that can be entered into a capability maturity matrix.

Based on the DRIVE capability maturity model, Figure 5-10 provides an extract from the capability maturity matrix (showing two of the levels for three of the elements – note that five levels and eight elements exist in total).

You can demonstrate the shape of the organisation in capability maturity terms by highlighting the gear levels that best describe its performance on each pillar, as shown in Figure 5-11.

Acme Inc.'s position overall may be described as driving in third gear; its performance is slightly unbalanced, with three pillars lagging in second gear, while another pillar is ahead, in fourth gear.

Phases	2nd Gear	4th Gear
Pillars	Starting points defined and communicated, SD established, initial skills in place, short term wins achieved	Approaches fully deployed across the organisation, regular monitoring of performance with and able to demonstrate improvement activities, fully integrated with normal business and end to end value streams, CI is way of life,
Processes (Functions & Operations & CI)	The need for management of processes is acknowledged and some skills training has taken place. Mapping of as-is processes is being undertaken in key operational areas and process ownership is in its infancy. CI skills training is starting with pilot projects aimed at consolidating skills and proving methodologies. CI skills are still in the hands of 'experts' brought in to lead projects targetting problem areas.	There is a shift away from functional process ownership to integrated value stream ownership. This is also reflected in the metrics and management processes and in the personal reward system. Process improvement is switching focus from problem solving to CI and value add and everyone in the workforce has sufficient skills to be able to contribute to proactive improvement identification and delivery. Process management extends to all activities including support and management processes
Customer Centricity (Market/Product / Service devt & delivery)	there is a clear understanding of market, customer segments and the need to obtain real Voice of the Customer, although the implementation of this may be in its infancy. At the individual process level there is a move to identy inputs and output linked to suppliers and customers. Customer feedback mechanisms are in place and the end to end processes to identify customer requirements, design, deliver and maintain products and services are being reviewed.	The customer delivery value chains are understood and are being managed/optimised. Customer satisfaction is no longer the goal - exceeding expectations is the only acceptable level. Customers are seen as partners and , together with suppliers, are involved in joint improvement and collaboration projects. Products and services are designed to meet customer needs 'right first time' using methodologies such as Design For Six Sigma and rapid prototyping and customer relationship management is integrated across the supply chain with 'not our problem' a thing of the past. customer centricity is very clearly established in the fabric of the culture.
Metrics & Business Results	Top level goals are set and cascaded via the SD programme and metrics put in place to collect relevant data. There is some loose linkage to scorecards and divisional/site objectives but the focus tends to be on this years achievement rather than trends and targets. Cause effect linkage with process metrics is rudimentary	Visual management is widely used with a large part fo the workforce feeling ownership of the results. Process owners understand the relationship between input, in-process and out put metrics, linked to CTQs. Senior Executive dashboards concentrate on the vital few key metrics with predictor metrics monitored aggressively and corrective action instigated very early. Targets are set at all levels with a check in place the 'the sum of the parts will deliver the whole'. Performance overall is being sustained at a high level in many areas with segmentation used to identify and address weaker areas.

Figure 5-10: Extract from the DRIVE capability maturity matrix. © Catalyst Consulting Ltd.

Each organisation will have its own unique map – in this sense every organisation is indeed different. However, the individual cells of the overall matrix describe individual conditions that may occur in many organisations. Taken together, these two things 'square the circle' – even though every organisation may be different, many similarities exist between organisations.

Assess your own organisation's capability maturity using a suitable model, such as the one described above. Doing so enables you to determine the state from which the organisation is starting out, and whether it's a balanced state.

Putting together the road map

The capability maturity matrix can now model the journey the organisation needs to make to complete its transformation. You can identify the gear levels desired for each pillar at the different stages of the journey.

To ensure a smooth drive, try to broadly align the gear levels for each pillar as your transformation journey changes gear upwards.

Phases	1st Gear	2nd Gear	3rd Gear	4th Gear	Overdrive
Pillars	**Unstructured, tactical, recognise the need**	**Starting points defined and communicated, SD established, initial skills in place, short term wins achieved**	**Plans aligned to strategy, capability assessed, gaps identified, first tranche improvements delivered, ability to support BAU in toto and to launch transformation projects, culture compatible with CI roll-out.**	**Approaches fully deployed across the organisation, regular monitoring of performance with and able to demonstrate improvement activities, fully integrated with normal business and end to end value streams, CI is way of life,**	**Excellence systematically used for market advantage.** **Extended enterprise multiplier, Innovation and breakthrough, Thought leadership, outstanding results, CI culture spans extended enterprise**
Strategy – Business Vision & goals	There is no clear vision and strategic planning is either absent or fragmented	The leadership team have developed a vision and strategic plans but these are not shared and/or understood at lower levels and may even be kept 'secret'. Planning is seen as a 'once a year then file it' activity and is based on limited inputs regarding the internal and external environment	There is a clear vision and strategy and comprehensive plans, based on a full range of internal/external environment analyses, are deployed down to divisional/ business unit level with clear roadmaps to achieve them in place and monitored	A full strategy deployment process is in place with review and corrective action integrated. Everyone in the organisation knows how they are contributing to the vision and organisational goals are aligned to personal objectives. The strategy development and deployment process is reviewed and refined in the light of experience and best practice	The planning process is extended across the whole supplychain and demonstrates the agility to react swiftly to any change in scenario. New approaches have been identified and the organisation is acknowledged as world class in this area
Culture – Leaders & people Leadership and Ethics	There is no clear culture in the organisation. Individuals behave in different ways and send mixed messages as to what is important - or they say one thing and act in another way	Values have been identified and communicated across the organisation but there is little evidence of them being seem as drivers of behaviour. It is unclear how these values relate to the strategic goals. Managers pay lip service to CI activities but often at arms length and fire -fighting is still the norm.	There is a clear understanding of the Values and managers are encouraged to 'walk the talk'. Feedback mechanisms are in place to help identify where behaviours need to change and practical help/training is available to improve performance. Managers are approachable by all staff and are visibly seen to be engaging in CI activities	The values are integrated into staff development reviews and reward and recognition processes. There is an open culture that encourages honesty in identifying and remedying areas for improvement. Managers understand the need to 'walk the talk' and encourage feedback and employee surveys show a high level of trust in management. CI activities are seen as a fundamental part of the manager's role.	The Values permeate everything the organisation does. CI is the norm - everyone sees it as their role on a daily basis. There is an energy for change in the organisation and a sense of purpose. Leaders are in the forefront of CI activities and learning from mistakes is encouraged at all levels. Innovative approaches to employee engagement are pioneered.
People - People Development, Education and Training, Empowerment and Involvement, Environmental & Safety Systems	Approaches to skills planning and people management are ad hoc and vary across the organisation, often according to individual manager's preference. There are no formal approaches to ensure safety and environmental systems are give priority, beyond thoses required by law.	There are clear people management processes in place which are at least fifty percent deployed. There is a top level understanding of the skill requirements needed to deliver the strategy and evidence of training and development to deliver this. Some CI tools training has been undertaken to support initial projects and targets for environmental activity are set although often not regularly monitored. There have been safety audits undertaken to identify the risks particular to the organisation and action taken to mitigate these.	People management processes are fully deployed and are constantly monitored and refined to fit the culture needed to deliver the strategy and support the Values. Skills profiles are understood and are actively being delivered. People feel empowered to take a lead in CI activities and are rewarded accordingly. Workplace safety and environmental contributions will be well understood and promoted.	The focus is on what is needed to deliver tomorrow rather than today and people have a clear roadmap of what they need to do to support the transformed operation. Functional boundaries are regularly crossed. Morale is high and self motivation and empowerment are the norm. Everyone believes they have two jobs: doing the job and improving the way it is done. Peer pressure will encourage adherence to workplace best practice and to consideration of the wider community impact of all actions.	Everyone wants to work for this organisation - they may well have won 'best place to work' type awards and will have sustained world class employee satisfaction results. Externally they will be recognised as champions of corporate social responsibility and the employees will be proud to say who they work for. They will have no problem recruiting and retaining the best talent and will encourage thought leadership in all disciplines and at all levels of the organisation.
Partnership & supply chain	There is no coordinated approach to selection and managing of suppliers, nor to identifying and managing strategic partners	Suppliers are chosen and managed in a structured way and performance is monitored although the data is not always used to drive improvment. The emphasis on supplier management tends to be tactical and often relates to cost management	Strategic partnerships needed in both the short and long term are identified via the planning process but this thinking is not yet factored into BAU activity at all levels. There is some limited joint CI activity with suppliers and customers on a project by project basis usually driven by a need to fix a particular issue.	The definition of partnership extends beyond suppliers to encompass stakeholders of any description including industry bodies, community bodies, pressure groups and media. There is a clear link to the strategic goals and partnership management is owned at all levels of the organisation with clearly defined roles. CI is extended across the whole end to end value chain and synergystic improvement activities are undertaken. The emphasis for these initiatives has moved from firefighting to prevention, from tactical to strategic.	An enhanced Value chain across the whole end to end supply process is seen as a key differentiator and is actively driven through stretch targets and constant questioning of the current delivery paradigm. Strategic goals are shares with partners and metrics are aligned to cross organisational delivery. There are examples of innovative approaches to collaboration and high levels of involvement in industry fora.
Enabling Resources & Asset Mgt (& Asset Mgt – Finance, IT, Knowledge, information, Technology, Asset mgt incl. Buildings & Equipment, TPM, Security, Safety)	There is no coordinated approach to managing the various resources deployed in the organisation. Although there may be sporadic local initiatives these are not coordinates or sustained and the emphasis is usually around cost cutting or fire fighting. Where there are resource strategies they may introduce conflicts of interest	The SD process is starting to link top level strategic goals to lower level operational resource strategies in areas such as IT and infrastructure and there a link between investment and future direction although in the course of execution the alignment may be lost. In the workplace initiatives related to approaches such as TPM/5S are being pilotted. Assets are being tracked and rationalised.	The alignment of investment in resources is established and maintained and any conflicts of interest actively managed. The resource strategies are executed and assets exploited and workplace initiatives are being systematically deployed in a number of areas. Attention is moving to the value add opportunities presented by technology and knowledge mangement but this is in its infancy. Security of all assets, tangible and intangible is clearly managed.	There is a tight alignment of resource strategies to goals at all levels in the organisation and this is constantly reviewed and adjusted. Investment is clearly linked to the goals and values of the organisation. Workplace initiatives are totally embedded into normal business in areas such as safety, TPM, 5s as appropriate. Information is accurate, easy to use, integrated across the supply chain. Technology is being exploited in line with the risk profile of the business. A structure for knowledge management is established and is being populated and maintained.	Resources are seen as critical differentiators and are exploited with agility in innovative ways to gain competitive edge. There is clear evidence in thought leadership in several areas of resource management emanating from the organisation and if approapriate new technologies are being patented and used. Exploitaion of critical resources in managed across the entire supply chain in conjuction with all manner of partners
Processes (Functions & Operations & CI)	There is little understanding of process. Often it is confused with having written procedures . There will be sporadic pockets of process activity but nothing coordinated.	The need for management of processes is acknowledged and some skills training has taken place. Mapping of as-is processes is being undertaken in key operational areas and process ownership is in its infancy. CI skills training is starting with pilot projects aimed at consolidating skills and proving methodologies. CI skills are still in the hands of 'experts' brought in to lead projects targetting problem areas.	As part of the SD process critical process capability is identified for both the current and transformed operations. These processes are assigned senior level owners who understand and take responsibility for the full obligations of process ownership. Target levels of performance are set on process outcomes and on driver in -process and input variables.End to end Value stream maps are being produced and the implications assessed. Critcal constraints have been identified and CI activities focused on these areas. CI skills are being passed on to approx. 50% of the popoulation	There is a shift away from functional process ownership to integrated value stream ownership. This is also reflected in the metrics and management processes and in the personal reward system. Process improvement is switching focus from problem solving to CI and value add and everyone in the workforce has sufficient skills to be able to contribute to proactive improvement identification and delivery. Process management extends to all activities including support and management processes	Process thinking has become 'wing-to-wing' encompassing all aspects of the supply chain including integration with customer processes and metrics. Targets for value streams and processes are driven by benchmarking against world class levels of performance and in some areas this organisation is the pace setter. There is an agility in the organisation's management of processes which allows rapid response to changing environments.
Customer Centricity (Market/Product / Service devt & delivery)	Although end customers are identified and managed the emphasis is on fire fighting . Product development is driven by 'what we can do' rather than 'what the customer wants'. There is little formalanalysis of market trends and Voice of the Customer (VoC). Customer segmentation is rudimentary.	there is a clear understanding of market, customer segments and the need to obtain real Voice of the Customer, although the implementation of this may be in its infancy. At the individual process level there is a move to identy inputs and output linked to suppliers and customers. Customer feedback mechanisms are in place and the end to end processes to identify customer requirements, design, deliver and maintain products and services are being reviewed.	Market and customer analysis and feedback feature strongly in the strategy formulation and deployment processes. There are well established and maintained processes in place to mange all the activities involved in product/service from design to maintenance. Customer relationship management is seem as a key activity and is supported with well developed customer satisfaction data collection and analysis	The customer delivery value chains are understood and are being managed/optimised. Customer satisfaction is no longer the goal - exceeding expectations is the only acceptable level. Customers are seen as partners and , together with suppliers, are involved in joint improvement and collaboration projects. Products and services are designed to meet customer needs 'right first time' using methodologies such as Design For Six Sigma and rapid prototyping and customer relationship management is integrated across the supply chain with 'not our problem' a thing of the past. customer centricity is very clearly established in the fabric of the culture.	The organisation is pioneering new ways to design, deliver and support products and services. It has gained a reputation for excellent customer service which extends outside its own industry and is a regular contributor to thought leadrership in the areas of market and customer centricity. Customer feedback showssustained performance at world class levels
Metrics & Business Results	Measurement is ad hoc and probably focussed predominantly on financials. Even where data is collected it is not trended and/or analysed to understand	Top level goals are set and cascaded via the SD programme and metrics put in place to collect relevant data. There is some loose linkage to scorecards and divisional/site objectives but the focus	The scope of metrics encompasses all the elements necessary to track and deliver the transformational goals identified, including staff and customer satisfaction, societal and business results. BAU metrics are routinely analysed,	Visual management is widely used with a large part fo the workforce feeling ownership of the results. Process owners understand the relationship between input, in -process and out put metrics, linked to CTQs. Senior Executive dashboards	Benchmarking is used to set ever more stretch targets and the organisation is recognised as achieving world class levels of performance in a number of areas. The culture of the organisation is
Gears	1st	2nd	3rd	4th	5th

Figure 5-11: Example of a completed capability maturity matrix for Acme Inc. © Catalyst Consulting Ltd.

Plot the desired gear levels for each pillar at the end of each future planning period (or year, if appropriate). The descriptions in the individual highlighted cells of the matrix describe the outcomes you seek to achieve by those times. The succession of (annual) pictures of the matrix then becomes your road map for the transformation journey.

Figure 5-12 illustrates how the matrix develops and changes over time.

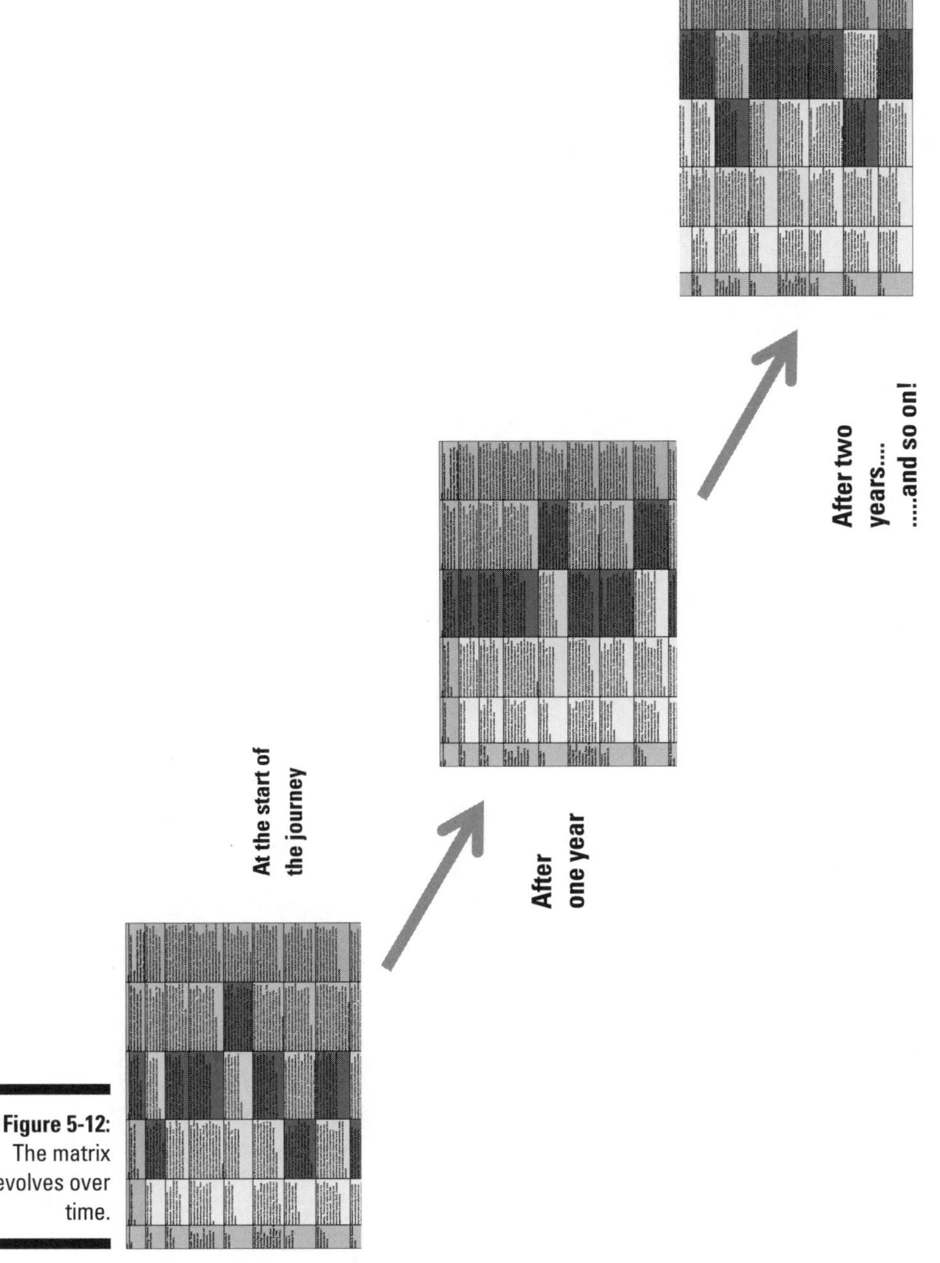

Figure 5-12: The matrix evolves over time.

Chapter 6

Establishing the Transformation Governance System

In This Chapter

- Getting organised for the journey
- Getting the programme office up and running
- Monitoring your progress

Having assessed your readiness for transformation and decided in principle to proceed, you now need to put in place appropriate organisational roles and structures to enable you to develop and manage the change. In this chapter we consider the roles of individuals and groups including transformation sponsors, the programme manager, the transformation board, a programme management office and workstream leaders. We also discuss how to develop a suitable transformation charter and how to monitor and control progress once the transformation is underway.

Leading by Example: Driving the Transformation

Transforming an organisation requires careful planning, implementing and steering. The DRIVE model described in Chapter 3 is clearly based on the analogy of driving a car on a journey; you'll arrive at your destination safely only if you have planned your route, fuelled (and maintained) your car, know where you're going, have navigated, steered and driven safely, and made any necessary corrections if you've taken a wrong turn.

Successful transformation involves a number of roles:

- **Overall transformation sponsor(s):** These are the senior leaders of the organisation, almost certainly led by the CEO or most senior individual. A transformation board comprising these sponsors is a useful forum for the ultimate governance of the transformation.
- **Programme or transformation manager:** A senior manager responsible for the day-to-day running of the transformation programme and answerable to the transformation board. They usually attend transformation board meetings.
- **Transformation programme management office:** The small team of people assisting the programme manager by providing professional and administrative support for the programme.
- **Workstream leaders:** The senior managers leading each workstream. It may also be appropriate for one of the senior leaders/members of the transformation board to act as a sponsor for an individual workstream.

A workstream is a subset of the overall transformation programme that can be usefully managed as a distinct entity in its own right. Typically, between one and four interdependent workstreams are evident in most transformations.

The following sections explore the roles of the transformation team further.

Agreeing the role of the transformation board

The first issue to address is whether one overarching transformation board or several are needed. If your transformation programme has just a single main workstream, one transformation board is clearly the order of the day. However, most transformations involve more than a single workstream so having a review board or steering group to oversee each of them makes sense. Because these workstreams are interdependent to a greater or lesser degree, the need still exists for an overarching transformation board responsible for overseeing the aggregate approach.

The roles of each oversight group must be defined and agreed upon, otherwise you risk overlaps or gaps and potential conflict between them.

Separating from operational management

The same directors or senior leaders may well constitute both the transformation board and the organisation's senior executive team or management board. The roles carried out by executive management on a day-to-day basis and within a business transformation process are somewhat different, however. Thus, as part of the management board senior leaders oversee the day-to-day operations of the business; as part of the transformation board they oversee the entire transformation programme.

Distinguish between the two by holding separate meetings with separate agendas, even if one follows on from the other on the same day. If appropriate, hold the meetings in different rooms to emphasise the distinction.

One clear difference exists between the two memberships: the transformation programme manager will probably not be a member of the management board nor attend its meetings; however, they'll regularly and routinely attend transformation board meetings and be a formal member of that board.

Establishing the Transformation Board Charter

Like the Transformation Charter described in Chapter 4, you need to create a Transformation Board Charter. This short document should include and set out the following:

- The members and chair of the transformation board, including officers responsible to it such as the transformation programme manager.
- Its terms of reference and scope (what it is and is not responsible for).
- Details of any subsidiary transformation steering groups, for example associated with individual workstreams, and their responsibilities in relation to the overall transformation board.
- Arrangements for meetings.
- Appropriate cross-references to the Transformation Charter.

The charter should be simple and avoid needless bureaucracy. However, writing it down, reviewing it and agreeing on it ensures that everyone involved is on the same wavelength and singing from the same song sheet. Just as strategy deployment is all about tightly aligning objectives and actions within the organisation to the breakthrough objectives, so the transformation board needs to tightly align the planning and oversight activities of the transformation itself.

Create light-touch charters for subsidiary steering groups of individual workstreams too. These documents help avoid overlaps or gaps in roles.

Identifying who else needs to be involved

As the key reason for the transformation board(s) is to oversee the transformation programme, progress and risk reviews will be the items most frequently on the agenda. These reviews will include overall workstreams and also the more critical projects making them up. To that end, the respective project leaders should present to the transformation board; they may well involve their project champions and members of their project teams.

As one of the other roles of the transformation board is to encourage and engage the organisation's key people in the transformation, offering the project leaders and their teams the opportunity to present their projects and demonstrate achievements is also an important vehicle for recognition and motivation.

Since the transformation process is critical to the organisation, the programme manager and transformation board may be being advised by outside consultants. These experienced Lean Six Sigma practitioners may play an active role in reporting to the board. In some cases, the lead consultant may also act as a member of the transformation board or of one of the subsidiary workstream steering groups.

Establishing the Programme Management Office

Behind the scenes, effective and efficient co-ordination, administration and support are required for the transformation programme. This is the role of the programme management office, which has the following responsibilities:

- To support the transformation board
- To provide administrative support for planning and execution of the transformation programme, including budget oversight
- To organise and support the formal transformation programme reviews
- To establish and operate an appropriate programme and project tracking and reporting system
- To identify, analyse and report significant divergences and variances from plan
- To provide professional guidance to all involved in the transformation programme and to ensure that professional integrity and appropriate standards and methods are applied

Selecting the manager

To head the programme management office, appoint a senior manager who is generally respected and well-regarded, and who's seen as a rising star in the organisation. Appoint the best person for this key role – not just the best available person.

The programme manager should report directly to the senior leader who has overall responsibility for the transformation, which is likely to be the CEO. So the programme manager will need to have, or be able to establish, a good working relationship with the CEO and other board members. They must lead the programme office efficiently and effectively and command authority and respect across all levels of the organisation.

The programme manager needs to be a very experienced project manager, and to be skilled in the arts of persuasion and influence. They also need to be tough, thick-skinned, and not afraid of confronting more senior managers.

The role of the programme manager is crucial. If finding and appointing the right individual doesn't cause some pain or discomfort somewhere in the organisation, then the correct individual has probably not been selected.

The individual successfully undertaking this key role is likely to be considered for promotion to a very senior role in the mainstream organisation once the transformation has been completed.

Assigning authority and responsibility

The programme manager represents the CEO, the transformation board and the transformation programme on a day-to-day basis. Their main tasks are to:

- Manage the programme office so that it provides the services required to administer and support the transformation programme
- Maintain the programme's tracking systems
- Select and manage the (small number of) staff in the programme office
- Sit on the transformation board as its administrator and facilitator
- Deliver the reports and analyses required by the transformation board
- Co-ordinate the efforts of any subsidiary review groups with those of the transformation board
- Communicate information about the transformation programme to the various stakeholders on behalf of the transformation board
- Influence and persuade staff at all levels in the organisation to support the transformation effort as required to the best of their ability

Tracking and Reviewing Progress

Keeping on track with the transformation process involves numerous reviews, tracking systems, and honest and efficient communication. This section gives an overview of the various means of monitoring and reporting using two different reviews.

Business reviews are focused on steering the transformation programme and making key decisions. Technical/professional reviews verify that the appropriate methodology, tools and rigour have been applied, meaningful facts and data have been collected and analysed, and correct conclusions have been drawn.

Business reviews

Senior leaders will have limited time and will be most concerned to know whether the transformation programme is on track to deliver the planned change by the agreed date. While it may be appropriate for them to review individual projects from time to time to demonstrate their involvement and to motivate and engage their staff, they're unlikely to have either the time or the inclination to go through the technical details of individual projects.

Organise periodic project fairs and exhibitions to showcase outstanding examples of constituent projects and to recognise the contributions of those involved. Senior leaders can visit these at times appropriate to them rather than using valuable collective review time that probably needs to be reserved for business reviews.

Technical/professional reviews

It's important to ensure that constituent projects, Lean Six Sigma or otherwise, are professionally managed, and that over time the organisation learns how to run them in an increasingly effective and efficient manner. Correct conclusions and outcomes are best ensured by using the appropriate methodologies and tools (DMAIC for a Lean Six Sigma improvement project, for example. Flip to Chapter 12 for more on this procedure). Without such tools the organisation risks jumping to conclusions before the real causes of problems or issues are understood, which in turn leads to developing inappropriate or ineffectual solutions and outcomes. Post-project reviews and the control phases of projects need to be adhered to if gains are to be sustained. One key guardian of such professional practices is the technical/professional review.

In Lean Six Sigma projects it is appropriate for the project leader to informally review adherence to such professional practice with a Master Black Belt or equivalent ahead of presenting progress at a formal tollgate review. This prior review assures the tollgate review team that the information presented to them is reliable and meaningful, and that appropriate business conclusions and decisions can be based on it and the project steered accordingly. For more information on tollgate reviews, see *Lean Six Sigma For Dummies* (Wiley).

Other aspects of reviews

Reviews can be either regular and scheduled or ad hoc and exceptional. They can also be either formal or informal. Although we give most consideration to formal reviews here, you need to recognise that quick short informal reviews have their place too, particularly to communicate and reassure champions and sponsors that things are generally on track, or to inform them that they need to provide some support.

Use regular informal reviews with project champions or programme sponsors to set their expectations, manage relationships, and save valuable time and effort during the more formal review sessions.

Working out how frequently progress should be reviewed and reported

While it makes good business sense to have a regular reporting and review cycle, there's also no doubt that unforeseen events can trigger the need for unplanned reviews and exceptional reporting.

Regular planned reviews and reports

Most organisations will have monthly financial reporting cycles for their normal business, and the accounting, reporting and internal review systems will typically be based on these. Much of the financial information relating to the transformation programme will be produced through the normal accounting process and reporting cycles. Overlaid on these may be more significant quarterly and annual reporting cycles, including the annual business planning cycle, and these will also impact on the review of the transformation programme.

Align the transformation review cycle with the normal regular business reporting and review cycles. Doing so ensures that an effective routine is maintained across the organisation, and that both 'normal' business and the transformation programme are appropriately managed by key leaders and staff.

In this approach, all projects and key activities within the transformation programme will be monitored on a monthly basis and status indicators and summary information collated. The programme office will review and analyse this information and produce the appropriate reports for formal review by the overall transformation board and any subsidiary review boards.

Unplanned 'trigger' events

Of course, not everything will run smoothly to plan. External events may affect the transformation process or issues may arise with individual constituent projects, often when least expected. Should a major problem occur with constituent projects or misalignments between workstreams, for example, the programme office will assess the scale and urgency of the issue involved. It determines whether an exceptional review is required or if the problem can be handled through the regular review system. Depending on the circumstances, a more in-depth review of the particular project may be called for.

External events may emerge from a variety of sources and directions and a possibility exists that they're identified outside of the day-to-day transformation activities. A takeover bid, for example, will probably be received by the chairperson, CEO or company secretary and may be a confidential issue for some time and thus concealed from less senior players in the transformation effort. Key changes in the marketplace may be picked up and assessed by the marketing or sales staff, or changes in the economic outlook by business analysts in the organisation.

At the appropriate point the programme manager will be consulted and involved, and a decision taken on whether to undertake an exceptional review of the overall transformation programme or of a particular workstream within it. Any significant reviews and decisions are likely to require an exceptional meeting of the transformation board. If extremely urgent, a virtual meeting may be held or the programme manager may consult members individually so that any urgent decisions can be expedited as required ahead of the next planned meeting.

Choosing programme/project tracking systems

A suitable tracking system is essential to support the programme. Most organisations tend to start out using an approach based on Excel spreadsheets. This may be suitable if the number of constituent projects and elements is relatively small (perhaps less than about 50); however, for larger scale programmes a number of professional IT packages are available. The advantages of an Excel spreadsheet-based system include:

- It is initially inexpensive and involves little effort to set up
- It can easily be configured to meet a wide range of requirements
- Internal expertise is likely to be readily available
- A wide range of reports can be simply developed from it

But the limitations include:

- Version control and backup may be harder to manage
- Co-ordination across different workstreams may be challenging
- Complex macros may need to be developed to meet specific requirements
- Linkage to strategy deployment and planning may be limited

A professional specialist package may be considerably more expensive but is likely to offer the following advantages:

- Full support and reporting to strategy deployment and planning
- Intelligent and configurable database to maintain project and programme records and details
- In-depth search and query routines
- Standard (but adaptable) reports relevant to both strategy deployment and programme/project tracking and review
- Cloud-based storage, access and version control
- Professional updates and maintenance
- Ability to effectively and efficiently handle large volumes of information relating to hundreds or even thousands of projects, and to co-ordinate interdependencies across workstreams and operations
- Appropriate security and access controls

Whatever system you use, efficient tracking is required to capture and maintain a range of information for each constituent project. This information includes the name and reference number of the project, the name of the project leader, key elements of the project charter, milestones, interdependencies, progress to date, including phases completed and signed off at a formal review, a RAG (Red, Amber, Green) status assessment (described in the 'Taking Corrective Action' section later in this chapter), and relevant summary notes.

An example of a good tracking report is shown in Figure 6-1. It is simple and straightforward to use, and the colour coding of the status of each project makes it easy to rapidly identify those projects with issues as well as gain a clear overall picture of progress.

Figure 6-1: An example of a simple project tracking report.

Project No	Project Name	Project Lead	Project Sponsor	Business Area	Approval Status	Project Start	Due Close	Initiative Phase	Stage	Status	Progress				
LI001	Project Lock	J Femann	R Wills	PSC ESPC/ITMS	Approved	20-May-11	TBA	1	1. Define	On Target	D	M	A	I	C
LI002	Project D.R.I.V.E	M Fish	M Baddeley	PSC ESPC/ITMS	Approved	24-May-11	TBA	1	2. Measure	On Target	D	M	A	I	C
LI003	Project ACR	K Ford	M Baddeley	PSC ESPC/ITMS	Approved	26-Apr-11	30-Jun-11	1	2. Measure	On Target	D	M	A	I	C
LI004	Project T.E.A.M	T Levan	N Coombs	OCC Contract to Cash	Approved			1	2. Measure	On Target	D	M	A	I	C
LI005	Project Concorde	C Quinn	K Byrde	PSC BoZ	Approved			1	3. Analyse	On Target	D	M	A	I	C
LI006	Project Query	T White	D Beck	OCC Contract to Cash	Approved			1	1. Define	On Target	D	M	A	I	C
LI007	Project GSR	S Kasinath	A Cotterill	PSC ESPC/ITMS	Approved	21-Apr-11	31-Aug-11	1	2. Measure	On Target	D	M	A	I	C
LI008/PG0001	Project ROAR	P Field	G Berge	PSC BoZ	Approved	1-May-11	31-Dec-11	1	1. Define	On Target	D	M	A	I	C
LI009/WW1	Project COST	G Berge	K Byrde	PSC BoZ	Approved	3-May-11	31-Dec-11	1	1. Define	On Target	D	M	A	I	C

- Each Project Defined, Approved and Tracked to completion.
- Visual picture of DMAIC Stage
- Start and Projected Close dates
- Status of Project

Understanding interdependencies and constraints

Interdependencies between constituent workstreams and projects, as well as resource constraints arising from managing them (such as subject matter experts within the organisation), should be identified during the strategy deployment process (see Chapter 9). These interdependencies need to be recorded in the programme tracking system and monitored through the review arrangements. The programme office is ultimately responsible for identifying and analysing the impact of slippages in one area on other constituent activities and alerting the relevant people so that appropriate corrective action can be taken.

Aligning workstreams

The strategy deployment process should identify and initially align the constituent workstreams within the transformation programme. But this alignment will need to be maintained throughout the execution of the transformation programme, particularly at critical points and times.

Apply critical path analysis to each individual workstream. Identify critical interdependencies, required start and finish times of significant milestones, and the impact of delays or incomplete performance outcomes on other workstreams. Explicitly review the performance of these individual workstreams within planned programme reviews and promptly take appropriate corrective action if and as required. In extreme cases it may be necessary to repeat the strategy deployment process to realign the workstreams if one goes dramatically off course.

Taking Corrective Action

A useful tool for working out if a project or workstream needs corrective action is based on a traffic light analogy: RAG – Red, Amber or Green (see Figure 6-2). Thus:

- **Red** = STOP – take appropriate corrective action now before proceeding any further.
- **Amber** = CAUTION – look more closely and proceed with care.
- **Green** = ON TRACK – carry on.

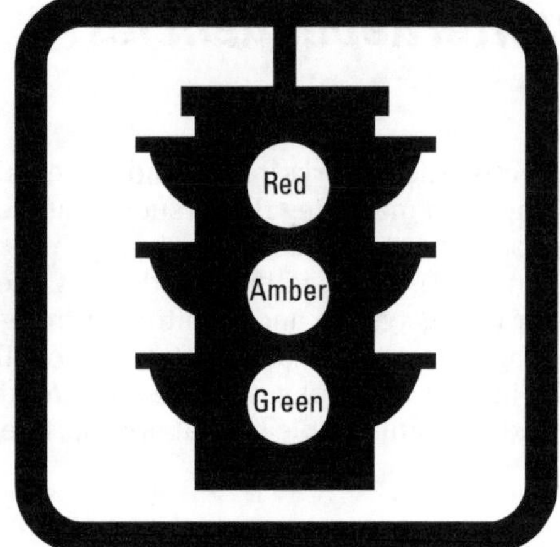

Figure 6-2: The Red, Amber Green (RAG) traffic light analogy.

These three choices reflect three different situations. RAG is also a useful way of assessing the status of any constituent element or project in the transformation process and colour coding its status in the tracking report. Colour coding the entries on all the projects and elements immediately makes visible those which require immediate review and corrective action, those which might do so shortly, and those which are well on track. Furthermore, looking at the overall pattern of colours, the report reader can immediately sense the extent to which the programme as a whole is on track or in jeopardy. The colour-coding pattern over successive months or reporting periods reveals how rapidly corrective action has or has not been taken; it visibly demonstrates the ongoing control or otherwise of the overall transformation programme.

RAG is just one example of a Lean Six Sigma visual management tool.

Initiating action

Preparing for contingent action makes good sense. If a project is Amber, you have time to prepare remedial action and thus the project will not suffer a delay. However, you still need to consider who needs to press the action button and when.

It's the responsibility of the individual project manager to properly progress their individual project (or other action or element in the transformation programme). It's the responsibility of the appropriate review team to ensure that the agreed action is in place – or otherwise to demand it. Appropriate corrective action should already have been taken for a project coded as Red before it's picked up by the programme manager or the transformation board as part of the review process.

Managing interdependencies

The interdependencies in a transformation programme are analogous to steps on the critical path in an individual project. Preventive management thinking – designing the approach to avoid the possibility of a problem occurring – comes into play here and you need to identify and anticipate interdependencies between workstreams and between individual projects. The more significant they are, the more attention needs to be paid to them. If possible, build in some backup or alternative approach to minimise risk if something goes wrong (prevention). If doing so isn't possible, consider in advance what actions might be needed if and when the more likely and foreseeable things do go wrong or are delayed; you'll then be in a position to take faster corrective action (contingency).

Managing interdependencies is very much a two-way street and the responsibility of both parties involved. The project or workstream manager whose element is slipping or non-performing should identify this situation and promptly take corrective action, including updating the other dependent project or workstream manager. That way, they can also take appropriate corrective action if needed. But it is also the responsibility of the dependent manager to anticipate such possibilities, develop contingency plans, and keep in close contact with the first manager, particularly at the more critical times. The programme office and the programme manager also have a role to play here in working with both parties to minimise risks stemming from interdependencies. Effective communication is key.

Updating plans

Hopefully corrective action will be prompt and a project or workstream will be back on track as quickly as possible. But if this is not the case, the plans themselves may need to be reviewed and revised.

Establish up-front the extent of any deviations from plans that can be reasonably accommodated without requiring the plans themselves to be modified (other than cosmetically). Use RAG at a programme level to oversee the transformation as a whole. Green implies that review or changes to plans aren't necessary, Amber signals that review and changes to plans may be needed depending on the outcome of corrective actions, and Red indicates that review and changes to plans are now required.

The extent to which changes to plans are required also determines how the organisation should proceed from here. Relatively modest changes may be accommodated by agreement through the normal review process; the changes will ultimately be authorised by the transformation board. The programme manager and the programme office are responsible for updating the plans and communicating the changes accordingly. Larger changes may require a reiteration of the strategy deployment planning and catchball process (see Chapter 8) to re-secure tight alignment of agreed changes across the workstreams and throughout the organisation. For obvious reasons, changing plans to this degree shouldn't be embarked upon lightly.

Walking the Talk

The Grand Old Duke of York he had ten thousand men. He marched them up to the top of the hill and he marched them down again. And again. And again! Some transformation! You can almost imagine his men looking at their strategy deployment map in a state of confusion, and wondering just where they were, where they were meant to be, and where on earth they were heading for next.

During the transformation process the leaders need to be believable and believed. The transformation message needs to be credible and honest. If not, flaws in the message and shortfalls in communication will eventually be exposed and the programme will rapidly fail. No matter what the temptation, take time to plan properly based on real facts and analysis. And communicate honestly the reasons for the planned changes and the impact they'll have on those affected – only then will the transformation programme have a realistic chance of success.

The transformation programme by definition is important, indeed essential, to the organisation. So any action, signal or behaviour suggesting otherwise contradicts its significance. Ultimately people will be judged by their actions rather than their words, so the body language of those involved needs to be appropriate and consistently reflecting the transformation message. Prioritising normal operational or personal activities ahead of the transformation effort, skipping transformation review meetings, or checking emails during meetings definitely sends the wrong message.

Informal communication is arguably more important than formal communication. The behaviour of every person and every team in the transformation process speaks loud and clear, particularly those of the senior leaders on the transformation and workstream boards, and those in authority such as the programme manager and the programme office staff.

Leadership need to ensure that employees receive the right training, coaching and support. Where practical, leaders should take part in training themselves to show how important it is. Introducing the training sessions, for example, or even delivering part of a programme sends clear messages to the organisation as a whole.

Nothing is more confusing than an inconsistent message. All the tight strategic alignment counts for nothing if the transformation message and the body language of those implementing the transformation are inconsistent. Throughout the period of transformation, staying on message is essential to staying on track.

Part III

Planning the Transformation Journey

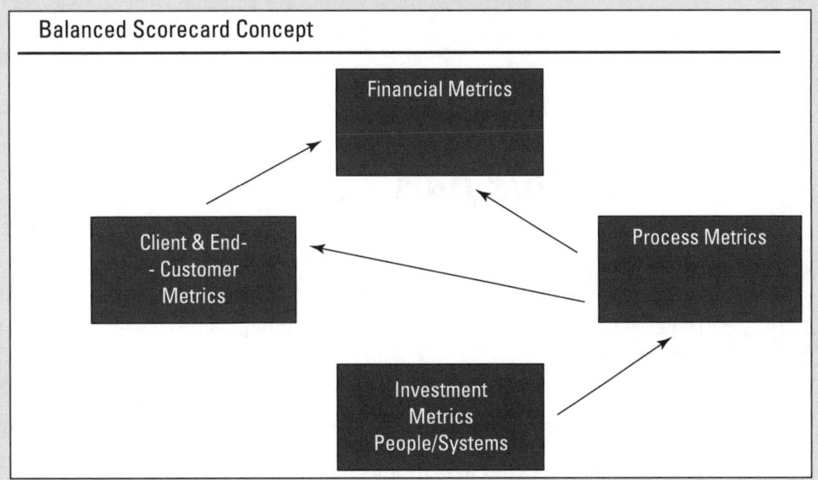

Find out more about lean six sigma business transformation at `www.dummies.com/extras/lssbusinesstransformation`.

In this part . . .

- See how to accommodate both Business Breakthroughs and Business Fundamentals and how to deploy them.
- Develop an effective and rapid approach to deploy the business strategy.
- Gain insight into how Strategy Deployment is implemented and adopted by organisations.
- Learn more about effective organisational structures and the roles of key stakeholders.

Chapter 7

Understanding Business Breakthroughs and Fundamentals

In This Chapter

- Reviewing your business initiatives
- Recognising business breakthroughs
- Focusing on business fundamentals
- Considering key performance indicators

Once you have in place your Transformation Charter, an assessment of your readiness for the intended transformation programme, a suitable approach to administering and governing it, and an understanding of the vital few objectives that will be central to the transformation, you are ready for the next stage. You now need to more clearly separate out the professional day-to-day management of the ongoing business from that of the transformation programme, and to establish the appropriate approach to deploying your transformation efforts.

Avoiding Initiative Overload

Most organisations seem to suffer from initiative overload. There's almost always too much going on and insufficient time and other resources to do the day job and handle all the initiatives that either come down from top management or are imposed by external stakeholders.

It makes good sense to review all the current initiatives and determine whether they're all really necessary or appropriate at this time. Ideally, you should have done so as part of your assessment of your organisation's readiness for transformation, but if not, consider undertaking a specific review.

Our experience suggests that most organisations find that they can rationalise several initiatives, defer others, and close down some that are no longer really needed.

You can use various capability maturity assessment methods to review initiatives, but conducting this review is always best done through a facilitated senior leadership workshop. Obviously, you can simply review the initiatives as a separate exercise, but doing so is unlikely to be as effective.

You're likely to have initiatives that remain important and which you want to continue that aren't necessarily a part of the transformation as such. You need to consider the resourcing implications of continuing these initiatives in parallel with the intended transformation programme.

Over time, all organisations build up clutter and then need to take stock and remove what's surplus to current requirements and tidy up what remains. The situation is just the same with initiatives.

Recognising that more is less

A practical limit exists to what anyone can do in any given period of time. If your list of things to do is too large, many of those items won't get done, but that doesn't stop you worrying about doing them. You may become trapped in a vicious circle, in which you cannot focus on things you can achieve because you're spending too much time worrying about those you can't. Having too many things to do may encourage you to do things piecemeal even when several items are interrelated, which results in wasted effort because you potentially carry out the same activities more than once if they relate to different items on your list. You may also risk doing things in the wrong sequence, which may result in rework.

The logical thing to do is to step back and review the list of things to be done, rationalise them by removing overlaps and duplications, and re-sequence them in an appropriate new order. Of course, you also need to remove from the list any items that have been overtaken by events or are of dubious benefit. Now more is less and less is more – in the sense that more is likely to be actually achieved with a shorter rationalised and prioritised list than a longer rambling one. And so it is with organisational initiatives.

Weeding out unnecessary initiatives

Of course you can simply list all the initiatives, and review and prioritise them. But doing so misses a key point – that many of them may no longer be necessary or appropriate. We've run many facilitated workshops with senior leadership teams using the EFQM Excellence Model framework (see Chapter 5) to help them self-assess their management system. Inevitably, as the leadership team members work together and discuss the entire picture (and not just those aspects for which they're individually responsible), they become aware of all the initiatives, current and planned, and where they fit (or don't) within their management system and the organisation's desired future state. Time after time these senior leaders have realised that many of their cherished initiatives are no longer relevant or are simply parts of a bigger picture and can better be reconstituted in a more rational way with different priorities. The key point to note here is that such workshops aren't directly focused on rationalising initiatives; that happens almost coincidentally as a result of their collective understanding of what the organisation's real priorities need to be.

Ideally, this review should be integrated with your review of readiness for transformation.

Avoiding succumbing to scope creep

Scope creep is the natural tendency to attach additional aspects to projects for seemingly good reasons – perhaps you forgot something or an event triggers the need for some new detail. Applying the principle of 'more is less' here suggests that scope creep left unchecked risks compromising your ability to effectively focus on the real things that matter for the success of your intended transformation.

Resist scope creep and ensure that you review the scope of your transformation programme and its constituent projects on a regular basis with a view to maintaining or indeed reducing it rather than allowing it to creep upwards and outwards.

Considering a second phase of transformation is preferable to allowing the scope of the initial phase to creep beyond manageable bounds.

Identifying Business Breakthroughs

In this section we consider how breakthrough differs from ongoing day-to-day management and how many breakthroughs you can practically handle. *Breakthrough objectives* are those intended to achieve a dramatic rather than gradual improvement in performance, and require a consistent, sustained and focused effort that's synergised and synchronised across the organisation (breakthrough objectives are covered in Chapter 4). Breakthrough activities are those associated with such objectives and are likely to make significant changes to the ways in which an organisation, department or key business process operates.

Distinguishing breakthroughs from daily management

The business transformation may be vitally important to you but you can't afford to take your eye off managing the rest of the business as the transformation progresses. Accordingly, managing these two aspects separately makes good sense.

In this context, *daily management* refers to the ongoing operation of the organisation, delivering products and services to its customers, and managing the relationships it has with its various constituent stakeholders. People still need to be employed, engaged and empowered to develop products, deliver those products and provide support to their customers – internal or external. The supply chain still needs to be managed, and all the everyday processes and activities need to take place to ensure that the business continues to survive and prosper. Short-term goals still need to be met and budgets adhered to. Anticipating success tomorrow as a result of the transformation doesn't apply; today's customers still need to be served, today's staff and suppliers still need to be paid, and today's investors and shareholders still need to be rewarded. Tomorrow's daily management may well look different after the transformation, but you still have to deal with today's version first.

Managing today's business through managing by process is the best approach to daily management. Managing through process means understanding today's processes, assigning process owners, and having key performance indicators (KPIs) in place and monitored with an appropriate scorecard; we go into further detail in the 'Establishing Key Performance Indicators' section later in this chapter. Associated gradual continuous improvement using Lean Six Sigma tools and projects is also a key component of effective daily management – not all improvement needs to be dramatic.

Consider the tale of the tortoise and the hare – the tortoise won the race by slowly and consistently proceeding forwards. A place exists for both ongoing continuous improvement and transformation.

Irrespective of whether your organisation is managed by process, value stream or function (such as operations, finance, HR, and so on), daily management requires continuity and a separate focus during the transformation process. We discuss further organising for ongoing continuous improvement in Chapter 10. We also consider organising the governance system for transformation in Chapter 6, and Chapters 9 and 13 go into more detail on organising the separate transformation streams.

Working out how many breakthroughs you can handle

In short – only a very limited number. The 'more is less' thinking applies here too. If you try to handle too many breakthroughs, the resources (people and time) required will detract either from managing them effectively or from undertaking professional daily management. If you try to handle too few breakthroughs, or breakthroughs too limited in scope, you won't see the dramatic change in performance you're seeking. But attempting to handle more than two or three real breakthrough objectives at any one time can lead to the initiative overload we describe earlier in this chapter.

Until your organisation has sufficient practical experience of managing through breakthrough objectives, limit the number under consideration to at most two or three. Scaling up from success is better than failing as a result of losing focus and valuable time (perhaps a full year) by attempting to take on more than you can handle. Even if the initial breakthrough is less dramatic, the improvement will nonetheless be a major step on your transformation journey.

Determining the Business Fundamentals

Much of the organisation's time must be devoted to keeping the business running; that is, carrying out the value-adding activities of the key business processes that fulfil the organisation's purpose. These are the business fundamentals.

Maintaining a routine

Because routine tasks require much less thought you can save your mental effort for those things that aren't routine. That's the idea here – you need to concentrate the organisation's efforts on the breakthrough you're seeking, but you also have to keep the everyday going; the company still has to satisfy today's customers and pay its bills. So if you can standardise the day-to-day stuff, you can have it both ways: carrying on business professionally and profitably while planning and executing the transformation process.

Since all work is a process, as illustrated in Figure 7-1, in principle all you need to do to manage the organisation's routine is to manage its processes.

Too often organisations are managed functionally in silos – going up and down the organisation – whereas the key processes go across the organisation if they are to deliver to the customer what they want, as illustrated in Figure 7-2. You need to manage by process or value stream rather than by function if you want to stay on top of day-to-day routines.

All Work is a Process

A series of steps and actions that produce an output for the customer:

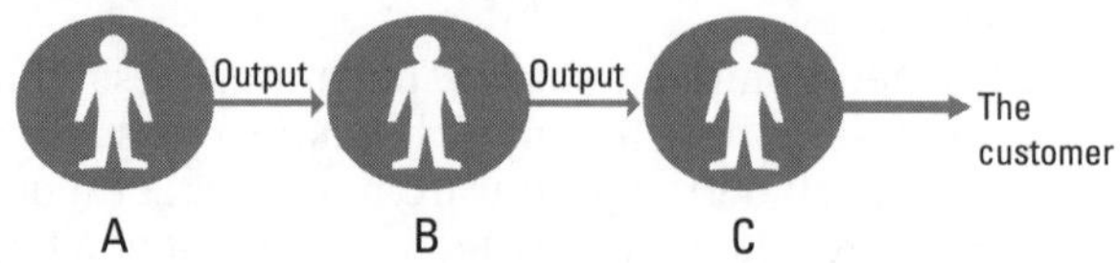

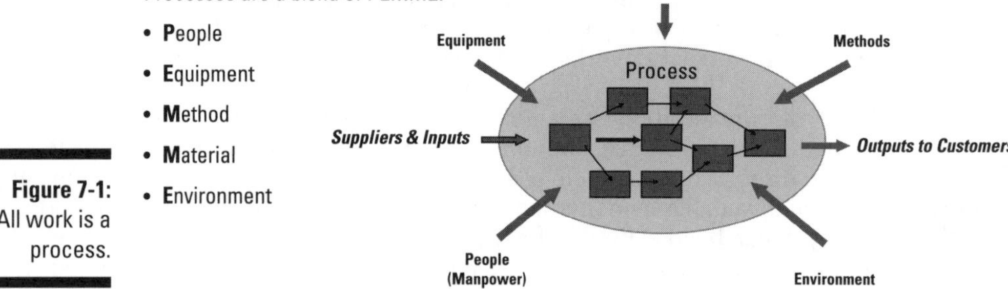

Figure 7-1: All work is a process.

Processes Tend to Flow Across the Organisation

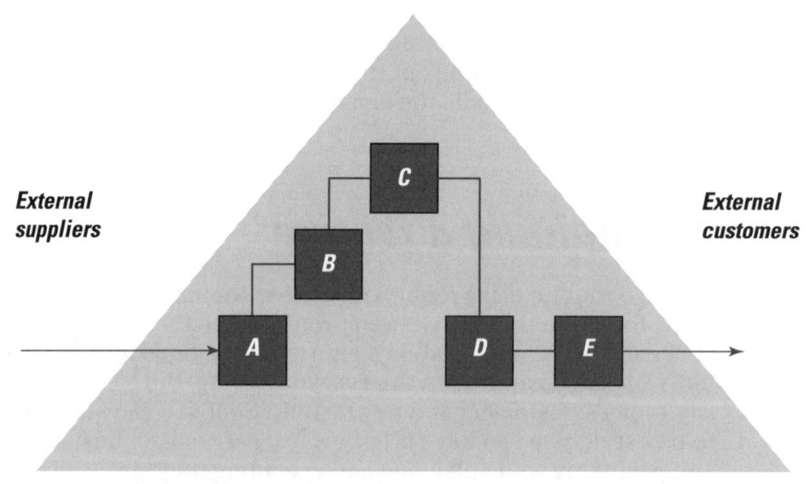

But all too often there's a silo mentality ...
Silos create disconnects and sub-optimisation, as well as impairing service delivery and performance

Figure 7-2: Processes tend to flow across the organisation.

Managing the key processes

A process is managed when:

- It's owned
- It has a clear customer-focused objective with prioritised customer requirements (the CTQs – 'critical to quality' issues that must be met for the customer to be satisfied)
- A process map is in place documenting how the process is expected to be carried out
- An effective data collection plan exists, balancing input, process and output measures – and that data is being collected and used to monitor and control the process
- It's stable and only affected by random/common cause variation
- It meets customer-focused objectives (CTQs) or an improvement plan is in place to make sure it does so
- It's been error-proofed to minimise the risk of it losing control or failing to meet CTQs
- A control plan exists to ensure that it's appropriately maintained

A process is professionally managed only when all of these requirements are met. Clearly, managing a process requires significant effort; you thus need to focus on just those key processes essential to the organisation's success. Processes improved using Lean Six Sigma tools should be in a managed state by the time the control phase has been signed off. A process doesn't necessarily need to be improved before it can become a managed process – but it does help!

Process owners

Figure 7-3 identifies the different roles of the process owner and process manager.

While only one process owner can exist there may be several process managers, as the same process may operate in different parts of the business or in parallel with different groups (for example, production cells or self-managed work teams) focusing on different products or customers. Having one owner with overall responsibility for the process's design, performance targets and improvement enables standardised consistent operation across the organisation.

Distinct Process Roles

Process Owner	Process Manager
Overall responsible for:	Operationally responsible for:
• Process design, operation and performance	• Continually monitoring the process (or parts of) within his / her area
• Ensures process design reflects needs (of customers and other stakeholders)	• Accountable for the performance of the process in achieving targets
• Sets targets for its performance	• Provides appropriate performance data
• Ensures adequate resourcing	
• Ensures continuous process improvement	
• Benchmarks with other organisations	
• Manages and resolves interface and integration issues	

Figure 7-3: The distinct roles of the process owner and process manager.

Usually the process owner will be a named individual; however, a collective group of leaders may act together as the process owner. In this case there's still just one process owner, albeit in the form of a group of people formally acting together.

The process architecture

The process architecture is how the collective of key processes is configured to support the organisation. It can be expressed as a high-level map showing which processes are recognised as key to the business, how they relate to each other, and which people are the process owners. Some processes will be common to all businesses (for example, 'managing people'), whereas others will be specific to certain types of organisation (for example, 'manufacturing products' is appropriate for a manufacturing business but probably not to a service sector organisation). Some processes assume much greater importance in some organisations than in others; for example, 'manage compliance' assumes greater significance in a tightly regulated sector such as pharmaceuticals or financial services than it might in logistics. Figure 7-4 shows the standard framework developed by the APQC (American Productivity and Quality Center), which you can use as a starting point to develop your own process architecture.

Figure 7-5 shows an example of a configured process framework for one of the authors' organisations, Catalyst.

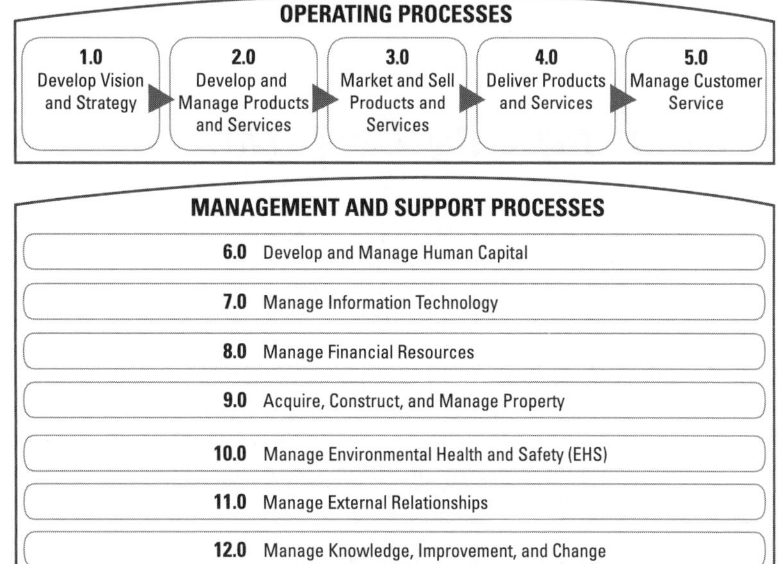

Figure 7-4: AQPC's generic process architecture.

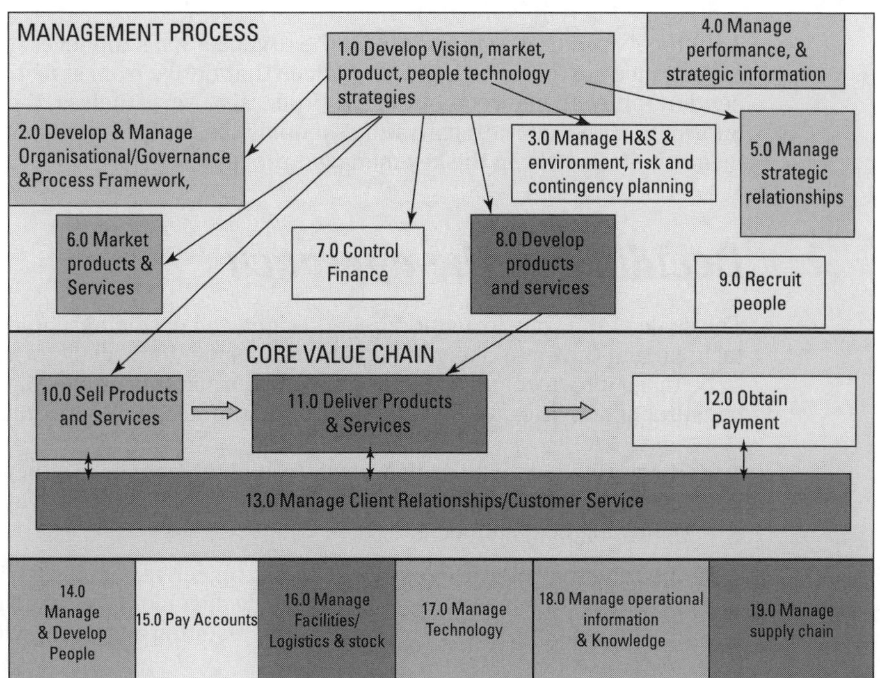

Figure 7-5: Catalyst's process architecture.

Review and update (if necessary) your organisation's process architecture on a regular basis as part of your annual planning cycle. This review should also check that all of the processes you've identified have named process owners and are managed processes (see the 'Managing the key processes' section earlier in this chapter).

Establishing Key Performance Indicators

Each managed process should have a balanced set of input, output and in-process measures. The output measures are *lagging indicators* (that is, measures that report after the event or transaction has been completed) that indicate how effective and efficient the process is – the extent to which it meets the requirements of its customers and of the business. The input and in-process measures are *leading indicators* (that is, measures that report before the event or transaction has been completed) that should enable the process owner to determine whether the process will continue to deliver the desired output. These measures collectively comprise many of the key performance indicators of the enterprise and will be included on the organisation's scorecards and dashboards.

Leading indicators have the advantage of identifying issues earlier than lagging indicators, thereby potentially allowing corrective action to be taken before the customer is impacted.

Additional measures may appear on the organisation's top level scorecard, for instance customer satisfaction indices that derive from stakeholder perception rather than directly from the processes. Nevertheless, the process information on that scorecard will essentially be comprised of key performance indicators from the key managed processes.

Deciding on the approach

The scale of the transformation being sought, the period available for undertaking it and the state of ongoing daily management are all factors that need to be taken into account. In relation to transformation and the alignment of constituent activities, you can achieve a quantum leap in performance by:

- Focusing on just one or two breakthrough objectives but then deploying the associated activities across and throughout the organisation in a tightly aligned manner, *or*
- Ensuring that you progress all business objectives across a wide front in as consistent a manner as possible using alignment mechanisms that are less demanding, but accepting that the resulting alignment will be less precise, *or*
- Creating a suitable combination of these two approaches.

A number of different mechanisms have evolved or been developed over the years that progressively more tightly align objectives and actions; these include management by objectives, the balanced scorecard and Hoshin Kanri (originating in Japan but more commonly known in the West as policy deployment or strategy deployment. See the later section 'Understanding the notion of Hoshin'). Before we look at these, however, let's take a small diversion to consider a 'softer' mechanism that aligns the behaviours of people and, indirectly, their actions and activities.

Acknowledging the value of values

Having commonly agreed company values in place which are consistently practised is a powerful alignment mechanism that works throughout the culture of the organisation. Rather than being airy-fairy, this approach ensures that everyone is trained to understand how the organisation's espoused values apply to very real everyday circumstances and decisions. Many organisations seek to adhere to a written set of corporate values, which might typically include:

- Put the customer first
- Treat people with respect
- Demonstrate integrity in all business dealings
- Treat the company's money as though it is your own

Both everyday and major decisions can be seen in the light of these values. You need to be aware, however, that abiding by such values may require resolving inherent contradictions dependent on circumstances. For example, applying the fourth value, 'Treat the company's money as though it is your own', may suggest that employees should choose the lowest cost alternative when procuring supplies and facilities from a range of bidders; however, doing so may involve a business practice that isn't totally above board, thus breaching the value of conducting business with appropriate integrity. Posing such dilemmas to staff, asking them to consider and discuss the decisions they'd make, and then comparing their responses to those of the organisation in line with its espoused values, is a powerful means of driving the alignment of behaviour and decision-making across and throughout the enterprise.

In itself, alignment through commonly applied values is probably insufficient for a successful transformation – but it is a helpful step. Combined with the 'harder' (that is, more formalised) mechanisms for aligning objectives and activities, this approach can leverage the tightness of the overall alignment of the transformation effort across the organisation. Indeed, many transformations include a workstream focused on changing the culture of the organisation.

Actively consider whether your organisation's values (as practised as well as espoused) are in alignment with your transformation efforts. If they're not, set up a workstream within your transformation programme to address this issue.

Weighing up the balanced scorecard

Chapter 5 looks at strategy maps and how they and the balanced scorecard can be used to review strategy, particularly in terms of its comprehensiveness and how well it's described and articulated. Taken together, strategy maps and the balanced scorecard can illustrate how an overall objective can be decomposed into a series of subsidiary actions and objectives, each with their own measures and targets, and how these impact the various stakeholders represented by the financial, customer, process, and learning and growth quadrants, as illustrated in Figure 7-6.

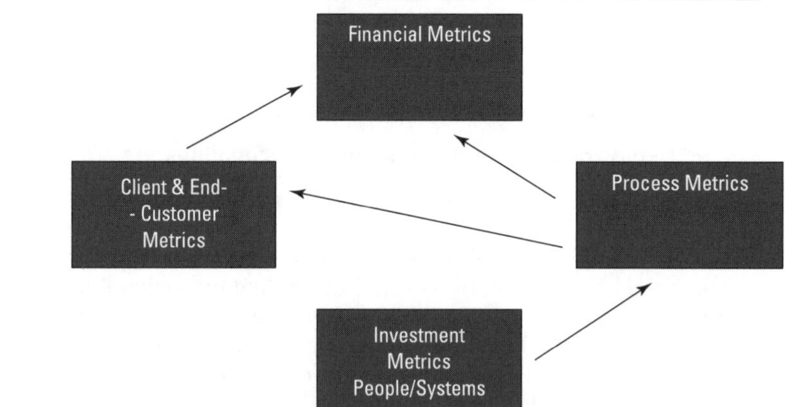

Figure 7-6: The balanced scorecard.

If the strategy is complete and self-consistent the various metrics shown on the balanced scorecard should exhibit suitable cause-and-effect linkages, which can also be shown as strategy maps across the scorecard.

The balanced scorecard concept can be applied across and down the organisation. The different parts of the enterprise each have their own scorecards linked to the organisation's top level scorecard. Together with the associated strategy maps, this approach can be used to decompose and link the objectives of the different parts of the business.

This approach is very visual and has the advantage that all the objectives have to include suitable metrics and targets. Appropriately linked, the system of scorecards should enable a fair degree of alignment of objectives across the organisation.

The system of scorecards, however, is arguably more likely to be the result of an effective strategy deployment exercise than the vehicle for actually facilitating and undertaking it. That said, the process of developing the scorecards is likely to force the organisation to adopt an appropriate approach to strategy deployment.

Looking at management by objectives

Management by objectives (MBO) is a process of defining objectives so that management and employees agree to them and understand what they need to do to achieve them. It espouses the principle that, when people have actively participated in the setting of their objectives, they'll be better motivated to achieve them. Appropriately cascaded throughout the organisation, MBO can enable a fair degree of alignment between the top-level objectives of the organisation and the different levels of management involved in delivering them. Managers can ensure that the objectives of their subordinates (and the groups of people they themselves manage) are linked to the organisation's overall objectives.

You can create objectives relating both to breakthrough and daily management. Although logical in theory, MBO in itself is unlikely to secure the degree of alignment of objectives being sought for your transformation efforts. By the time the objectives have cascaded a few times and reached people in different functions, small differences in alignment are likely to have multiplied and random impacts come into play unless the process has been subjected to stringent external moderation.

Understanding the notion of Hoshin

Hoshin Kanri (or simply Hoshin) is a strategic planning and management system, which was popularised in the late 1950s in Japan based on concepts developed by Professor Yogi Akao. Translated into English it can be read as 'Golden Arrow' or 'Strategic Direction'. Hoshin was introduced into the US and Europe in the 1980s via organisations with Japanese subsidiaries such as Xerox and Hewlett-Packard, and its usage has accelerated more recently through its link with the Toyota Production System (TPS) and widespread application of Lean by that company. Hoshin is more typically referred to as 'policy deployment' or 'strategy deployment' in Western organisations. The notion of Hoshin is intended to help an organisation:

- Focus on a shared goal
- Communicate that goal to all leaders
- Involve all leaders in planning to achieve the goal
- Hold participants accountable for achieving their part of the plan

It assumes that daily controls and performance measures (daily management) are already in place. Hoshin planning involves the following seven steps:

1. **Identify the key business issues facing the organisation.**
2. **Establish measurable business objectives that address these issues.**
3. **Define the overall vision and goals.**
4. **Develop supporting strategies for pursuing the goals (in the lean organisation, this strategy includes the use of lean methods and techniques).**
5. **Determine the tactics and objectives that facilitate each strategy.**
6. **Implement performance measures for every business process.**
7. **Measure business fundamentals.**

Closely associated with Hoshin is the catchball process (described in detail in Chapter 8) that tightly aligns the strategies, tactics and objectives down and across the organisation.

The separation of daily management and the focus on just a very few key objectives is consistent with the approach we recommend for planning and deploying transformation. Chapters 8 and 9 go into significantly greater detail on how Hoshin-based strategy deployment is applied in practice, and Figure 7-7 illustrates the different levels of strategic alignment that can be achieved using either MBO or Hoshin strategy deployment.

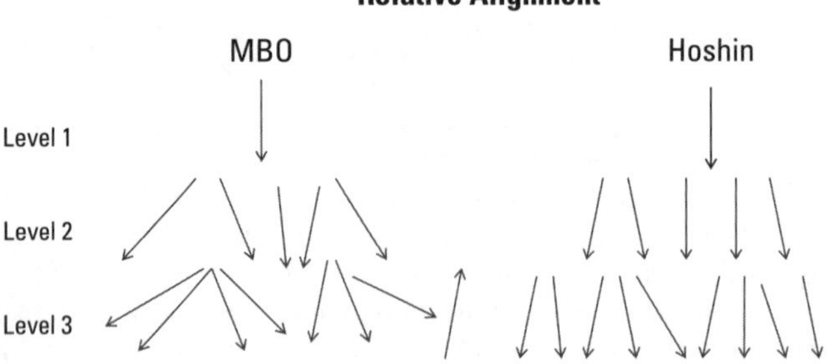

Figure 7-7: Tightness of alignment using MBO or Hoshin.

Chapter 8

Planning for Strategy Deployment

In This Chapter

- Introducing the strategy deployment process cycle
- Looking at your critical objectives
- Building the strategy deployment architecture
- Getting to grips with catchball
- Developing the X Matrix

This chapter covers the Improve phase of DRIVE, whereby you plan the enactment of your transformational business strategy using strategy deployment tools and methodology.

The DRIVE model is a systematic approach to ensuring a successful business transformation journey. It involves five phases – Define, Review, Improve, Verify and Establish. We introduce how to drive the Lean Six Sigma transformation journey by deploying business strategy using the DRIVE model in Chapter 3.

Making Strategy Deployment Happen in Practice

Strategy deployment (SD) has been adapted from the Japanese strategic planning and management system called Hoshin Kanri, and has evolved based on best practices established in deploying strategies in companies over the past 15 years. We introduced the concept of Hoshin Kanri in Chapter 2 when we discussed planning for the transformation.

Strategy deployment is a rapid, systematic and sustainable approach to successful strategy execution. It realigns resources around the 'critical few' initiatives and makes sure that people are working on the right things. It provides a direct link between strategic thinking and tactical action. It breaks strategy down into actionable steps and engages and aligns everyone with the organisation's strategy. It uses standardised tools, monitors results, and tracks and corrects deviations.

Many organisations seem to struggle with strategy execution, finding it difficult to focus tactical initiatives on achieving strategic objectives. As a result, people waste time and resources on the wrong things.

Linking back to strategy

Preparing for the SD process during the strategy review process is described in Chapter 5. It involves reviewing the strategic plan and developing the strategic essentials. The strategic essentials provide the starting point for SD and are clear, single-dimensional statements that summarise the long-term (three to five year) business strategy. They're often expressed very simply, for example 'grow sales', 'reduce costs', 'develop people' and so on. However, they should have some measurable and verifiable end goal to aim for, such as 'number one in the market' or 'produce upper-quartile returns'.

Typically, the strategy review will identify three to four strategic essentials.

Choose only a few strategic essentials – three or four is typical. You need to make sure that when they're broken down into short-term (annual) goals called focus areas and cascaded, the organisation has a manageable number of initiatives to achieve.

Following the strategy deployment steps

Strategy deployment follows the Plan–Do–Check–Act (PDCA) cycle that is described in detail in Chapter 1. So how does SD work?

The SD process, illustrated in Figure 8-1, is initiated as part of the organisation's annual business planning when the leadership team scans and reviews its current strategy plan. The *Plan* phase starts when it develops the general statements of direction for the organisation in the medium to long term – the strategic essentials. Chapter 5 discusses reviewing the strategic plan and developing strategic essentials.

The leadership team define the medium- and long-term critical objectives and the shorter-term focus areas. These are then cascaded to the next level of management, which breaks the focus areas down into short-term process improvements. We recommend using the catchball process to gain consensus and alignment (described in detail in the 'Playing Catchball' section later in this chapter). Teams are then assigned to establish detailed action plans, targets and metrics so that achievement of the process improvements can be effectively managed.

The *Do* phase involves mobilisation of the necessary resources to implement the process improvements using appropriate Lean Six Sigma methods (DMAIC or DMADV), which are covered in Chapter 1.

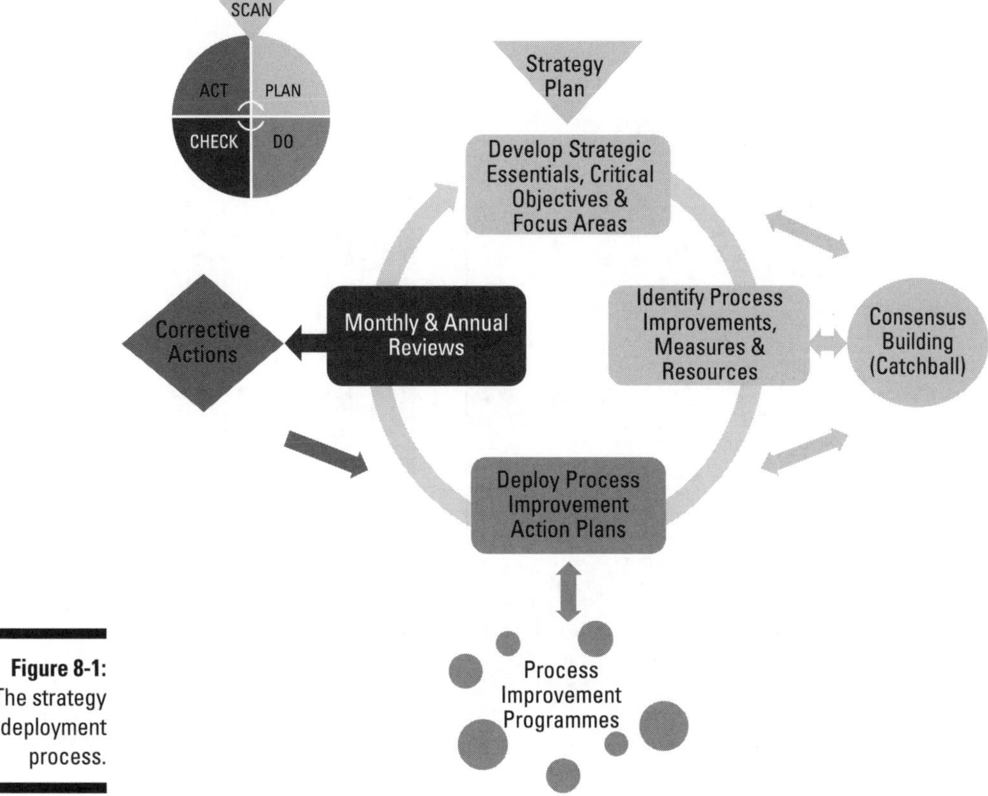

Figure 8-1: The strategy deployment process.

As these improvements are completed they're managed as part of the everyday management system. This system focuses on the operation and monitoring of workflow by managing performance and looking for further improvement opportunities. This approach is described in more detail in Chapter 12.

The *Check* phase involves monthly reviews to establish the progress being made by the improvement teams. If the planned progress is not being achieved, improvement teams will need to follow a formal corrective action or countermeasures process – the *Act* phase – to understand the root cause(s) of the issues and put in place an appropriate recovery plan.

Progress is also reviewed by the leadership team as part of the annual business planning process. This could result in changes to the focus areas, with corresponding new process improvements agreed for the following year.

To support the SD process, we recommend the use of four documents, as shown in Figure 8-2:

- The X Matrix
- Action plan

- Tracking chart
- Countermeasure

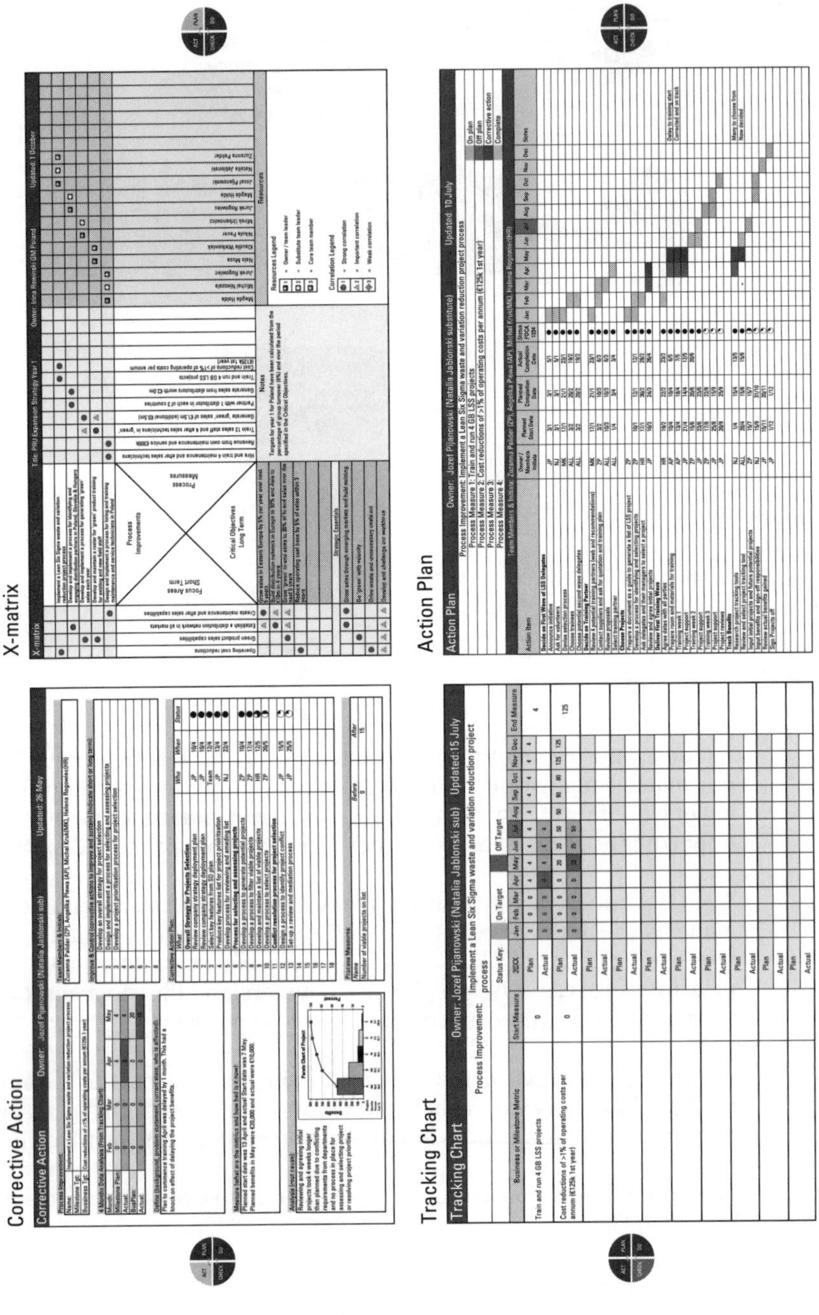

Corrective Action

X-matrix

Tracking Chart

Action Plan

Figure 8-2: The strategy deployment document set.

The purpose of the X Matrix, and how to use it, is covered later in this chapter in the section, 'Introducing the X Matrix'. The action plan, tracking chart and countermeasure are covered in Chapter 9. It suffices to say here that they logically follow the PDCA process to help drive improvement.

Decomposing and Cascading the Critical Objectives

We must next establish the critical objectives. The critical objectives break down the strategic essentials into a number of measurable goals that need to be achieved over the medium to long term – see Figure 8-3.

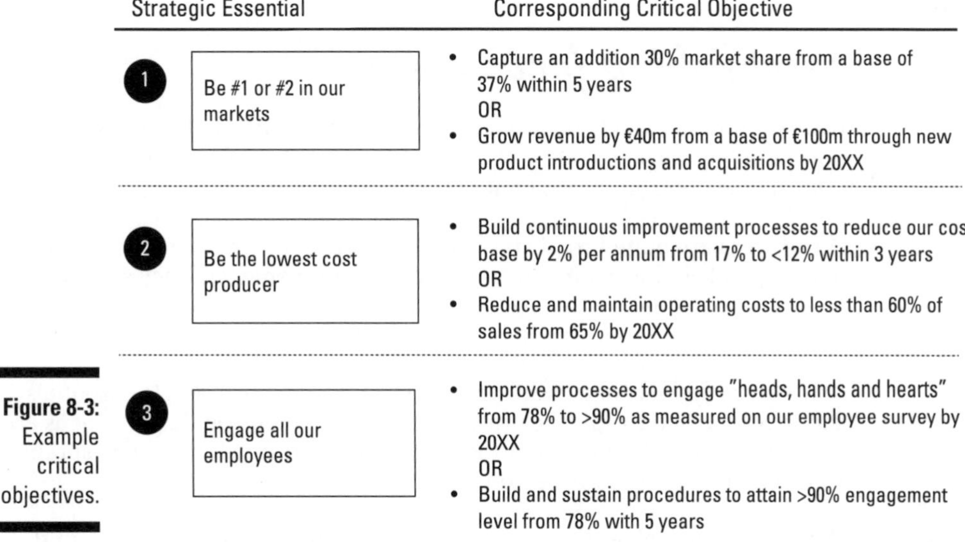

Figure 8-3: Example critical objectives.

The critical objectives should stretch the organisation, but how to achieve them may not be immediately clear. The critical objectives express the strategic essentials in **S**pecific, **M**easurable, **A**chievable, **R**elevant and **T**ime-bound (SMART) ways.

They should specify defined goals with a 'from–to' structure, and represent a significant performance improvement challenge (a breakthrough). The critical objectives typically cross functional boundaries and may well involve several processes. Critical objectives have medium- to long-term goals, typically from two to five years.

Targeting your critical objectives

A lot of thought needs to go into defining the critical objectives, and they should focus on achieving the strategic vision for the business. Consider benchmarking your organisation against other companies to establish the required levels of performance improvement the strategic objectives are meant to achieve.

Don't base your critical objectives solely on your competition or industry. Think about the vision, and ask yourself what the desired situation or the organisation would look like and then allow that to be your driver.

A mistake companies commonly make is focusing on current best-in-class results. Critical objectives need to be focused on achieving projected world-class performance.

Establishing focus areas

We must now establish *focus areas*, which are the critical objectives broken down into logical steps. More than one focus area may be needed for each critical objective, but try to limit them to two or three.

Focus areas are quite broad statements of intent and are themselves capable of being broken down into several process improvements. They should be measurable and are usually expressed in the form 'from x to y', as shown in Figure 8-4. Focus areas should be short term – 12 months or less.

Focus areas are part of a multi-step plan to achieve the strategic essentials and they'll be tied to specific critical objectives. When you define a focus area, try to ensure that it's customer-focused. Also make sure it has a measurable and verifiable end goal, based on the 'from–to' structure.

Make sure that each focus area is capable of being cascaded throughout the organisation.

Specifying process improvements

When the focus areas are agreed on, you can then identify the specific process improvements needed. These break down the focus areas into manageable projects (as shown in Figure 8-5).

	Critical Objective	Corresponding Focus Areas
	Capture an additional 30% market share from a base of 37% within 5 years	• Develop & implement customer & market analysis processes within 6 months • Improve existing NPD processes to launch new products from 36 months to less than 20 months within 1 year • Develop indirect sales channels from 15% to >20% by December 20XX
	Build continuous improvement processes to reduce our cost base by 2% per annum from 17% to <12% within 3 years	• Develop & initiate a Lean Six Sigma transformation process this year • Design & deploy processes for continuous improvement to reduce operating costs by 2% per annum within 12 months
	Build and sustain procedures to attain >90% engagement level from 78% within 5 years	• Improve processes to engage "heads, hands and hearts" to >80% as measured on our employee survery this year • Develop & implement talent management processes within 12 months • Develop & implement rewards & recognition processes by the end of Q3

Figure 8-4: Example focus areas.

	Focus Area	Corresponding Process Improvements
	Develop indirect sales channels from 15% to >20% by December 20XX	• Develop & implement a distributor certification process by year end • Design & implement a new sales capture and assessment process by September • Develop & implement sales training tools and techniques by end of Q3
	Design & deploy processes for continuous improvement to reduce operating costs by 2% per annum within 12 months	• Design & launch a continuous improvement opportunity identification process by Q4 • Develop & implement a training and project delivery process for Lean Six Sigma this year • Run projects to deliver cost savings this year
	Develop & implement talent management processes within 12 months	• Develop & Implement a talent recognition process by Q2 • Design & commence a first wave talent training process this year • Develop a career path talent management process by Q3

Figure 8-5: Example process improvements.

A process improvement should be a sustainable process and not a one-off action because you need to ensure that you're building long-term capability. Several process improvements can exist for each focus area and the objectives of each must be SMART. A multi-functional team needs to be set up to develop a detailed action plan for the achievement of process improvements.

Process improvement plans need to strike a balance between being too detailed and narrow and too broad and nebulous.

To ensure the organisation doesn't have too many projects to run and manage, choose only the top three or four process improvements required to achieve the critical objectives.

Creating the Strategy Deployment Architecture

The strategic essentials, critical objectives and focus areas define what the organisation will work on. That information now needs to be cascaded across and down the organisation. How this cascading is deployed depends on the nature of the focus areas and the structure of the organisation.

You may find building up a simple flow diagram useful (see Figure 8-6) to show how the strategy architecture will be divided throughout the company. In decentralised companies, regions and functions will usually be given autonomy to decide how they will cascade SD within their own operation. We recommend that SD be cascaded through only one or two levels.

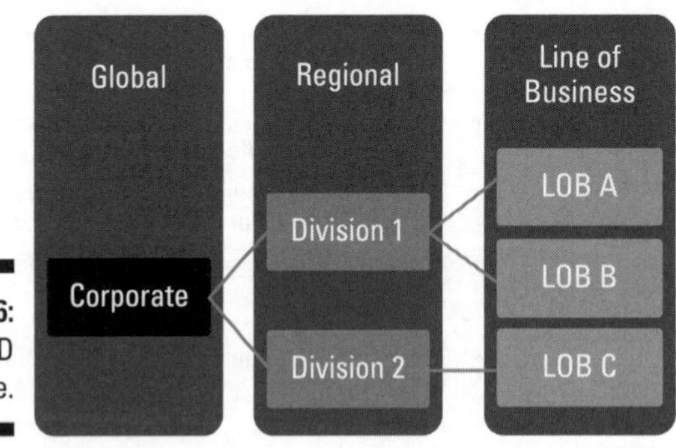

Figure 8-6: Example SD architecture.

Cascading to the point of impact

The SD must be cascaded to the people involved with the specific processes identified for improvement – the *point of impact* (see Figure 8-7). Typically, the point of impact is a significant process, for example a new product introduction process, and involves a cross-functional team working together to design and implement a new process, or improve an existing process if one is already in place (albeit with problems).

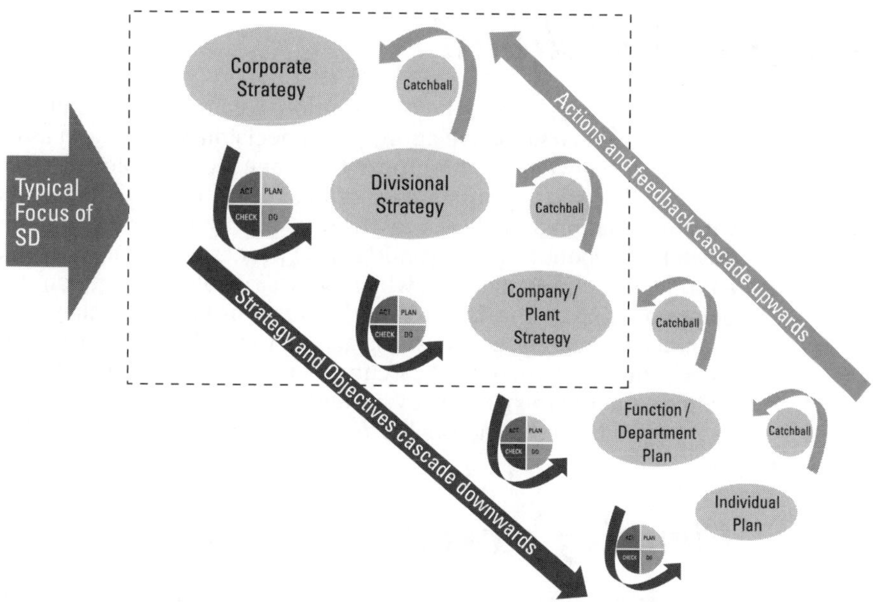

Figure 8-7: Cascading to the point of impact.

Creating the strategy deployment roll-out schedule

When the SD architecture and cascade structure have been defined, an SD roll-out plan should be created (see Figure 8-8), identifying the individual SD events and dates, as well as the resources assigned.

SD Events	Dates	Resources Assigned
Completion of Reflection and finalised Strategy Summary document		
Consensus and Communication completed		
Improvement Planning & Action Planning Event 3 days		
Planning catchball period/schedule		
Deployment Planning Event 2 days		
Monthly Review Schedule		

Figure 8-8: Example SD roll-out schedule.

Playing Catchball

To help gain buy-in from the organisation, a game of catchball is a good idea. *Catchball* is a participative approach to decision-making, and assists the shaping and development of the actions needed to deploy the transformation strategy. The strategic essentials, critical objectives and focus areas, together with information and ideas, are 'thrown' and 'caught' back and forth, up and down throughout the organisation. This process is normally conducted as a formal structured meeting, which allows people to reflect on the issues before passing on the 'ball' to another team or layer of management, for example. Ultimately, consensus is gained throughout the organisation. As well as helping to secure buy-in, catchball should be used throughout the organisation as a tool to spur discovery and new ideas. Although not necessarily easy, try to keep the catchball process simple and control the timescales.

Planning a catchball meeting

For your catchball meetings to run smoothly and efficiently they need to be designed to achieve a particular purpose. You can use a *terms of reference* document (see Figure 8-9) to let people know why they are required and what you expect of them. This document should include the purpose of the meeting, required attendees, the agenda, and information inputs and expected outputs from the meeting.

TEAM NAME	Division 'XYZ' Sales Growth Team	
MEETING PURPOSE	To 'catchball' the Process Improvements and Targets for the sales growth Focus Area	
ATTENDEES	Division 'XYZ' sales growth team & sales growth focus area owner	
TIME & LOCATION	10:00 in meeting room 1	
DURATION	1 hour	
AGENDA	Review Process Improvements for sales growth Review Targets and Process Measures Critique meeting	
INPUTS Sales X-matrix	**OUTPUTS** Update X-matrix Points to communicate	**RULES** Start on time Come prepared Keep an open mind Stick to the point

Figure 8-9: Terms of reference document for a catchball meeting.

Apply the input–process–output (IPO) model to planning a catchball meeting. Everyone should be clear about the Inputs they are expected to make, the meeting Process itself and the Outputs expected from it. To ensure that participants are prepared for the meeting, distribute any necessary documents a few days in advance and ask them to review them. Remember to book a room for your catchball meeting and to provide the necessary equipment for presentations, such as flipcharts, paper, sticky notes and pens, and so on.

Running a catchball meeting

Enter a catchball meeting with an open mind and use discussion and dialogue (see Figure 8-10).

The senior management of an organisation often find that catchball provides an opportunity to coach subordinates. Coaching can get them thinking more deeply about their plans and actions and how they might link to the longer-term objectives and focus areas of the organisation. The catchball process also provides an opportunity for you to learn more about your organisation and the capabilities already in place. For team members it's an opportunity to show what they can do and to learn more about the wider aspects of the business.

Wherever possible, use data and facts during the catchball sessions. People's unsupported opinions can quickly lead into argument and debate, and possibly a win or lose situation.

Compliance	Debate	Discussion	Dialogue
• Do as asked or told • Typically one-way communication— no discussion required except for questions about clarity of direction • Influence through position of power	• A structured argument– purpose is to win argument • Winning is achieved by showing the merit of a position and the denigration of the opponent's position • Influence through a win/lose equation	• A civil discourse • Exchange of information and positions on topics • Positions may be influenced but are typically held based on expertise or role	• A discourse guided by a spirit of inquiry • Communication purpose is to understand how we think and the assumptions we hold about a topic • Communication serves to make explicit the "tacit knowledge" in a group

Figure 8-10: Communication process for catchball.

Setting the catchball meeting agenda

A typical agenda for a catchball meeting should include:

- Introductions (if required).
- An outline of the purpose of the meeting.
- A restatement of strategic essentials, critical objectives and focus areas.
- A review of documentation relating to the subject of the meeting, such as the current status of a process improvement.

Build consensus throughout the meeting through open discourse, and record any changes and areas of agreement. Conclude the meeting by summarising the outcomes and thank the team for their time.

If conflict arises and starts to dominate the meeting, put the issue in a 'parking' area for later resolution. It's important to stay focused.

Following on from a catchball meeting

Following a catchball session it is important to update the relevant stakeholders. Refer to any RACI charts (which we discuss in Chapter 3) to ensure the relevant communication requirements are met, and issue the minutes of the meeting promptly, ideally within 24 hours.

Introducing the X Matrix

The X Matrix is so named because of its shape – see Figures 8-11 and 8-12 later in this section. It offers the unique advantage of allowing you to 'visualise' your strategy deployment design by illustrating it on one piece of paper.

The document records the decisions (and supporting discussions) needed to communicate and execute an effective strategy.

Identifying the what, how, how much and by when, and who

The X Matrix enables you to see the direct link from the focus areas, which is *what* you need to do to achieve the critical objectives, to the process improvements, which provide *how* you will do it. Each process improvement will have its own metrics that provide the goals in terms of *how much and by when*, as well as the resources – that is, the teams *who* will be involved in the process improvement. See Figure 8-11 for how these elements of the X Matrix interrelate.

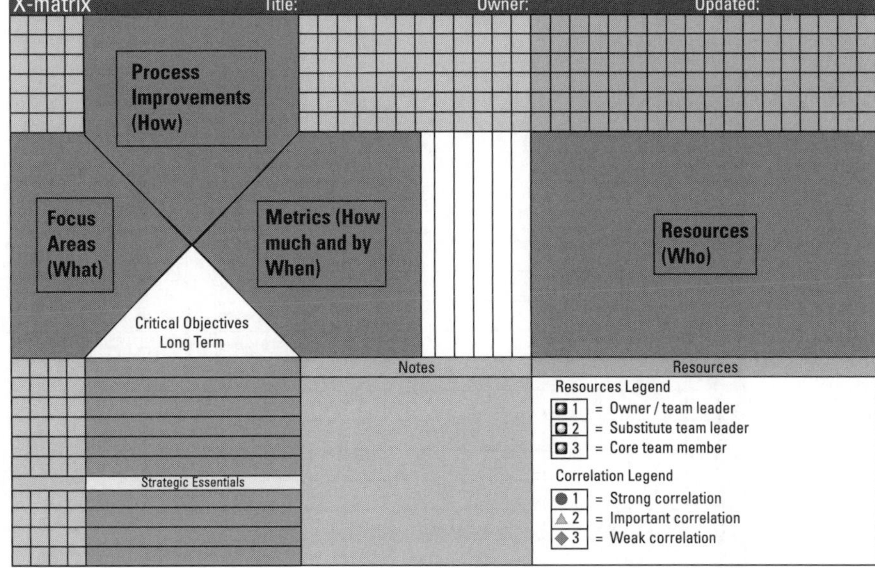

Figure 8-11: The X Matrix: the what, how, how much and by when, and who of SD.

Looking at the components of the X Matrix

The X Matrix is constructed during the SD planning phase and then updated as required during implementation. It has the following components, as illustrated in Figure 8-12:

- **Strategic essentials (1):** The top three or four key things that must get done in the medium to longer term.
- **Critical objectives (2):** The strategic essentials expressed as objectives.
- **Focus areas (3):** The shorter-term key areas to focus on in order to achieve the critical objectives.
- **Process improvements (4):** The individual improvements within the focus areas, which typically involve developing or improving one or more processes.
- **Process measures (5):** The metrics needed to track the progress and achievement of the process improvements. Two types of process measure exist:
    - Milestone metrics show progress in the implementation of the process improvement.
    - Business metrics show how the process improvement will impact business performance.

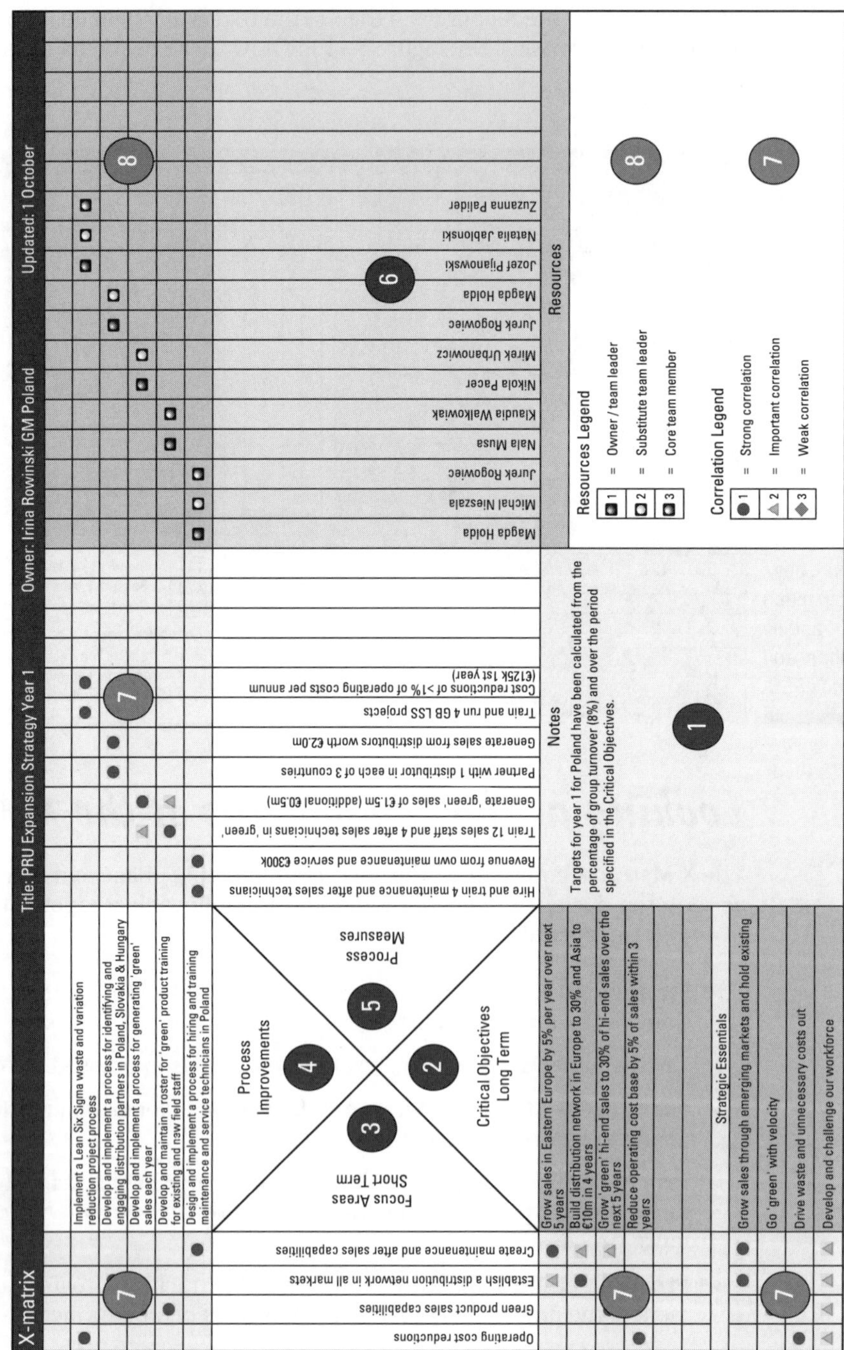

Figure 8-12: Components of the X Matrix.

More than one of each type is possible, but using just one of each that has a clear correlation with the desired improvement is best.

- **Resources (6):** The team leader or deputy, specialists and advisors (if involved) are listed. They're responsible for achieving the process improvement. Other resources are usually shown on the detailed action plan.
- **Correlation matrices (7):** These show the linkage between the strategic essentials, critical objectives and focus areas; focus areas and process improvements; and process improvements and process measures.
- **Resource correlation matrix (8):** This shows the linkage between process improvements and the key resources responsible for their delivery.

Working out how to use the X Matrix

Using the DRIVE model to plan your organisation's transformation journey (as described in Chapter 3), you'll have prepared a first draft X Matrix in the Prepare stage of the Improve phase. You'll then have updated it during the Shape stage. The X Matrix then needs to be reviewed and updated at the end of each step of the SD process.

Understanding the interrelationships and correlations between components is vital. Without this knowledge and awareness, you will be unaware of potential knock-on effects of various initiatives and you run the risk of sub-optimisation of the process improvements – see Figure 8-13.

Establishing process measures

Once the process improvements have been agreed, you need to establish the measurements that will be used to assess improvement performance.

Two types of process measure exist: milestone measures and business measures (see Figure 8-14). Each process improvement may have either or both types and may have more than one of each to fully describe it:

- **Milestone measures:**
    - Provide a means of assessing progress towards implementation.
    - Should be objective, not subjective.
    - Do not need to link to focus areas or critical objectives.
    - Could show the percentage completion or a quantity, for example X out of Y achieved.

  So, if a process improvement is 'Develop and implement a training and project delivery process for Lean Six Sigma this year,' a corresponding milestone metric might be 'Train 15 Green Belts and three Black Belts in the next year.'

X-matrix — Title: PRU Expansion Strategy Year 1 — Owner:

Focus Areas Short Term (columns F1–F4):
- F1: Develop capability to continuously improve and reduce operating cost base
- F2: Establish a distribution network in all markets
- F3: Define and implement 'green' hi-end sales capability in all markets
- F4: Develop and implement a maintenance and after sales capability in emerging markets

Process Measures (columns M1–M8):
- M1: Hire and train 4 maintenance and after sales technicians
- M2: Revenue from own maintenance and service €300k
- M3: Trian 12 sales staff and 4 after sales technicians in 'green'
- M4: Generate 'green' sales of €1.5m (additional €0.5m)
- M5: Partner with 1 distributor in each of 3 countries
- M6: Generate sales from distributors worth €2.0m
- M7: Train and run 4 GB LSS projects
- M8: Cost reductions of >1% of operating costs per annum (€125k 1st year)

F1	F2	F3	F4	Process Improvements	M1	M2	M3	M4	M5	M6	M7	M8
●				Implement a Lean Six Sigma waste and variation reduction project process							●	●
	●			Develop and implement a process for identifying and engaging distribution partners in Poland, Slovakia & Hungary					●	●		
		●		Develop and implement a process for generating 'green' sales each year			▲	●				
		●		Develop and maintain a roster for 'green' product training for existing and new field staff			●	▲				
	▲		●	Design and implement a process for hiring and training maintenance and service technicians in Poland	●	●						

F1	F2	F3	F4	Critical Objectives Long Term
	●	▲	●	Grow sales in Eastern Europe by 5% per year over next 5 years
	●	▲	●	Grow sales through distribution in Asia by €10m per year over next 3 years
		●		Grow 'green' to >30% of hi-end sales over 5years
	▲	●	▲	Train and sustain all sales and field staff in "green" and distribution skills within 2 years
	●	▲	▲	Build and sustain a distribution network in Europe to >30% of sales within 5 years
●				Continuously reduce operating cost base by 2% of sales per year over next 3 years

F1	F2	F3	F4	Strategic Essentials
	●	▲	●	Grow sales through emerging markets and hold existing
		●		Go 'green' with velocity
	▲	●	▲	Develop and challenge our workforce to compete in a 'green' environment
●				Drive waste and unnecessary costs out

Notes

Targets for year 1 for Poland have been calculated from the percentage of group turnover (8%) and over the period specified in the Critical Objectives.

Correlation between elements of the X-matrix use the legends:

●	1	Strong correlation
▲	2	Important correlation
◆	3	Weak correlation

Figure 8-13: X Matrix correlation.

- **Business Measures:**
  - Show a cause-and-effect relationship with a specific process improvement.
  - Aid the achievement of critical objectives by ensuring that business measures related to a process improvement result in the successful achievement of critical objectives over time.

	Process Improvement	Corresponding Process Measures
	Design & implement a new sales capture and assessment process by September	Milestone Metric • 10 key milestones from action plan to hit by September 20XX Business Metric • Grow sales from €2m to €2.5m by September 20XX
	Develop & implement a training and project delivery process for Lean Six Sigma this year	Milestone Metric • Train 15 greenbelts and 3 blackbelts per year • Run at least 1 project per greenbelt and 2 per blackbelt this year Business Metric • Reduce operating costs from 17% to 15% by end of Q4
	Design & commence a first wave talent training process this year	Milestone Metric • Complete the 4 key traning processes and 1 training wave by year end 20XX Business Metric • N/A

Figure 8-14: Example process measures.

So, if the related process improvement is 'Design and implement a sales force competence assessment and improvement process,' a corresponding business measure might be 'Sales force competence index increases from 5 to 7.5 by 31 December.'

Sorting out the human resources

With defined process improvements and performance metrics in place, you need to identify the key players in the teams responsible for each process improvement. These are typically the team leader, and any essential or core team members.

You may find that process improvements are related to end-to-end processes that span organisational functions, in which case it will be necessary to identify a key resource from within each area.

Add the names of the relevant individuals to the X Matrix or action plans as appropriate, and use a correlation symbol to denote the specific process improvement they'll be working on – see Figure 8-15.

We cover the roles of the individual process improvement team members as we start to implement SD in Chapter 9.

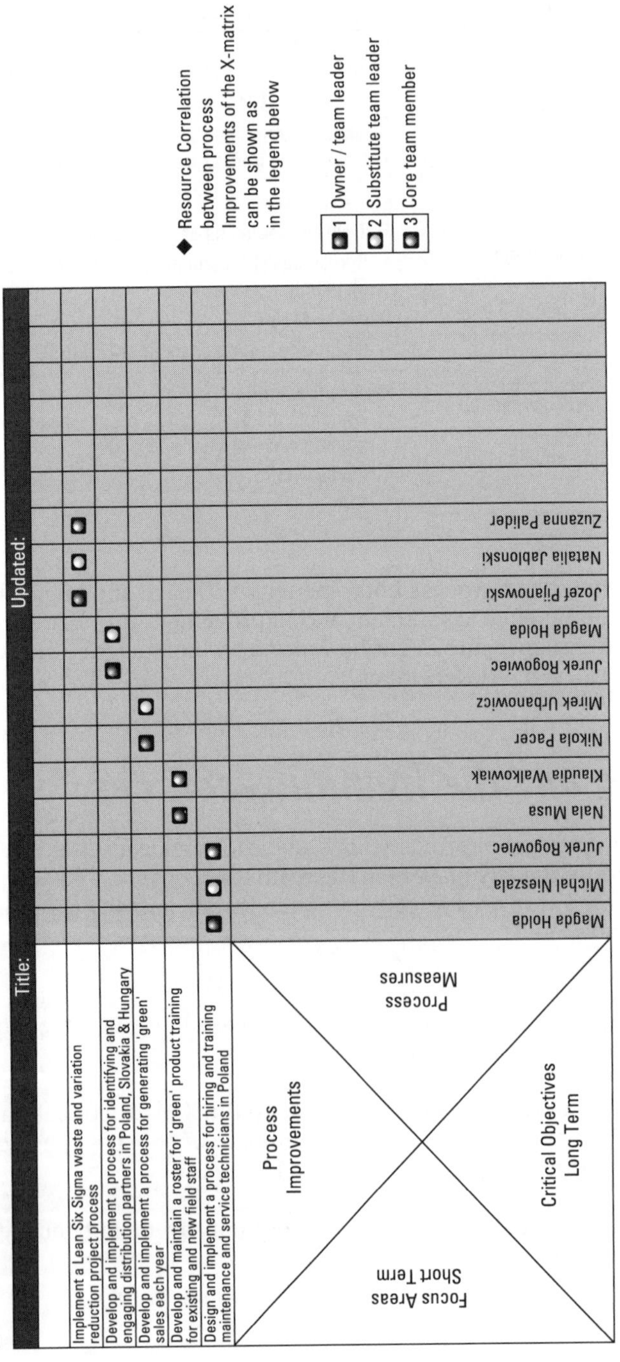

Title:

Updated:

Implement a Lean Six Sigma waste and variation reduction project process

Develop and implement a process for identifying and engaging distribution partners in Poland, Slovakia & Hungary

Develop and implement a process for generating 'green' sales each year

Develop and maintain a roster for 'green' product training for existing and new field staff

Design and implement a process for hiring and training maintenance and service technicians in Poland

Process Improvements

Process Measures

Focus Areas Short Term

Critical Objectives Long Term

Magda Holda

Michal Nieszala

Jurek Rogowiec

Nala Musa

Klaudia Walkowiak

Nikola Pacer

Mirek Urbanowicz

Jurek Rogowiec

Magda Holda

Jozef Pijanowski

Natalia Jablonski

Zuzanna Palider

◆ Resource Correlation between process Improvements of the X-matrix can be shown as in the legend below

1 Owner / team leader

2 Substitute team leader

3 Core team member

Figure 8-15: Resource correlation.

Chapter 9

Implementing Strategy Deployment

In This Chapter

- Getting the deployment underway
- Keeping sight of the daily operational issues
- Reviewing and reporting your progress
- Understanding the need for countermeasures

In Chapter 8, we looked at planning for strategy deployment (SD). This chapter focuses on its implementation and adoption by the organisation. Once underway, it's important to review and maintain progress using countermeasures to get back on track should things slip.

Starting SD Implementation

The strategy deployment process is led by senior leadership and has two basic components, as illustrated in Figure 9-1. The first is an annual planning process, which identifies the focus areas for improvement during the next 12 months, determines the pace of improvement needed, and assesses the human resource support required to meet the objectives. The catchball process (described in Chapter 8) comes into play here, and focus areas are deployed down to the point of impact where the actual process improvement and related action plans are created to achieve a particular critical objective. Some adjustments might be needed to ensure that the plan is achievable given the resources available. The annual plan also assesses the Lean Six Sigma maturity of the organisation, and identifies the tasks needed to take it to the next level.

The second component of the SD process is a monthly SD meeting focusing on how planned improvements are progressing. The time during these meetings is spent reviewing progress against the overall improvement plans. In too many organisations, however, these meetings seem to focus on not losing ground and the maintenance of business performance at current levels.

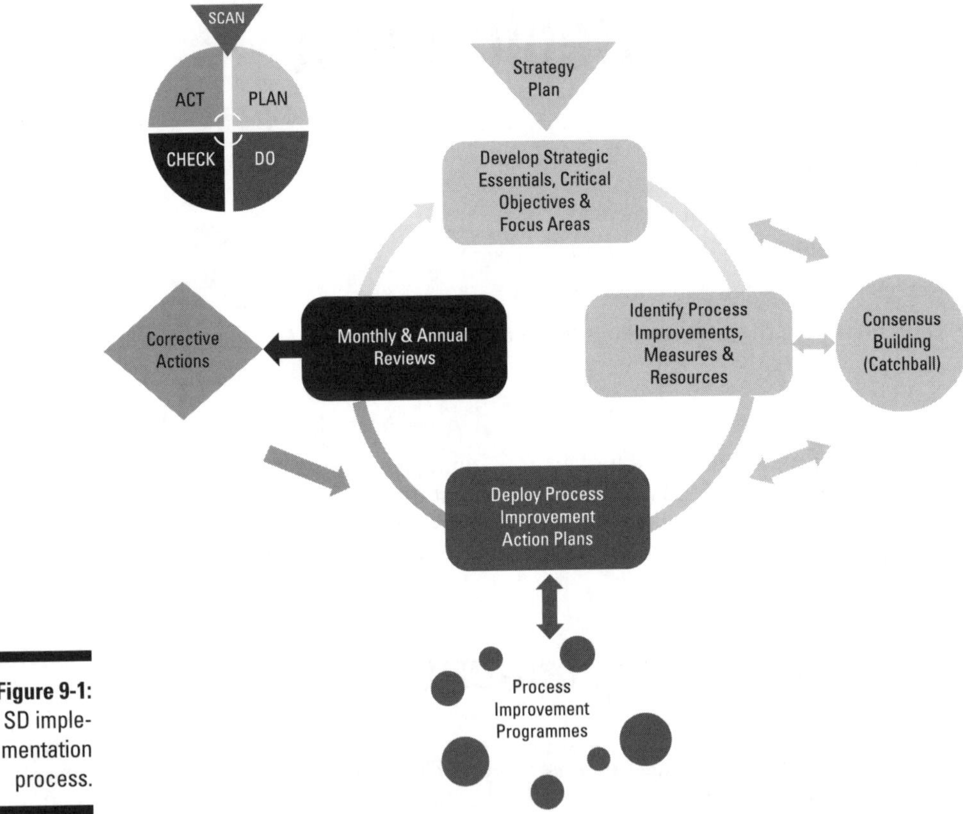

Figure 9-1: SD implementation process.

A monthly SD meeting needs to address whether incremental improvement targets have been met and, if not, what corrective action has to be taken to address the situation; if goals have been met, whether anything has been learnt that can be shared with the rest of the organisation; and, based on last month's performance, whether improvement targets are likely to be met for the coming month and, if not, what must be done to get back on track.

The monthly SD meeting brings all leaders together to focus on improvement rather than fire-fighting; it provides a chance to share learning that can be disseminated throughout the organisation to help shape its future.

Setting improvement targets and striving to meet them every month imposes a tremendous sense of discipline. The knowledge that improvement is expected pushes everyone to seek ways to increase their focus on improvement tasks. In turn, this is likely to encourage greater use of Lean Six Sigma tools to enhance performance, and the sharing of learning about what's working and what's not.

One of the most difficult aspects of a business transformation from the perspective of an organisation's leadership is that painting a vision of what the organisation will look like with another year of Lean Six Sigma learning and improvements under its belt is challenging. After all, no one in the organisation has been 'there' before – you must create your own future state. One of the things that enables leadership to achieve the future state is the push provided by the challenge of meeting the annual process improvement goals and the corresponding pull from the people who want to make it happen.

Developing the X Matrix in further detail

Chapter 8 discusses how to develop the short-term focus areas and process improvements from the longer-term vital few critical objectives. In fact, several process improvements may be required for each annual focus area.

Chapter 8 helps you develop the X Matrix. Once it's established you need to create and implement action plans for each process improvement, and put tracking charts in place to ensure you remain on target (see Figure 9-2).

You may also need to conduct further catchball sessions following creation of the action plans to ensure that they'll result in the required process improvements (the catchball process is covered in Chapter 8). It's also possible that you'll need to return to the X Matrix to ensure the planned improvements are achievable based on available budgets and resources.

The monthly SD review meeting is used to oversee progress and agree on corrective actions for getting improvement projects back on track.

In Chapter 8 we recommend the use of four documents to be used in the SD process:

- The X Matrix
- Action plan
- Tracking chart
- Countermeasure

Chapter 8 describes the X Matrix, and how to use it. Here, we discuss the action plan and tracking chart documents, and we'll explore the countermeasure documents later in this chapter, in the section 'Driving Results with Countermeasures'.

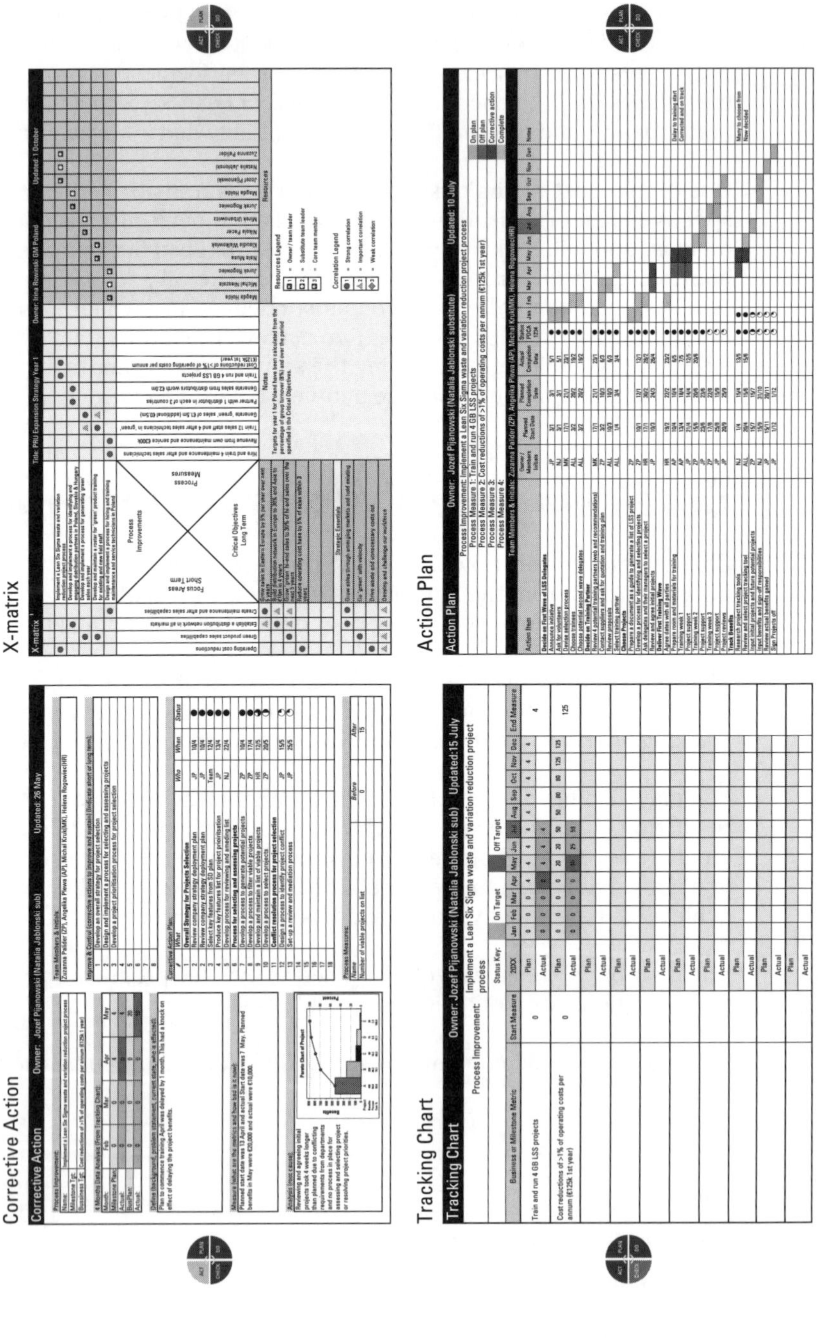

Figure 9-2: SD process documentation.

Creating effective action plans

The action plan is used to deploy strategy. The action plan is developed by the process improvement team and is owned by a workstream owner. The role of the workstream owner may be assumed by a business leader, value stream manager, process manager or functional manager depending on the point of impact of the specific process improvement. We discuss how to cascade SD to the point of impact in Chapter 8.

An action plan is necessary for each process improvement identified in the X Matrix. The example shown in Figure 9-3 shows an X matrix with two process improvements, A and B, each with its own action plan.

The action plan must contain sufficient detail to enable staff to follow it through and monitor progress. It provides a detailed list of the actions necessary for the successful implementation of a process improvement and identifies each person's responsibilities and the due dates for each task.

The action plan is a live document and should be reviewed and updated frequently by the team leader.

The action plan should include the following information (as illustrated in Figure 9-4):

- **Owner/team leader (1):** The name of the owner/team leader responsible for implementing the plan.
- **Process measures (2):** The milestone and business measures relevant to tracking this particular process improvement, copied from the X matrix.
- **Team members (3):** The names of team members, together with their initials.
- **Status legend (4):** It is recommended that a combination of colour and hatching is used to provide a visual representation of progress for the timing plan. For example, Green is on plan but not yet complete, Red is off plan and requires a corrective action, purple has been successfully dealt with using a corrective action, and light blue represents an action completed on time.
- **Headings (5):** These should include Action Item, Owner's/Team Leader's/Team Member's Initials, Planned Start Date, Planned Completion Date, Actual Completion Date, PDCA Status and Timing Plan with notes.
- **Detailed actions (6):** A 'to do' list of detailed actions, responsibilities, timing and status.
- **PDCA status (7):** Status of action using Plan (P), Do (D), Check (C) and Act (A) as the completion criterion. Zero (0) or blank means the action item has not yet been planned, Plan means a plan is in place for the action item, Do means the action item has been completed, Check

means the action has been checked for effectiveness and Act means mark the action as completed if it's worked or re-plan and take appropriate action steps if it hasn't.

- **Timing plan (8):** A chart of the timing and status of the actions, with notes for information if required.

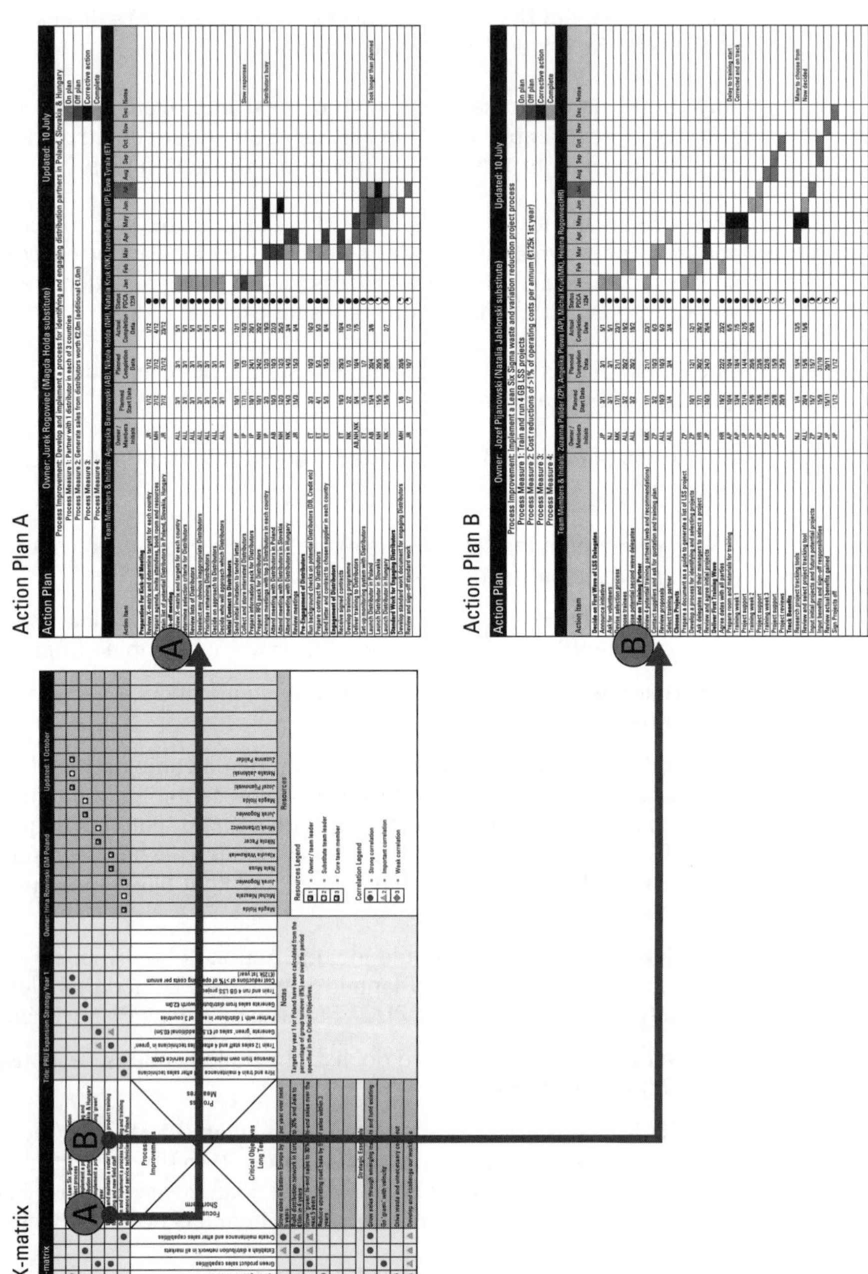

Figure 9-3: Relationship between X Matrix and action plans.

Action Plan (1) **Owner: Jurek Rogowiec (Magda Holda substitute)** **Updated: 10 July**

Process Improvement: Develop and implement a process for identifying and engaging distribution partners in Poland, Slovakia & Hungary

(2)
Process Measure 1: Partner with 1 distributor in each of 3 countries
Process Measure 2: Generate sales from distributors worth €2.0m (additional €1.0m)
Process Measure 3:
Process Measure 4:

(4) Key: On plan; Off plan; Corrective action; Complete

(3) **Team Members & Initials: Agnieska Baranowski (AB), Nikola Holda (NH), Natalia Kruk (NK), Izabela Plewa (IP), Ewa Tyrala (ET)**

(5) Action tem	Owner/ Members Initials	Planned Start Date	Planned Completion Date	Actual Completion Date	Status PDCA 1234	(7)		Mar	Apr	May	Jun	Jul	Aug	Sep	Oct	Nov	Dec	Notes
Preparation For Kick-off Meeting																		
Review X-matrix and determine targets for each country	JR	1/12	1/12	1/12	●													
Prepare agenda, invite attendees, book room and resources	MH	7/12	7/12	4/12	●													
Obtain list of potential Distributors in Poland, Slovakia, Hungary	JR	7/12	21/12	23/12	●													
Kick-off meeting																		
Review X-matrix and targets for each country	ALL	3/1	3/1	5/1	●													
Determine selection criteria for Distributors	ALL	3/1	3/1	5/1	●													
Review lists of Distributors	ALL	3/1	3/1	5/1	●													
Deselect any obvious Inappropriate Distributors	ALL	3/1	3/1	5/1	●													
Prioritise remaining Distributors	ALL	3/1	3/1	5/1	●													
(6) Decide on approach to Distributors	ALL	3/1	3/1	5/1	●			(8)										
Decide who will approach which Distributors	ALL	3/1	3/1	5/1	●													
Initial Contact to Distributors																		
Send Initial Invitation to tender letter	IP	10/1	10/1	12/1	●													
Collect and store interested Distributors	IP	17/1	1/3	16/3	●													Slow responses
Prepare Information pack for Distributors	IP	10/1	24/1	20/1	●													
Prepare RFQ pack for Distributors	NH	10/1	24/2	20/2	●													
Arrange meetings with top 3 Distributors in each country	IP	3/3	12/3	19/3	●													Distributors busy
Attend meeting with Distributors in Poland	AB	10/3	10/3	22/3	●													
Attend meeting with Distributors in Slovakia	NH	12/3	12/3	25/3	●													
Attend meeting with Distributors in Hungary	NK	14/3	14/3	3/4	●													
Review meetings	JR	15/3	15/3	5/4	●													
Pre-Engagement of Distributors																		
Run background checks on potential Distributors (DB, Credit etc)	ET	3/3	10/3	10/3	●													
Prepare contract for Distributors	ET	4/1	5/3	5/3	●													
Send letter and contract to chosen supplier in each country	ET	5/3	15/3	6/4	●													
Engagement of Distributors																		
Receive signed contracts	ET	19/3	29/3	10/4	●													
Develop training programme	NK	2/2	1/3	1/3	●													
Deliver training to Distributors	AB.NH.NK	5/4	10/4	7/5	●													
Set-up montoring system with Distributors	ET	1/5	1/7		◑													
Launch Distributor in Poland	AB	15/4	20/4	3/6	◑													Took longer than planned
Launch Distributor in Slovakia	NH	15/5	20/5		◔													
Launch Distributor in Hungary	NK	15/6	20/6	2/7	◑													
Standard Work for Engaging Distributors																		
Develop standard work document for engaging Distributors	MH	1/6	20/6		◔													
Review and sign-off standard work	JR	1/7	10/7		◔													

Figure 9-4: Architecture of an action plan.

Using speedy tracking charts

Tracking charts, or bowling charts as they're sometimes known, provide a visual system for tracking the progress of milestone and business measures in relation to implementation of a process improvement. Tracking charts are created, updated and owned by the workstream owner and monitored and audited by the leadership team at SD review meetings.

One tracking chart must be created for each process improvement.

Figure 9-5 illustrates how each process improvement may have one or more milestone and business measures, which are shown on the X Matrix in light and dark hatching, respectively.

The following information should be on the tracking chart (as illustrated in Figure 9-6):

- **Owner/team leader (1):** The name of the owner/team leader responsible for the results.
- **Process improvement (2):** The title of the process improvement being tracked.
- **Milestone or business metric (3):** A description of the metric to be tracked.
- **Start measure (4):** The measured and verified value of the milestone or business metric at the start of the deployment process.
- **Key (5):** Green for on target and red for off target. Amber isn't needed as progress is either on or off!
- **End measure (6):** The target value of the milestone or business metric at the end of the deployment process.
- **Plan (7):** The planned target for the milestone or business measure at each review period.
- **Actual (8):** The measured and verified actual value at each review period.
- **Blank rows (9):** Left empty for other milestone or business measures as required.

Note that the measures reflect the planned timing based on the action plans and, in Figure 9-7, it takes three months before results start to show due to preparation work.

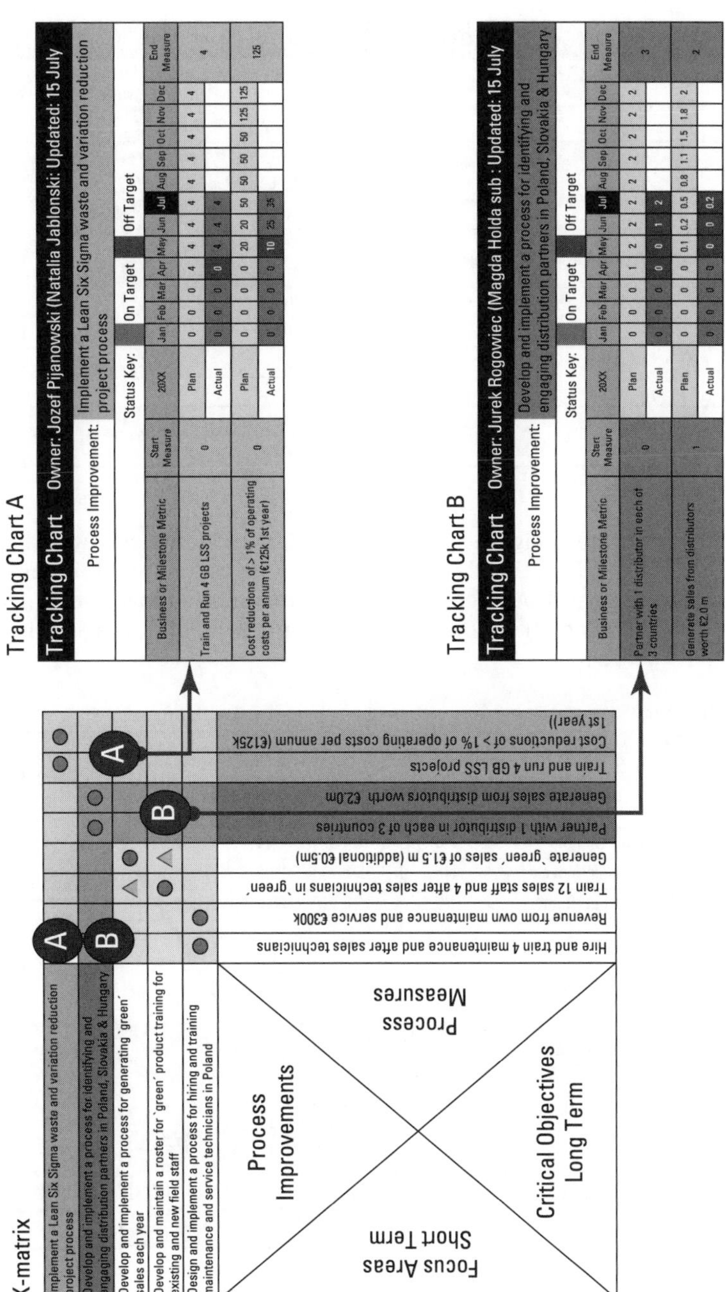

Tracking Chart Owner: Jozef Pijanowski (Natalia Jablonski: Updated: 15 July

Process Improvement: Implement a Lean Six Sigma waste and variation reduction project process

Status Key: On Target Off Target

Business or Milestone Metric	Start Measure	20XX	Jan	Feb	Mar	Apr	May	Jun	Jul	Aug	Sep	Oct	Nov	Dec	End Measure
Train and Run 4 GB LSS projects	0	Plan	0	0	0	4	4	4	4	4	4	4	4	4	4
		Actual	0	0	0	0	4	4	4						
Cost reductions of > 1% of operating costs per annum (€125k 1st year)	0	Plan	0	0	0	0	20	20	50	50	50	50	125	125	125
		Actual	0	0	0	0	10	25	35						

Tracking Chart Owner: Jurek Rogowiec (Magda Holda sub : Updated: 15 July

Process Improvement: Develop and implement a process for identifying and engaging distribution partners in Poland, Slovakia & Hungary

Status Key: On Target Off Target

Business or Milestone Metric	Start Measure	20XX	Jan	Feb	Mar	Apr	May	Jun	Jul	Aug	Sep	Oct	Nov	Dec	End Measure
Partner with 1 distributor in each of 3 countries	0	Plan	0	0	0	1	2	2	2	2	2	2	2	2	3
		Actual	0	0	0	0	0	1	2						
Generate sales from distributors worth €2.0 m	1	Plan	0	0	0	0	0.1	0.2	0.5	0.8	1.1	1.5	1.8	2	2
		Actual	0	0	0	0	0	0	0.2						

Figure 9-5: Tracking charts for each process improvement.

Tracking Chart (1) Owner: Jurek Rogowiec (Magda Holda sub) Updated:15 July

(2) Process Improvement: Develop and implement a process for identifying and engaging distribution partners in Poland , Slovakia & Hungary

(3) (4) (5) Status Key: On Target Off Target (6)

Business or Milestone Metric	Start Measure	20XX	Jan	Feb	Mar	Apr	May	Jun	Jul	Aug	Sep	Oct	Nov	Dec	End measure
Partner with 1 distributor in each of 3 countries	0	(7) Plan	0	0	0	1	2	3	3	3	3	3	3	3	3
		(8) Actual	0	0	0	0	0	1	2						
Generate sales from distributors worth €2.0m	1	Plan	0	0	0	0	0.1	0.3	0.5	0.8	1.1	1.5	1.8	2	2
		Actual	0	0	0	0	0	0	0.2						
		Plan													
		Actual													
(9)		Plan													
		Actual													
		Plan													
		Actual													

Figure 9-6: Architecture of a tracking chart.

In the example in Figure 9-7, the action item to launch a new distributor in April is missed, so this development appears as 'off target' in the corresponding tracking chart. As a consequence of this missed target, planned sales revenue from this distributor, expected to appear in May, is also missed.

Action Plan

Action Item	Owner / Members Initials	Planned Start Date	Planned Completion Date	Actual Completion Date	Jan	Feb	Mar	Apr	May	Jun	Jul
Launch Distributor in Poland	AB	15/4	20/4	3/6							
Launch Distributor in Slovakia	NH	15/5	20/5								
Launch Distributor in Hungary	NK	15/6	20/6	2/7							

Tracking Chart

Business or Milestone Metric	Start Measure	20XX	Jan	Feb	Mar	Apr	May	Jun	Jul	Aug	Sep	Oct	Nov	Dec	End Measured
Partner with 1 distributor in each of 3 countries	0	Plan	0	0	0	1	2	3	3	3	3	3	3	3	3
		Actual	0	0	0	0	0	1	2						
Generate sales from distributors worth €2.0m	1	Plan	0	0	0	0	0.1	0.3	0.5	0.8	1.1	1.5	1.8	2	2
		Actual	0	0	0	0	0	0	0.2						

Figure 9-7: Tracker timing reflects the action plan.

Managing Breakthrough Improvements

Breakthrough improvements aim to create significant performance improvements or changes in the way an organisation, department or key business process operates. These activities are typically directed at overcoming the critical business issues the organisation faces in the next two to five years. In the broadest sense, these issues may relate to profitability, growth or market share; toward a specific issue such as a quality problem; or in support of a new product or service introduction.

One of the biggest challenges organisations face is deciding what to *stop* doing. Many organisations have literally hundreds of programmes or initiatives in progress at any particular time. Many of these are 'pet' projects or were initiated some time ago and probably aren't even directed towards achieving the current long-term strategy!

All specific improvements or changes to be made by the organisation should contribute directly to the business objectives. These are the critical objectives chosen by the leadership team.

Strategic deployment is about focusing on the vital few process improvements and using the critical few metrics to measure how you're progressing.

SD makes a distinction between 'targets' and 'business fundamentals'. All other metrics that your organisation prefers to measure drop to the status of business fundamentals during the SD process.

Getting Back to Business Fundamentals

Realistically, much of the organisation's time must be devoted to keeping the business running; that is, carrying out the value-added activities of the key business processes that achieve the organisation's purpose. Monitoring of these day-to-day value-added activities needs to occur within all parts of the organisation so that process owners are able to take real-time corrective action for continuous process improvement. These selected monitoring points are the business fundamental measures. Ideally, they link to the CTQs (critical to quality requirements) that we discuss in Chapter 3.

Keeping a handle on the day-to-day work

For the success of the SD process, it's essential to put in place a daily routine management system that enables you to complete your SD action plans and day-to-day work activities.

The daily management system supports SD by providing the key performance indicators that support or refute progress in the process improvement efforts. By carrying out effective root cause analysis of problems in the workplace, the system should also help provide a valuable reality check for the monthly reviews.

In order to work appropriately, however, the daily management system needs managers to work on their processes together with the people actually carrying them out (see Chapter 3 on working effectively with others).

Managing for daily improvement

Managing for daily improvement (MDI) is a process designed to promote a disciplined, consistent focus on the team's priority results and the process elements critical to driving those results – hour by hour, day by day – and is typically operated by managers.

MDI comprises four key components (as illustrated in Figure 9-8):

- **Leader's standard work:** This provides a structured and repeatable routine for managers and supervisors. The aim is to help them drive a change of thinking and behaviour that moves from purely focusing on results to a focus that includes the process and opportunities for improvement.
- **Daily accountability process:** This involves a structured daily routine for teams to create control charts, which we discuss in Chapter 3, review data and information, and identify any actions needed. This process might involve creating a control chart, or determining corrective actions (countermeasures) and follow-up.
- **Visual controls:** Part of visual management, these present a process's current condition and performance (refer to Chapter 2) and could form part of an activity board.
- **Abnormality management:** This is a process and on-going approach to ensure a rapid response to abnormal or sub-standard operating conditions and links to a control plan (refer to Chapter 3).

Managers and supervisors need to understand that MDI cannot be delegated. They must become coaches and teachers and help their staff solve problems by removing barriers for them. The programme management office function (see Chapter 10) must ensure that the necessary infrastructure is in place to instruct the managers/supervisors in the use of MDI tools.

MDI must be defined, understood and visible.

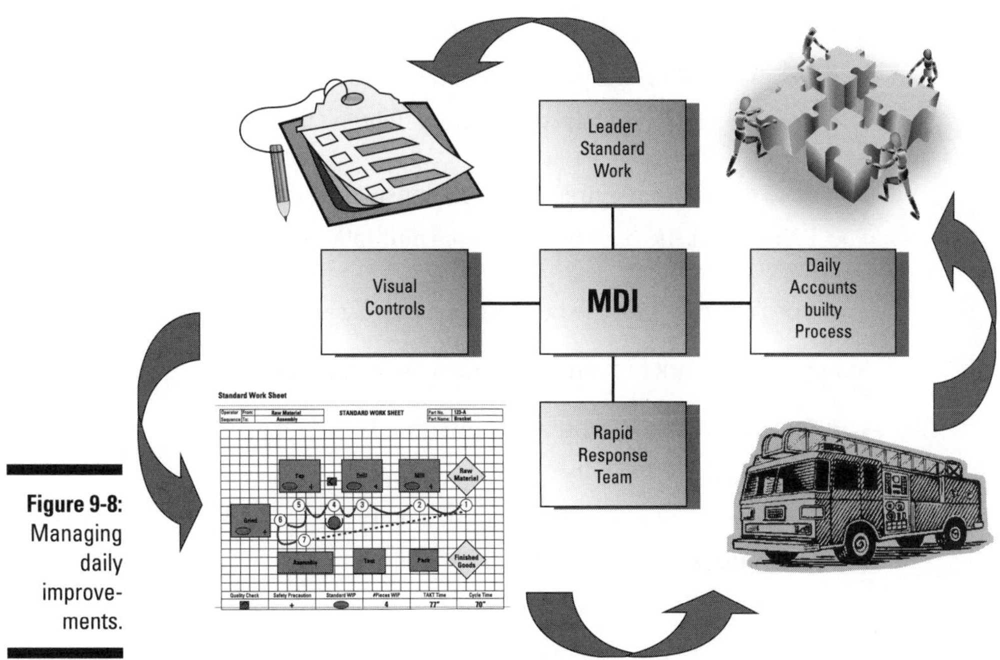

Figure 9-8: Managing daily improvements.

Carrying out standardised work

Standardised work is detailed in a document called a standardised worksheet, which we discuss later in this section. It provides a visual system by which process workers develop and follow a series of predefined process steps. Standardised work instructions represent current best practice, often referred to as 'the one best way'.

In an environment of continuous improvement, the one best way won't be the one best way for long! It will be replaced by a new one best way following each enhancement to the process.

Standardised work helps minimise process variation both in terms of how the work is done and in the degree of variation in the performance results. Standardisation helps reduces waste, eases problem solving and enhances productivity within a particular job or set of jobs. Visual work instructions provide a convenient way for supervisors to check operators' actions and add discipline to the organisational culture.

Standardised work instructions:

- Define interaction between people and the environment when processing products or services

- Detail operator actions and work sequences
- Provide routines to ensure operations are performed consistently
- Detail best known and understood processes
- Provide a basis for improvement by defining the normal and highlighting the abnormal
- Take customer requirements into consideration
- Expect that the operator performs multiple repetitive operations within a work sequence
- Does not promote the building of unnecessary inventory

Standardising work provides numerous benefits, such as:

- Development and capture of employee knowledge
- Enhanced productivity
- Maintenance and improvement of quality
- Reductions in waste, cost and variability
- Easier training of new operators
- Reductions in injury and strain
- Provision of a baseline for improvement activities

Workers become empowered to develop best practices – new one best ways – that make processes easier and more efficient. Standardised work ensures these best practices aren't lost over time and are available to set the standard for all employees (new and old) to live by.

The key to standardised work is actually using the document describing each process rather than letting it sit on a shelf gathering dust. For that reason, the work instructions must be easy to use. They need to be visible and as simple as possible.

Make sure the work instructions are easy to update so that they keep pace with process changes.

The standardised worksheet in Figure 9-9 visually details an operator's work sequence. Where appropriate, it also shows the operator's movements and motions within the physical work area.

The standardised worksheet shows the standard work in process (WIP) requirements, gauges and safety conditions, which are useful details when visually detailing operator assignments. They also comprise an audit tool for supervisors. The standardised worksheet is also useful in helping to train new operators assigned to an area.

Standard Work Sheet

Operator	From:	Raw Material
Sequence	To:	Assembly

STANDARD WORK SHEET

Part No.	123-A
Part Name:	Bracket

Tap

Drill

Mill

Raw Material

Grind

1 2 3 4 5 6 7

Assembly

Test

Pack

Finished Goods

Quality Check	Safety Precaution	Standard WIP	#Pieces WIP	TAKT Time	Cycle Time
	+		4	77"	70"

Figure 9-9: The standardised worksheet.

If a process isn't documented, there's no process. The more consistently the work is actioned, the better the quality and the more stable and predictable the process and results. Without a standard, no improvement can be made.

Sticking to the Plan

Using the PDCA process, you need to develop and complete action plans. To make your action plans as effective as possible:

- Take time to plan well.
- Use the collective skills and knowledge of the team to first set out the broad headline steps that need to be taken.
- Fill in the details under each broad headline.
- Assign responsibilities and dates.
- Set a review schedule, say weekly, and update as required.

Action plan steps should follow a structured approach. If an existing process needs to be improved, use DMAIC or PDCA. If the process does not yet exist, or is too badly broken to repair and improve, then a new design is required and you should use DMADV.

Chapter 1 describes the PDCA cycle and the DMAIC and DMADV processes.

Ensuring Effective SD Progress Reviews

Monthly reviews are a fundamental part of the SD process and are important for maintaining momentum. They help to resolve issues and keep the organisation on track in terms of achieving the strategic essentials.

The monthly review is an opportunity to gain consensus on direction, to align/realign the organisation and to resolve resource conflicts. From time to time, improvement efforts may need to be redirected towards achieving strategic essentials.

From the outset, set a schedule for reviewing strategy deployment progress.

Not setting a schedule will result in delays and missed targets.

Timing SD review meetings

Once the SD documentation – the X Matrix, action plan, tracking chart and countermeasure documents – has been updated, you need to conduct a review at a local level with the teams and process improvement owners. Next review the key items or summary with the leadership team and/or focus area owners. Use the standard SD documentation, *not* individual PowerPoint slides! The time needed for each review will vary but, for local reviews, plan on 20–30 minutes per process improvement and, for leadership reviews, set aside 20–30 minutes per focus area and 10–15 minutes per process improvement.

Establishing everyone's roles

Process improvement owners, team leaders and team members need to attend the monthly SD reviews and they need to perform the following roles.

Role of managers/process improvement owners

Reviews are excellent opportunities to develop people. Use questioning to challenge accuracy and completeness of thinking in a way that acts to move people towards their ultimate goal. Use coaching methods to encourage team members to think through and solve their own problems. Ensure that you:

- Conduct lively SD reviews that test team members' understanding.
- Don't try to solve the team's issues; instead, encourage the members to solve their own by:
    - Making sure that they understand the situation (with data).
    - Checking that no resource conflicts exist.

- Evaluate the effectiveness of action plans and corrective actions.
- Expect high performance and challenge the team. Treat good try 'misses' as opportunities for learning.
- Decide when to take action and what type of action to take.

Role of leaders/focus area owners

The leadership will need to have the ability to use Socratic questioning and coaching methods to encourage process improvement owners to think through and solve their own problems. You need to provide training in Socratic questioning and encourage its use throughout the organisation.

Critical thinking scholar and author, R.W. Paul, identifies six types of Socratic questions:

1. Questions for clarification	• Why do you say that? • How does this relate to our discussion?
2. Questions that probe assumptions	• What could we assume instead? • How can you verify or disapprove that assumption?
3. Questions that probe reasons and evidence	• What would be an example? • What do you think causes . . . to happen? Why?
4. Questions about viewpoints and perspectives	• What would be an alternative? • What is another way to look at it?
5. Questions that probe implications and consequences	• What generalisations can you make? • What are the consequences of that assumption?
6. Questions about the question	• What was the point of this question? • Why do you think I asked this question?

Role of team members

Reviews allow you to develop team members' understanding and abilities. They should welcome challenges and questions as opportunities to show what they know but not be afraid of stating that they don't know but will find out. To encourage team member participation in review meetings:

- Prepare well
- Update all documents
- Know your data, critical action points and issues
- Encourage lively discussion

- Present solutions not problems
- Present an honest and open view
- Expect to be challenged and to be helped with good try 'misses'
- Decide when to ask for help and what type of help you require

Setting the SD review meeting agenda

The following items are typically on the SD review meeting agenda:

- Update action plans, tracking charts and corrective action plans
- Local management/process improvement owners' reviews with teams
- Leadership team/focus area owners' review with local management/process improvement owners

The timing for each meeting will depend on the number of action plans and the number of missed measures needing to be addressed.

The monthly review needs to address the following questions:

- Are targets being met using sustainable business processes?
- Will good results be sustainable in the future?
- Which processes are achieving results?
- What processes aren't achieving good results?
- What is causing bad results?
- Are adequate resources assigned to SD projects?
- Are improvement processes adequate?
- Is the knowledge and capability of individuals being stretched?
- Is a learning organisation and culture being created?

Reporting

For reviews with local management and process improvement owners, the focus is on the tracking chart, action plan and corrective actions (as required). For the leadership/focus area owner reviews, the focus is on the strategy summary, X Matrices and tracking charts, while the action plans and corrective action plans are held in reserve if further explanation is required.

X Matrices, action plans, tracking charts and corrective action plans are the documents required for monthly reviews, as illustrated in Figure 9-10.

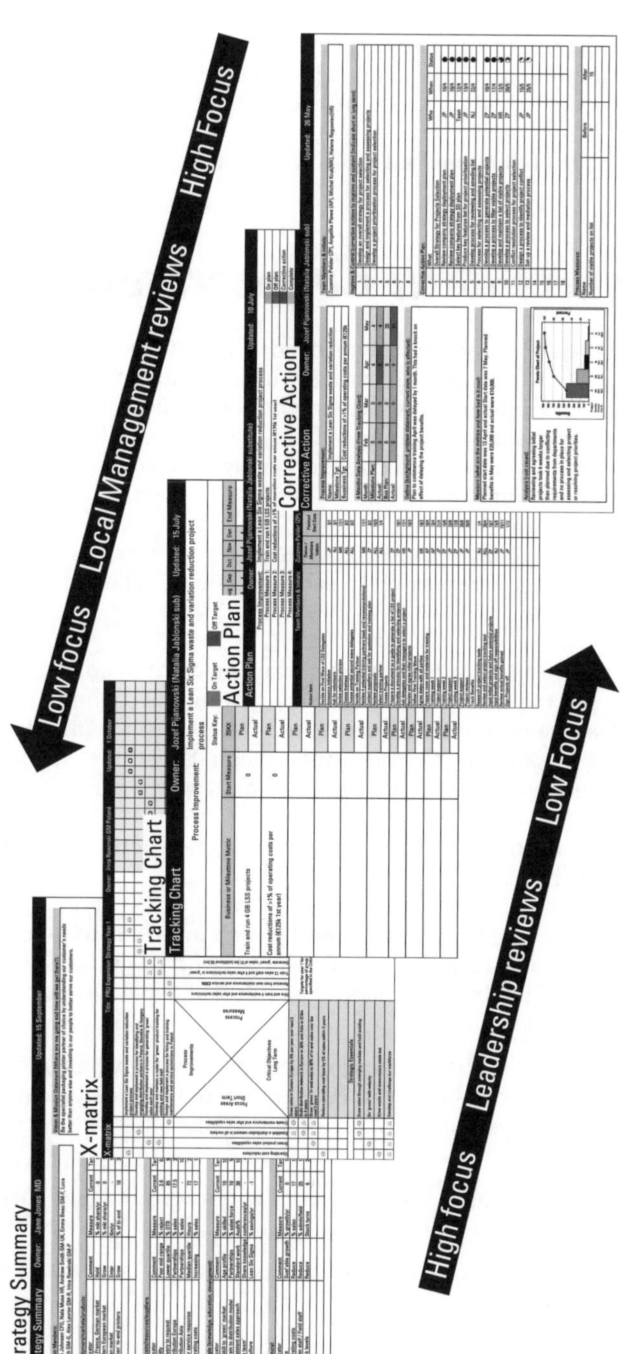

Figure 9-10: Documents required for monthly reviews.

Discouraging the use of supplementary documents as being able to succinctly describe status and corrective actions is a valuable lesson in itself. Electronic versions of documents should also be encouraged.

Limit the number of documents and avoid death by PowerPoint.

Driving Results with Countermeasures

Countermeasures identify the actions needed to reduce or eliminate the root causes of problems that are preventing you from reaching your goals. They employ a structured problem-solving methodology such as DMAIC and can be used when progress is declining or likely to decline. Effective corrective actions involve both short-term containment action to protect the customer and long-term permanent solutions.

You need to create countermeasures whenever your process improvements are moving off plan and report on the actions you're taking in the SD monthly reviews.

For every measure that's off target on a tracking chart, a corrective action plan must be put in place (see Figure 9-11). This applies whether you miss a milestone measure or a business measure. However, since milestone and business measures are often related or connected, just one corrective action plan can be used even if both measures are off target.

Let's take a look at the architecture of the corrective action plan with reference to Figure 9-12:

- **Name of process improvement and which metric is to be corrected (1):** If both milestone and business measure are off target and need correction, then use the business metric as this will usually be more important to the business.
- **Use the data from the tracking chart (2):** showing when and by how much the target has been missed. Again, if both milestone and business measures have been missed, the business measure is usually the better one to use.
- **Define (3):** A succinct description of the background and current problem as a result of the missed target.
- **Measure (4):** A measure of how bad the situation is now and where that data came from.
- **Analysis (5):** A root cause analysis of the problem. Show data, graphs and evidence, where possible.

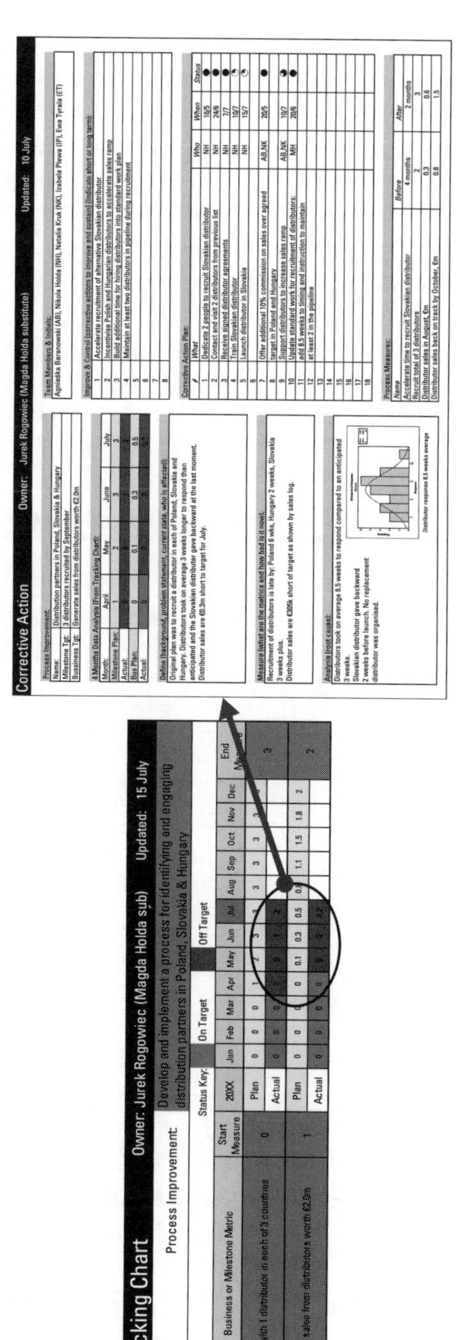

Figure 9-11: A corrective action for every miss.

- **Team members and initials (6):** Include all members of the corrective action team who may, or may not, be the same as those in the process improvement team. (The owner and substitute are shown in the header bar.)
- **Improve and control (7):** Identify whether improvements are designed to get back on target and ensure that the action plan doesn't go off target again. State whether improvements are short term or long term.
- **Corrective action plan (8):** A description of the individual actions – who is responsible for each action, when they are to be completed, and current status in PDCA format.
- **Process measure (9):** Additional measures that will be used to track progress in relation to getting back on target. Typically, process measures will be different from the milestone and business measures used for overall tracking.

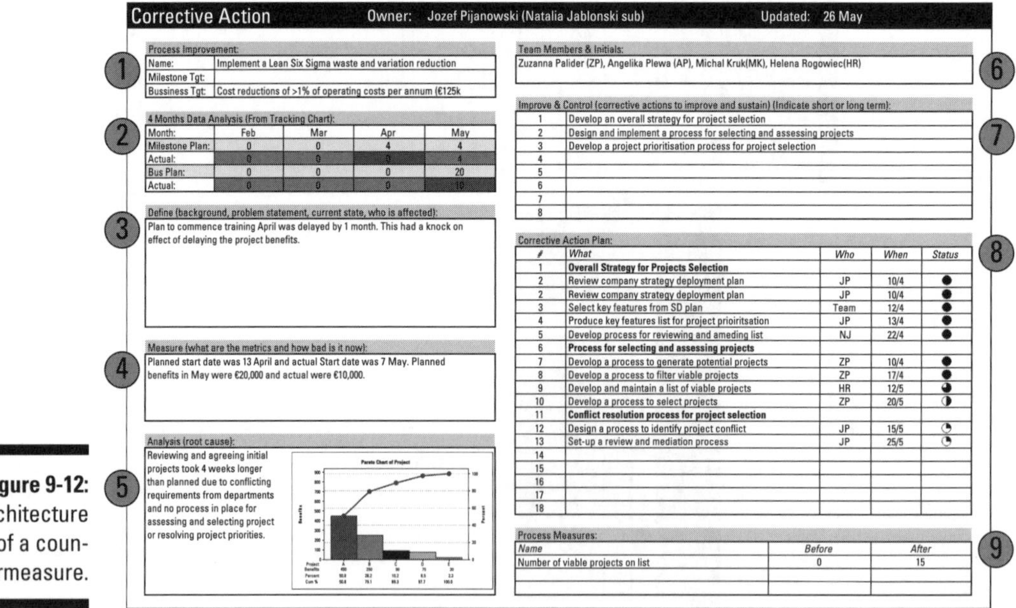

Corrective Action Owner: Jozef Pijanowski (Natalia Jablonski sub) Updated: 26 May

1 Process Improvement:

Name:	Implement a Lean Six Sigma waste and variation reduction
Milestone Tgt:	
Bussiness Tgt:	Cost reductions of >1% of operating costs per annum (€125k

2 4 Months Data Analysis (From Tracking Chart):

Month:	Feb	Mar	Apr	May
Milestone Plan:	0	0	4	4
Actual:	0	0	0	4
Bus Plan:	0	0	0	20
Actual:	0	0	0	10

3 Define (background, problem statement, current state, who is affected):

Plan to commence training April was delayed by 1 month. This had a knock on effect of delaying the project benefits.

4 Measure (what are the metrics and how bad is it now):

Planned start date was 13 April and actual Start date was 7 May. Planned benefits in May were €20,000 and actual were €10,000.

5 Analysis (root cause):

Reviewing and agreeing initial projects took 4 weeks longer than planned due to conflicting requirements from departments and no process in place for assessing and selecting project or resolving project priorities.

6 Team Members & Initials:

Zuzanna Palider (ZP), Angelika Plewa (AP), Michal Kruk(MK), Helena Rogowiec(HR)

7 Improve & Control (corrective actions to improve and sustain) (Indicate short or long term):

1	Develop an overall strategy for project selection
2	Design and implement a process for selecting and assessing projects
3	Develop a project prioritisation process for project selection
4	
5	
6	
7	
8	

8 Corrective Action Plan:

#	*What*	*Who*	*When*	*Status*
1	**Overall Strategy for Projects Selection**			
2	Review company strategy deployment plan	JP	10/4	●
2	Review company strategy deployment plan	JP	10/4	●
3	Select key features from SD plan	Team	12/4	●
4	Produce key features list for project prioiritsation	JP	13/4	●
5	Develop process for reviewing and ameding list	NJ	22/4	●
6	**Process for selecting and assessing projects**			
7	Devolop a process to generate potential projects	ZP	10/4	●
8	Develop a process to filter viable projects	ZP	17/4	●
9	Develop and maintain a list of viable projects	HR	12/5	◕
10	Develop a process to select projects	ZP	20/5	◑
11	**Conflict resolution process for project selection**			
12	Design a process to identify project conflict	JP	15/5	◔
13	Set-up a review and mediation process	JP	25/5	◔
14				
15				
16				
17				
18				

9 Process Measures:

Name	*Before*	*After*
Number of viable projects on list	0	15

Figure 9-12: Architecture of a countermeasure.

Follow these guidelines when devising corrective actions:

- Clearly state the problem using data and facts only.
- Use a structured problem-solving method such as DMAIC or DMADV.
- Don't insert a solution in the problem statement.

- Establish the current situation.
- Use tools to establish the real problem, real/root cause, solution(s) and controls.
- Solve problems at the lowest possible level in the organisation.
- Test whether completed actions have the desired effect on the problem.

Getting the Most from Visual Management

How do you develop processes that help people understand if 'their' process is getting better or worse? What you need is a system that drives ownership, awareness and accountability for each process from the lowest possible level in the organisation to the highest level in the organisation. In other words, you need visual management.

Visual management is likely to be one of the key fundamentals to successfully transforming an organisation. It provides both real-time and predictive information on the health of your business and is a key enabler for supervisors, managers and executives.

Visual management is a key component of managing daily improvements and provides real-time information and feedback regarding the performance of a business process. It communicates the shared vision of the business and how each individual contributes to success, and provides workers with a clear and common understanding of goals and metrics. Visual management presents the same information to everyone, maintains focus on the critical few metrics, and drives ownership and accountability from the lowest possible level in the organisation.

Benefits of visual management include:

- A cleaner and safer workplace
- Less wasted time
- Improved quality
- Enhanced morale
- Standardisation of work
- Abnormalities and waste become clear to everyone
- A move from 'specialist' understanding to an environment in which everyone understands

Visual management is common in the everyday world but not in the work environment. Too often, you must 'talk to somebody' to find out what's going on – are you ahead, behind, better than yesterday, better than last month?

You need to get away from using computer-generated reports emanating from meetings taking place in conference rooms. How will you fully understand a situation if you don't see it for yourself? How will you get to its root cause? To be customer-driven, you must understand your customers' needs and problems, using all of your senses to gather process data.

Ultimately, you need to use visual management as a predictive management tool so that you can identify a potential problem and take action to correct it – before it happens.

For more on visual management, Lean Six Sigma For Dummies (Wiley).

Chapter 10

Establishing a Continuous Improvement Organisational Structure

In This Chapter

- Sorting out a continuous improvement framework
- Adhering to standards while remaining flexible
- Taking a look at the continuous improvement group
- Summarising the roles of various stakeholders

In this chapter we discusses how to organise the continuous improvement activities that may either form one of the parallel transformation workstreams or follow on after the transformation has been undertaken (whether fully or partially).

A workstream is a clearly defined and scoped sub-programme of change within the overall transformation or a programme of non-transformational change following on from it.

Setting Up the Structure for Continuous Improvement

Continuous improvement is both an integral part of and a downstream activity following on from business transformation.

The transformation will include a number of Lean Six Sigma projects and other improvement activities. These will need to be managed within the context of the overall transformation programme, and it is often convenient to think of them as constituting one of the individual workstreams that make up the transformation. But, just as importantly, the business continues to develop even after the core transformation has been successfully concluded, and continuous improvement activity needs to occur to further enhance the performance of the organisation.

The continuous improvement workstream has itself to be programme-managed as part of the overall transformation effort, and you need to establish a continuous improvement organisational structure that's integrated with the transformation during that phase and continues afterwards. The components of the continuous improvement organisational structure are:

- A continuous improvement programme manager (or managers) responsible for the integrity of the programme and ensuring a consistent professional approach across the organisation.
- A continuous improvement programme management office responsible for supporting and administering the programme, including organising training for those involved and tracking the progress of the constituent projects.
- Continuous improvement experts, typically known as Master Black Belts, responsible for providing expert analysis and coaching support in the selection and execution of projects.
- Lean Six Sigma project leaders, known as Green Belts (if part time) or Black Belts (if full time). Green Belts tend to lead those projects scoped within an individual function or department; Black Belts usually lead the more complex and longer cross-functional projects spanning the organisation.

Depending on the scale of the transformation, the roles of the transformation programme manager and of the continuous improvement programme manager may be assumed by the same person or different individuals. If different, the continuous improvement programme manager is likely to report to the transformation manager. Likewise, the respective programme management offices may be integrated or otherwise separate but tightly interconnected.

The size of the organisation and the scale of the transformation will be important factors in determining whether the continuous improvement organisational structure is centralised or decentralised (see Figure 10-1). Ultimately, though, the style and culture of the organisation is likely to be the biggest determinant. This is perhaps best illustrated using some examples.

A UK insurance company that's a subsidiary of a global group will have a centralised transformation programme management office responsible for centralised aspects of continuous improvement. For decentralised continuous improvement, individual business functions will have their own continuous improvement leaders and (part-time Green Belt) project managers; widespread continuous improvement activity will take place. In contrast, an otherwise similar competitor with a smaller-scale continuous improvement programme operates centralised continuous improvement, with full-time Black Belt project managers located in the central programme management office.

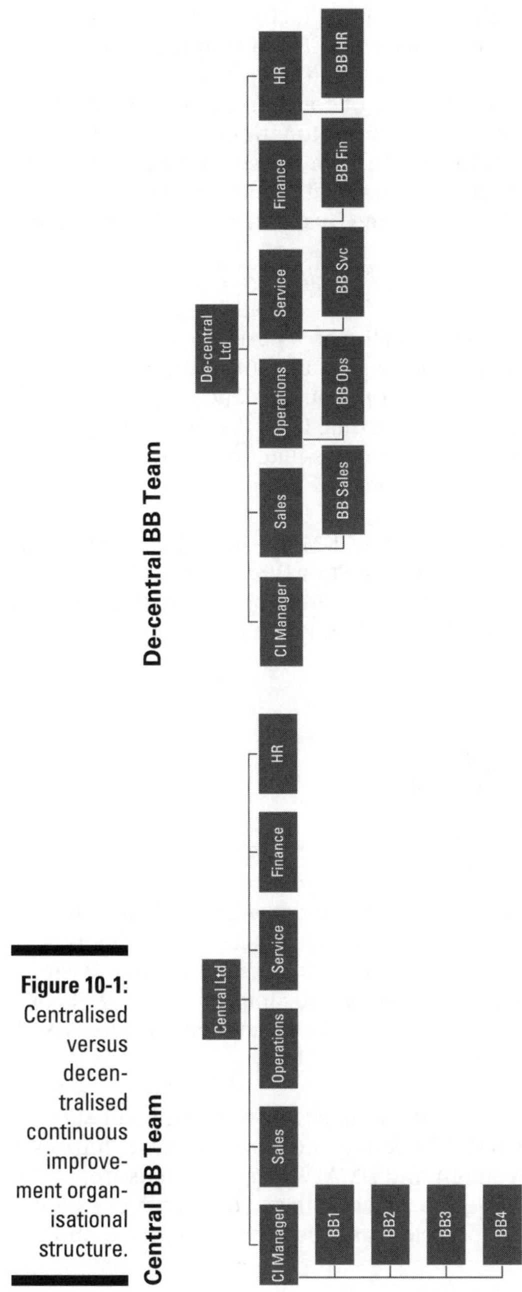

Figure 10-1: Centralised versus decentralised continuous improvement organisational structure.

Contrasting the two approaches, the determining factor for the organisations appears to be the number and choice of continuous improvement projects selected. In the first example, widespread continuous improvement deployment occurred and the majority of continuous improvement projects were (single) functional in nature; cross-functional projects were managed through the transformation structure. In the second example, the continuous improvement focus was on cross-functional projects and the organisation had yet to expand its programme to smaller-scale improvement activities.

Green Belt continuous improvement projects led by people improving processes within their normal area of responsibility on a part-time basis are essentially (single) functional projects and are suitable for being organised decentrally. Black Belt projects tend to be more complex and cross-functional in nature and led by individuals seconded full time from their normal operational roles; such projects, as a result of their cross-functional nature, are more likely to require centralised organisation.

Consider the likely mix of projects (for example, DMAIC Green Belt ones within an individual function, cross-functional Black Belt or DfSS ones, and Kaizen events), together with the scale of the overall programme before determining whether to adopt a centralised or decentralised continuous improvement organisational structure.

Creating Standards while Maintaining Flexibility

Irrespective of whether you adopt a centralised or decentralised structure, it's essential that a common standardised approach is taken to continuous improvement across the organisation. Without it, no cross-functional leverage will be possible and pockets in which continuous improvement stalls or progresses spasmodically are likely to exist – in short, a recipe for chaos and limited variable deployment.

To create a common standardised approach, use the standard Lean Six Sigma project methodologies of DMAIC (Define, Measure, Analyse, Improve and Control) for process improvement and DMADV (Define, Measure, Analyse, Design and Verify) for design projects unless you have very good reasons to do otherwise. These are world class, best practice, tried and tested approaches.

The following actions are key to creating your desired standardised approach:

- **Agree and use standard continuous improvement terminology (the 'lexicon') across the organisation.** Over the years your organisation may well have developed its own jargon and words for certain things. 'Champion' or 'sponsor', or other words and phrases, may already have well-established meanings that are different from their typical use by other organisations adopting Lean Six Sigma. If that's the case, define your continuous improvement terminology carefully and apply it across the enterprise to avoid any confusion of meaning.
- **Develop and deliver common Lean Six Sigma training (and coaching support) to all those involved in continuous improvement.** Ensure that you agree and organise a common training curriculum for staff involved in the transformation process. Of course, different levels of training will be needed for various groups (executive sponsors, project champions, Black Belts, Green Belts, Yellow Belts and so on). Depending on your needs, you may consider customised or generic training programmes, but you need to ensure, for example, that all Green Belts receive training on the same curriculum and are trained on the same core range of tools and techniques irrespective of what part of the organisation they work in.

  A point of qualification here: it may be appropriate to distinguish the curricula for 'Manufacturing' Green Belts and 'Service/Transactional' Green Belts. Some specific tools and techniques are more relevant to each group, in addition to those common to both. If you want your Green Belts to be able to support any part of your organisation, create a curriculum common to both. If that's not the case, you may feel it appropriate to have two 'flavours' of Green Belt training.

  If your organisation operates in many different countries, consider appointing different internal or external trainers to conduct the Lean Six Sigma training. However, be aware that different external providers may have their own materials and follow a different curriculum. You need to ensure that a common curriculum is adopted across the organisation, either by encouraging external providers to adopt common materials or by adapting or customising external providers' material for your own organisation.
- **Certify Yellow, Green and Black Belts (and possibly champions as well) to a common standard.** Learning how to lead Lean Six Sigma projects doesn't end as you come out of the classroom, it continues through being applied to real improvement projects. Hence a Green Belt, for example, is not fully fledged until they've undertaken their training and successfully applied it to deliver at least their first improvement project. It makes good sense to recognise this combination of learning and project experience through some kind of formal 'certification', which will likely also include an examination to confirm the individual's learning. Internal certification schemes can be developed, but nationally and internationally

recognised external Lean Six Sigma certifications are also available from the British Quality Foundation (BQF) and the American Society for Quality (ASQ), for example. The bar is set quite high for such certification and it's an excellent way to both recognise achievement and ensure common high standards across the organisation.

- **Implement a formal Lean Six Sigma certification scheme appropriate to your organisation.** Unless good reasons exist for doing otherwise, adopt a nationally or internationally recognised external certification scheme.
- **Standardise continuous improvement project tollgate reviews.** Individual Lean Six Sigma projects should be reviewed after each DMAIC phase. In essence, two types of review exist – a business review, where the intent is to verify whether the project is on track and on time to deliver the chartered improvements, and a technical review to validate that the methodology and appropriate tools have been properly used and correct conclusions drawn. Both are important, and are often combined, but it is the technical review that assures the common standard approach across the organisation. The previous bullet point described certification, but in essence the assessment review after the project has been completed could be regarded as the ultimate technical review of last resort – the certifier has to verify that the Green (or Black) Belt has indeed followed the methodology and used the appropriate tools throughout the entire project.
- **Facilitate best practice transfer and learning across the organisation.** Adopting common standards is not about securing the least common denominator; rather, it's about seeking common high standards and continuous learning and improvement.
- **Actively seek to identify and transfer best continuous improvement practice across the organisation.** Consider such vehicles as project fairs, recognition events, internal continuous improvement conferences and the like to facilitate this process.

Introducing the Continuous Improvement Group

Typically, the continuous improvement group will include an overall continuous improvement programme manager, some specialist support staff, both administrative and professional experts (Master Black Belts) and Lean Six Sigma project leaders (whether Green Belts or Black Belts). Project champions may also be considered part of the continuous improvement group.

The corporate continuous improvement group

We've considered the need for establishing common continuous improvement standards while maintaining flexibility. This is certainly a core part of the role of the corporate continuous improvement group. The corporate continuous improvement programme manager will typically be responsible for:

- Providing continuous improvement leadership across the organisation, and identifying and communicating the appropriate methodologies and toolkits.
- Supporting the corporate senior leadership team on all matters relating to continuous improvement.
- Organising training and coaching for the project champions and team leaders (the Belts).
- Organising an appropriate programme governance system covering the selection of projects through to their steering and completion, together with effective handover into the normal operating 'business as usual' and downstream process management.
- Communicating information about continuous improvement throughout the organisation, including the recognition of successful projects, and the sharing and transfer of best practices.
- Leading a small central continuous improvement programme management office that provides support and administration for the programme.
- Working very closely with the transformation programme manager during the transformation process and being responsible for the constituent continuous improvement workstreams.

Consider carefully whether the person assuming the transformation programme management role should also act as the continuous improvement programme manager or whether the latter position should be held by a separate individual who is functionally responsible to the transformation programme manager. To some extent this decision will depend on the scale and scope of the transformation programme and the personal capabilities of the individuals concerned.

The continuous improvement programme management office is likely to include a small group of support staff responsible for:

- Organising the logistics for Lean Six Sigma training and project/programme reviews.
- Maintaining the project tracking and governance systems.
- Organising other continuous improvement events and managing day-to-day continuous improvement communications.

Depending on the degree of centralisation, a small group of Black Belts/ Master Black Belts may also be necessary, responsible for providing Lean Six Sigma technical support across the enterprise, including:

- Leading the more complex continuous improvement projects, which might be cross-organisational and involve the customer or supply chains, or constitute an end-to-end process design.
- Providing coaching and advanced analysis support to other projects occurring elsewhere in the organisation.
- Leading the deployment of specific segments of the continuous improvement programme.
- Leading the mainstream internal Lean Six Sigma training programmes.

Divisional/regional continuous improvement groups

The decentralised continuous improvement groups will normally include the Green Belts responsible for leading projects within their own areas of responsibility on a part-time basis, together with their project champions.

Depending on the degree of decentralisation, the small cadre of Black Belts (and perhaps Master Black Belts) may be hosted within divisional/regional continuous improvement groups. At least some of these people will almost certainly have programme management responsibilities for the projects being undertaken in their own division or region as well as other responsibilities listed in the previous section. They'll be responsible for ensuring that corporate continuous improvement standards, methodologies and toolkits are used, but not for determining them in the first place.

Even if this cadre is decentralised, the more senior Black Belts and Master Black Belts will still form a virtual team across the organisation and will in effect operate within a matrix of responsibility; although directly reporting to their local divisional or regional management, they'll also have a functional reporting line to the corporate continuous improvement programme leader.

Appoint people to the more senior Black Belt and Master Black Belt roles who are comfortable managing within this matrix environment. If they're unable to operate effectively along both axes, the continuous improvement programme will likely suffer.

Understanding the Stakeholders

Earlier sections in this chapter introduced these roles; here, we briefly summarise their responsibilities and any other relevant information.

Business leader

The business leader has overall responsibility for the part of the organisation assigned to them, both for its longer-term strategic development and day-to-day operational performance. They're responsible for the people reporting to them within that part of the organisation and for its overall management. The business leader also sponsors and leads any transformation and/or continuous improvement programme relating to that part of the organisation.

Champion/sponsor

The project champion is the manager who commissions the continuous improvement project to improve a process important to them, probably within their sphere of responsibility, and to address an associated performance problem or opportunity. They're involved in selecting the project and the team members for it (including the project leader – Black or Green Belt). As the project progresses, the project champion continues to be involved by:

- Providing strategic direction to the team.
- Developing the first draft of the improvement charter and ensuring the scope of the project is sensible.
- Remaining informed about the project's progress and taking an active involvement in project and risk reviews.
- Providing financial and other resources for the project team.
- Helping to ensure the business benefits are realised in practice.
- Being prepared to stop the project if necessary.
- Helping to get buy-in for the project across the organisation.
- Ensuring appropriate reward and recognition for the project team in the light of its success.

The programme sponsor is the senior leader who commissions the overall continuous improvement programme and is ultimately responsible for its success. They're responsible for:

- Getting buy-in from the organisation as a whole and its external stakeholders.
- Establishing the continuous improvement programme and chairing the programme reviews.
- Providing financial and other resources for the programme.
- Being prepared to re-steer/re-direct the programme as and if necessary.
- Ensuring appropriate reward and recognition for those involved across the programme.

Although the terms 'champion' and 'sponsor' could be used interchangeably, we recommend that you reserve one of the terms for responsibility at the overall programme level and the other for that at the constituent project level. We use 'sponsor' for 'programme sponsor' and 'champion' for 'project champion' to avoid any misunderstanding between the two roles.

Value stream manager

Interchangeably also known as the 'process owner', this individual is responsible for the process or value stream. They need to ensure that the process is designed and managed to meet customer and stakeholder CTQs (critical to quality parameters).

The value stream manager, or process owner, may also often be the individual who acts as the project champion who commissions and sponsors any continuous improvement project relating to that process. (Though note that, if the project relates to just a smaller part of the value stream, it's possible that the project champion may report to the value stream manager.)

Functional manager

The functional manager is responsible for an entire business function such as finance, operations, marketing or HR, or for a department within a business function. They're responsible for the performance of the processes within their area on a line or operational basis. Many such processes may exist, but it's likely that the end-to-end value stream will cut across several functions or departments. The functional manager is thus responsible for operating processes consistently in line with the design required by the respective process managers, and for contributing towards any process improvement activity commissioned by them.

In essence, functional managers are responsible for the operation of a vertical slice of the organisation, whereas value stream managers are responsible for the end-to-end processes across the organisation. Clearly, functional managers and value stream managers need to work constructively together for both day-to-day operational management and transformation and continuous improvement to be effective.

Lean Six Sigma Black Belts

Black Belts are expert continuous improvement practitioners, whose role is to lead complex projects and provide expert support, using appropriate tools and techniques, to the various project teams within their scope of responsibility. They're often from different operational functions across the company, joining the Black Belt team from customer service, HR, marketing or finance, for example. The Black Belt role is usually full time and often for a term of two to three years; after this period, they return to operations. In effect, Black Belts become internal consultants working on improving the way the organisation works and changing the organisational systems and processes for the better. The Black Belt team may be centralised and report directly to the continuous improvement programme manager, or it may be decentralised and the various divisions, regions or functions will operate as a virtual team. This decision will depend on the culture of the organisation and the scale of the continuous improvement programme.

Black Belts will typically receive about four weeks of Lean Six Sigma training over a period of some months. In addition to the foundation training that Green Belts receive (see below), Black Belts will develop a solid understanding of all the main statistical and change management tools, and will become effective practitioners in the use of statistical software.

Lean Six Sigma Green Belts

Green Belts are trained to use the basic Lean Six Sigma tools and lead the more straightforward projects. They're normally part time and devote the equivalent of approximately a day a week (20 per cent of their time) to Lean Six Sigma projects. They're usually mentored by a Black Belt.

Green Belts continue to undertake their usual day job, the idea being that the improvement projects they lead will be related to their normal areas of responsibility. All managers have the responsibility for not only undertaking their job but also to improve the processes therein. In that sense, the part-time Green Belt role is already effectively part of their normal job; they're just being trained and empowered to improve those processes using the best practice approaches inherent in Lean Six Sigma. They will, by the very nature of their role, be decentralised across the organisation and remain in their normal host functions, divisions or regions.

Green Belts' basic Lean Six Sigma training typically lasts about a week and covers lean tools, process mapping techniques and measurement. It also provides a firm grounding in the DMAIC methodology and the basic set of statistical tools. Some Green Belts will also receive about a further week's training to cover the full body of knowledge required for ASQ certification, or to learn how to apply the more common statistical tools.

Part IV

Starting out on the Transformation Journey

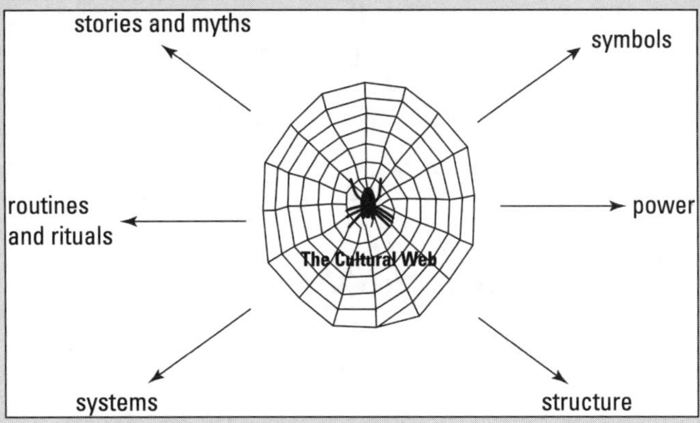

For a great bonus article about lean six sigma business transformation, head online and take a look at `www.dummies.com/extras/lssbusinesstransformation`.

In this part . . .

- Plan and achieve the cultural change necessary for successful business transformation.
- Deploy the Continuous Improvement tool-kit and embed the concepts of Kaizen into the organisation's DNA.

Chapter 11

Creating the Right Culture

In This Chapter

- Understanding your organisation's culture
- Working through the cultural transformation process
- Getting stakeholders on board
- Creating a vision of the desired company culture
- Developing leaders' and employees' skills

In order to achieve a Lean Six Sigma business transformation, you need to think about how the organisational culture should change for the new ways of working to be sustained. This chapter provides a pragmatic approach to planning a cultural change that will enable the business transformation to be both successful and sustained.

Culture, What Culture?

Every organisation has a unique culture, which will have developed over time. Culture can be simply described as the way people normally do things in an organisation and what they do when no one is around to tell them what to do. Employees and executives often take for granted the culture of their organisation, because they see and work with it every day. Individuals find it difficult to change their cultural mindset if they've worked for the same organisation for any length of time.

Cultures develop over time and are affected by:

- Events of the past
- The present climate
- The structure of the organisation
- Organisational aims
- The kind of people who work in the organisation

Many change initiatives fail as the result of insufficient awareness of cultural factors – and that's often the main reason why transformational change programmes fail to be sustained too.

Understanding what culture means

To be able to design the Lean Six Sigma change programme and bring about the required changes in employee behaviour, you must first understand the culture of your organisation. MIT professor Edgar H. Schein proposes that culture has three components:

- **Norms and values:** These are what's written on company literature, such as the mission statement, organisation charts, websites and business cards. These norms and values are then enacted in employee behaviours. However, some organisations do not practise what they preach and the enacted values may not align with those espoused.
- **Underlying assumptions:** These are the unwritten, unspoken things that happen within the organisation. They're what people really pay attention to. Assumptions are difficult to tackle because they're often subconsciously expressed and based on things that have happened in the past. For example, if a particular group of visitors comes to view an operation, could it mean that redundancies are in the offing? A Lean Six Sigma transformation programme will be derailed if people wrongly assume that layoffs are about to occur.
- **Artefacts and behaviours:** These are anything that can be seen, felt or heard in the company. These artefacts and behaviours can be viewed as a cultural web, as shown in Figure 11-1.

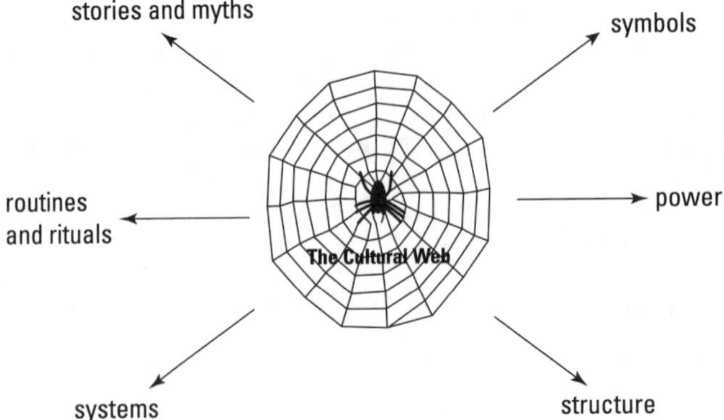

Figure 11-1: The cultural web.

The John Lewis Partnership has a unique set of values expressed in its mission statement: '. . .a visionary and successful way of doing business, boldly putting the happiness of Partners at the centre of everything it does.' This statement is the embodiment of an ideal, the outcome of nearly a century of endeavour to create a different sort of company, owned by Partners (its staff), and dedicated to serving customers with 'flair and fairness'.

To get a better understanding of the underlying assumptions operating within your organisation, listen to how other employees explain the culture to newcomers. What are the things that you must and mustn't do?

The cultural web can be broken down as follows:

- **Symbols:** Language and jargon demonstrating status.
- **Power:** Who has power within the organisation and whether their approach is autocratic or democratic.
- **Structure:** How the company is actually organised; for example, whether it's tightly controlled or informal, hierarchical or organic.
- **Systems:** Whether the systems for maintaining control are focused on reward or punishment, and the number of such systems that exist.
- **Routines and rituals:** How established corporate behaviour is and how easy it is to introduce new ways of doing things.
- **Stories and myths:** Which members of staff are seen as heroes or villains and how these roles affect power and internal relationships.

Now that you recognise what organisational 'culture' entails, you can analyse that of your own company.

Assessing your organisation's culture

You can choose from a number of methods to examine your organisation's culture. For example, *interviews* and *focus groups* are powerful tools with which to gather first-hand information on how employees view the culture of their organisation, and to uncover possible resistance to change.

You can develop a set of questions based on the cultural web described in the preceding section. Think about the culture of your organisation and answer the following questions:

Symbols:

- What language and jargon are used within the organisation and on company literature?

- Are symbols readily accessible and understood both within and outside the organisation?
- What aspects of company strategy are highlighted in publicity material?
- What status symbols exist, such as company cars, business accounts or access to an executive dining room?
- Do particular symbols define the organisation?

Power:

- What core beliefs inform leadership?
- How strongly held are these beliefs (are those at the top idealists or pragmatists)?
- How is power distributed throughout the organisation?
- What are the main barriers to change?

Structure:

- Is the organisation structured along mechanistic or organic lines?
- Is the organisation structured hierarchically or horizontally?
- How formal or informal is the organisation?
- Does the company structure encourage collaboration or competition?
- What type of power balance does the organisational structure support?

Systems:

- What things are most closely monitored and controlled?
- Is emphasis on reward or punishment?
- Are controls related to past history or current strategies?
- Do many or few controls exist?

Routines and rituals:

- Which routines are emphasised?
- Which routines would look odd if changed?
- What behaviours do routines encourage?
- What are the key rituals?
- What core beliefs do these rituals reflect?
- What do training programmes emphasise?
- How easy is it to change routines and rituals?

Stories and myths:

- What core beliefs do company stories and myths reflect?
- How pervasive are these beliefs (at different levels throughout the organisation)?
- Do stories and myths relate to strengths or weaknesses; successes or failures; conformity or mavericks?
- Who are the heroes and villains?
- From which norms do the mavericks deviate?

Overall:

- What is the dominant culture?
- How easy will it be to change this culture?

A disadvantage of interviews and focus groups is that employees may not wish to openly express their views and opinions. If this is likely to be the case in your organisation, consider quantitative assessments instead. A *quantitative assessment* provides a snapshot of the organisation's shared values and behaviours. A number of commercially available surveys can help you to capture data on employee satisfaction, employee engagement and organisational culture indicators, for example. Some surveys are available online; others may be administered by third parties. The great advantage of this survey method is that the anonymity and confidentiality it offers should attract more open and honest responses from employees.

Have a look at the following quantitative assessments:

- **Creatrix (`www.creatrix.com`):** This is a diagnostic tool focusing on innovation as the primary driver. It helps to build the innovative capacity of an individual/team or organisation.
- **Business Improvement Review (`www.rapidbi.com`):** The BIR is a strategic diagnostic tool that looks at culture, processes and capabilities.
- **Organisational Culture Inventory™ (`www.humansynergistics.com`):** The OCI provides organisations with a visual profile of their current operating culture in terms of the behaviours that members believe are required to 'fit in' and meet expectations.

Identifying the leadership culture

Effective leadership is one of the most important aspects of a successful Lean Six Sigma business transformation. The leadership style and behaviours that are prevalent in your company can have a huge impact on organisational performance and employee morale. Several cultural surveys are available to help you gather relevant data, including the Leadership Survey published by the Leadership Circle (see Figure 11-2). This survey enables you to carry out a thorough examination of your organisation's leadership culture. The Leadership Survey:

- Establishes a compelling rationale to change leadership behaviour.
- Focuses leadership-development efforts.
- Identifies cultural challenges likely to be faced during a business transformation.
- Correlates leadership effectiveness to productivity, profits, turnover and other key metrics.

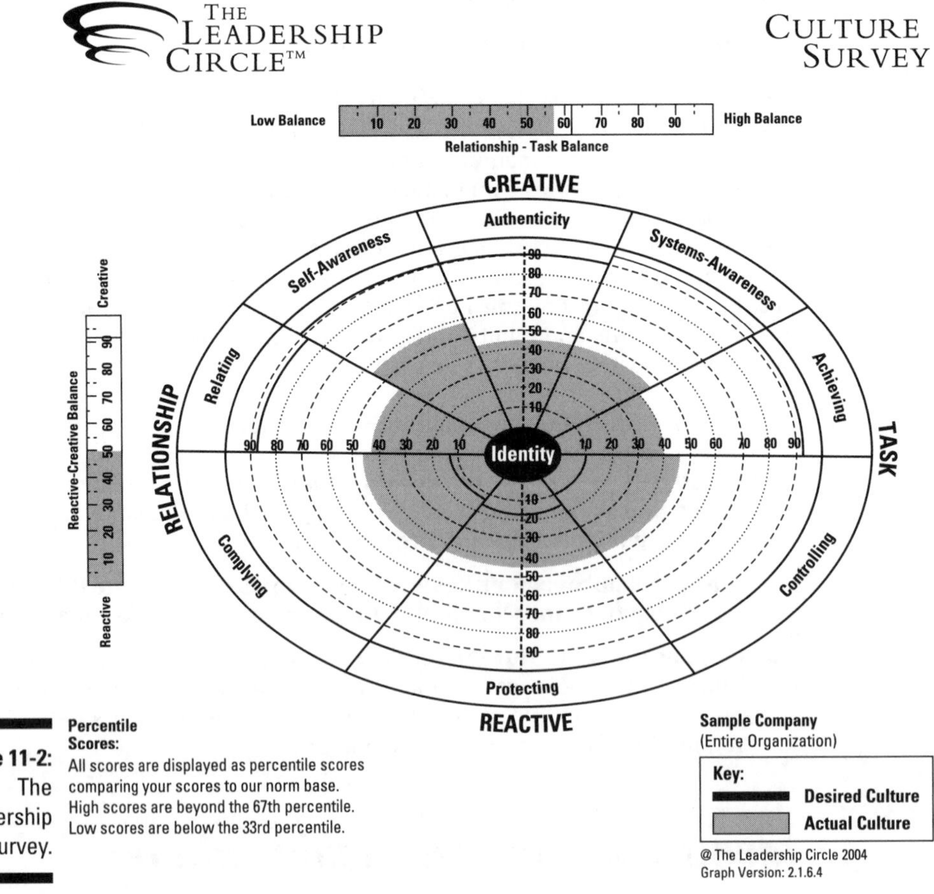

Figure 11-2: The Leadership Survey.

Initiating cultural change

To initiate a cultural transformation you need to consider which attitudes will have to shift, and how significant a change of viewpoint will be required from the average employee or manager.

What behaviours do we expect of the leaders involved in a Lean Six Sigma business transformation? Leaders must thoroughly understand what the organisation does, live the philosophy, and teach it to others. They need to support staff and the work they carry out, and take responsibility for the processes they operate.

Effective leaders must demonstrate the following key characteristics:

- Passion for Lean Six Sigma and its underlying principles and thinking
- Disciplined adherence to process accountability
- Project management orientation
- Ownership of the transformational change
- Balanced commitment to production and management systems
- Effective relationships with other business functions supporting the transformation programme
- Ability to measure processes and results separately

Leaders should also:

- Enjoy and respect people – help people feel good about themselves, see the good in each person and believe that everyone has something to contribute
- Think quickly and logically – be able to keep track of tasks and monitor the emotional climate of the group
- Be excellent communicators – be outstanding listeners, able to simplify themes, create clarity and engage and inspire people.
- Demonstrate warmth and inspire trust – convey warmth and friendliness, put people at ease and be non-judgemental
- Be goal orientated – focus on the end goal, ensure that decisions get made, push for tangible outcomes and be customer focused

The success of the business transformation process depends on the selection of good leaders. Employees will need role models and new heroes with whom to identify. Successful changes involve the creation of new myths built on heroic stories of the new ways of doing things.

You can act your way into a new way of thinking faster than you can think your way into a new way of acting.

Managing a Cultural Transformation

For the Lean Six Sigma transformation process to be successful, the culture of the organisation must change in order to embrace continuous improvement. Employees must feel empowered to make improvements to their business processes and work methods. To ensure that employees feel able to initiate improvements, you need to make sure that the organisational change process as a whole is effectively managed.

You need to be able to predict the issues and problems that must be addressed at each stage of the transformation in order to accelerate the change and minimise the pain. You also need to help people to let go of ingrained thinking and working and to embrace the new culture of continuous improvement.

Organisational culture is complex, powerful, deep and stable. If you want to alter it, the change process needs to be managed and will take time!

Kotter's eight steps to cultural change

Dr John Kotter's eight-step process is a very effective method for managing cultural change. You will need to continuously repeat the process to sustain an effective cultural change as the Lean Six Sigma transformation is deployed over time.

The eight steps are discussed below:

1. **Establish a sense of urgency:** You need to let stakeholders know why the Lean Six Sigma transformation must happen now and what the positive outcomes of immediate action will be – and the likely negative consequences of inaction.
2. **Form a powerful guiding coalition:** You have to assemble a powerful group of people who are committed to achieving the transformation. This should include leadership team sponsors, employees who enjoy and thrive on change, and Lean Six Sigma practitioners who will assist teams in making process improvements.
3. **Create a vision:** You must develop a future vision of the transformed organisation, linked to business strategy and the transformation plan (see the section 'Utilising a cultural transformation plan', later in this chapter).

4. **Communicate the vision:** Make sure that you communicate regularly with all stakeholders throughout the Lean Six Sigma transformation journey.
5. **Empower others to act on the vision:** You have to understand and remove unhelpful structures and systems to allow people to experiment and feel empowered.
6. **Plan for short-term wins:** Ensure that you establish process improvements that create short-term benefits. Publicly reward people for their involvement in the improvements.
7. **Consolidate improvements and produce still more changes:** Recognise and reward those able to promote and work towards the transformation vision. Sponsor new improvement projects to create a culture of continuous improvement.
8. **Institutionalise new approaches:** Continue to reward people who exhibit empowered behaviours that lead to the achievement of the transformation objectives.

You need to keep reviewing and iterating the process and thinking of ways to keep re-energising the organisation.

Lewin's three phases of change

Another useful way of thinking about change is to use the three-stage theory of change commonly referred to as Unfreeze, Change, Refreeze, developed by Kurt Lewin and illustrated in Figure 11-3. The following sections describe these three stages in detail.

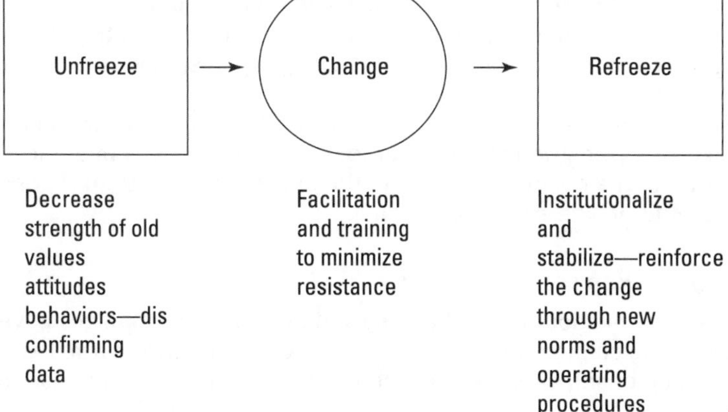

Figure 11-3: Lewin's three phases of change.

Stage 1: Unfreeze

In today's world of constant change, the unfreezing stage is probably the most important to understand. It is about getting ready to change. Unfreezing involves recognising that change is necessary and preparing to move away from your current comfort zone.

This first stage is about preparing employees for the change before the change takes place (and ideally creating a climate in which they actively want the change). The more people feel that change is necessary and urgent, the more motivated they are to make that change. If there's no sense of urgency and people don't understand why the change is needed, there's no stimulus to make an immediate change and the need for change itself becomes less important.

Unfreezing and boosting motivation for the change involves weighing up the pros and cons and deciding if the pros outnumber the cons before any action is taken. Lewin calls this process Force Field Analysis. *Force Field Analysis* helps you to understand the different factors (forces) for and against making a change that you need to be aware of (analysis). If the factors for change outweigh the factors against it, you'll make the change; if not, you won't.

This unfreezing stage involves moving yourself, a department, or an entire business towards motivation for change. You may find it useful to create Force Field Analysis diagrams for each stakeholder group.

Stage 2: Change

In order to start the cultural change you need to change behaviours through a process called transition. Transition is the inner movement or journey that you make in reaction to a change. You need to help stakeholders to move towards a new way of working.

People often find transition a difficult process because they're learning about upcoming changes and need to be given time to understand and work with them. It's vital that you support your team during transition, by offering training or coaching, and expecting and accepting mistakes as part of the process.

Using role models and allowing people to develop their own solutions also makes the transition stage easier for your staff. Keep communicating a clear picture of the desired change and the expected benefits so that people don't lose sight of where they're heading.

Stage 3: Refreeze

This stage is about re-establishing stability once the changes have been made. The changes are accepted and become the new norm. People form new relationships and become comfortable with their routines. This stage can take time.

Lewin's concept of refreezing is somewhat out of fashion. Instead, you need to see this final stage as being more flexible than a rigid frozen block. You must keep reviewing and reinforcing the cultural change to ensure that it's accepted.

The cultural change journey doesn't have an end; rather, it is an ongoing process.

Utilising a cultural transformation plan

A cultural transformation plan will be invaluable in successfully managing the cultural change. The objectives and goals of the cultural transformation plan should be aligned to the Lean Six Sigma programme plan. The cultural transformation plan must be built around the steps of change discussed above and provide a detailed plan of how the cultural change will occur and be sustained. See the sample cultural transformation plan in Figure 11-4.

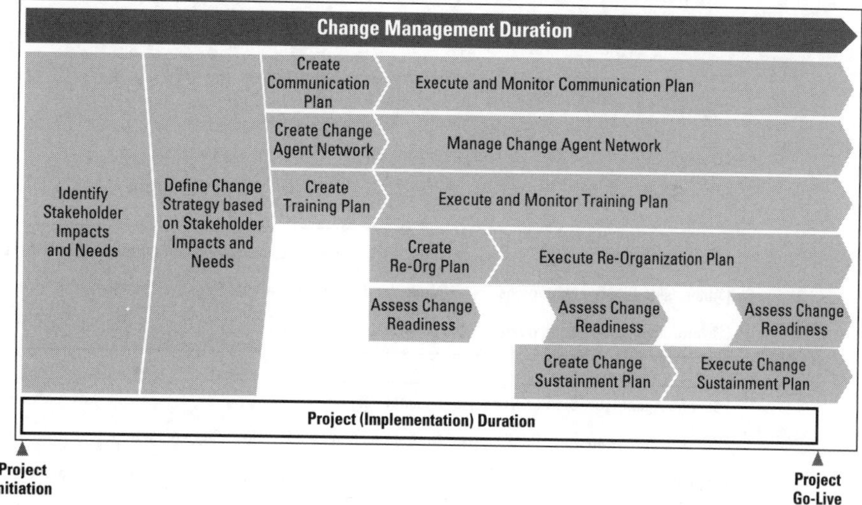

Figure 11-4: Sample cultural transformation plan.

The cultural transformation plan should include the following sections:

- Strategy and goals
- Stakeholders' impacts and needs
- Organisational structure
- Communication plan

- Training plan
- Rewards and recognition plan
- Risk management plan
- Sustaining the change plan

Cultural transformation plans should be aligned with the phases of the Lean Six Sigma transformation programme to ensure that the organisation is prepared for the introduction of each phase. Plans should be regarded as living documents and actively updated to reflect changes in the programme. All plans should be communicated to stakeholders.

Achieving Stakeholder Buy-in

Getting stakeholders on-board with the cultural transformation is vital (refer to Chapter 2 for more on stakeholders). You need to identify change managers who can work with employees at all levels of the organisation to gain their buy-in.

The key change management roles and their functions are illustrated in Figure 11-5.

Role	Function
Change sponsors	Have the authority, resources, and accountability to call for and support change
Authorising Change champions	Make the decision to change. Fund the change
Reinforcing Change champions	Confirm the change and support it out into the organisation
Change Agents (Six Sigma "Belts")	Facilitate change
Primary change agents (Black belt)	Operate as dedicated implementers of change
Supporting change agents	Assist with focused tasks during change implementation
Change Stakeholders	Change
Support Roles	
Change Masters	Teach the organisation how to manage change
	Support the use of an organised, systematic change management process

Figure 11-5: Change management roles.

Change managers need to build partnerships with all stakeholders – resistors and supporters, and those who are currently neutral. They must establish appropriate two-way communication with stakeholders and help them understand and agree to the cultural change that's needed.

Acknowledging resistance to change

The change phase of the cultural change is often the hardest for people to cope with as they're unsure of what's involved. Although they may acknowledge that cultural change is necessary, people may still have concerns or feel resistant to it for some or all of the following reasons:

- Fear of the unknown – change involves ambiguity and uncertainty.
- Old habits and ways of doing things are unthreatening and comforting – cultural change is an unknown entity.
- Concern over loss of status, job security, money, authority, friendships and personal convenience.
- Selective perception that change is incompatible with the goals and interests of the organisation.

Failure to build effective partnerships with stakeholders has consequences. A lack of awareness of stakeholders' concerns can eventually result in an unpleasant surprise – one you're not prepared for. Unacknowledged resistance can explode at any time and ruin the transformation process. Perhaps more importantly, you also miss tapping in to those stakeholders who are your supporters and, as a result, lose their potential leverage.

Dealing with resistance

Resistance to change is natural – after all, the unknown may involve danger. Most people prefer to stick with what they know so don't be surprised to encounter significant resistance. You need to uncover the source of such resistance so that you can take appropriate action.

Sources of resistance can be political, technical or cultural and can be expressed in the following ways:

Political:

- Will my department be made smaller?
- What makes them think they know how to run my department?
- Where's my next career move?

Technical:

- Will it work?
- How will it work?
- I can't see how it can save money.

Cultural:

- It's against my principles.
- No one asked my opinion.
- It's never been done like this before.

John Kenneth Galbraith's Law of Human Nature states that: 'Faced with the choice of changing one's mind or proving that there is no need to do so, almost everybody gets busy on the proof.' Rather than allowing stakeholders to develop entrenched resistance to the cultural change, you need to deal with their concerns promptly and honestly. Also bear in mind that resistance may be expressed at any stage of the transformation journey – not just at the start.

Stakeholders will be more ready to express organisational concerns than personal worries. Change agents thus need to develop supportive and open relationships with stakeholders so that they feel able to discuss their personal concerns regarding the anticipated change.

Developing the Vision for Change

The vision for change is a picture of your desired future, expressed in a way that resonates with all members of the organisation. The vision for change is shared with employees, customers, shareholders, vendors and candidates for employment, and creates shared meaning about what your organisation wants to look like – it becomes the rallying cry for the Lean Six Sigma transformation programme that seeks to capture hearts and minds.

You need to communicate the vision of the transformed business to all stakeholders in a way that is meaningful to them.

Everyone will have their own view of how the changes will affect them, so tailor your explanation of the vision so that it's relevant to individual stakeholders.

A change vision isn't the same thing as a corporate vision. The change vision provides a view of what the organisation will be like after you've implemented cultural changes and worked through the Lean Six Sigma transformation process.

A great change vision is easy for people to understand, is only half a page long, communicates its message in 60 seconds, and is intellectually solid, but also has emotional appeal and speaks to the broad range of people who ultimately have to change, regardless of their status.

The first step in developing the vision is creating a statement on the future state of the organisation. This is most effectively achieved by using *backwards visioning*, which involves a team creating a picture of the future, by imagining that the change has been successfully completed. If this were the case, what would they expect to see, both internally and externally, in terms of things such as behaviours, measures, rewards and recognition?

You need to regularly review the cultural transformation vision to ensure that it reflects both changes made to the Lean Six Sigma transformation programme, and progress made. From time to time you need to re-energise people to ensure the momentum of the transformation journey is maintained.

Getting Communication Right

Throughout the transformation process you need to develop effective communication with all the stakeholders involved. Everyone in the organisation needs to be aware of the progress that's being made, so a variety of communication channels must be developed.

Consider creating a communication network to reflect the involvement of key stakeholders, as shown in Figure 11-6.

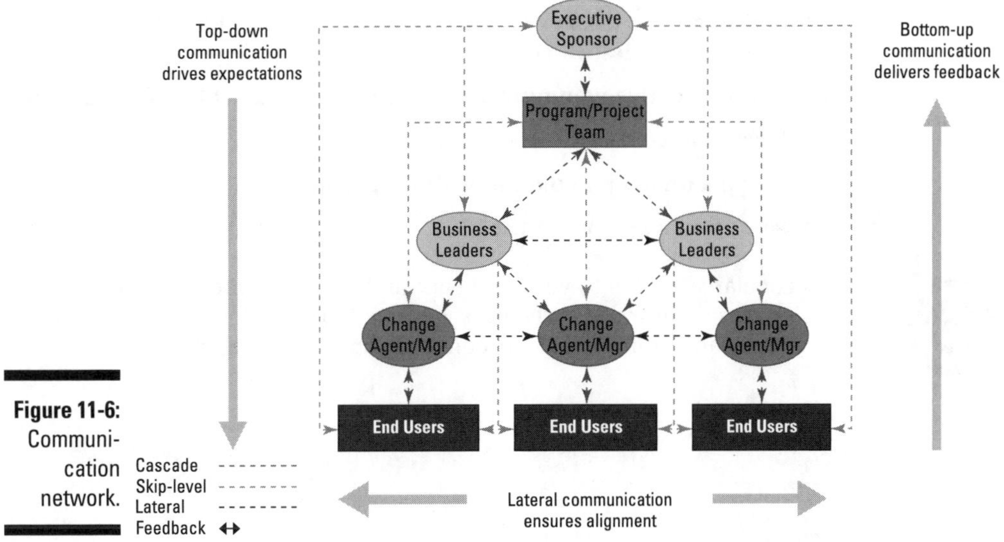

Figure 11-6: Communication network.

Working out what to communicate and when

Measured proactive communication offers advantages over deferred or delayed communication. Secrets are hard to keep, so you need to be open, especially with positive messages.

Either way, an open approach is likely to reduce rumours and misconceptions, and should lead to people trusting their leaders. What's more, steady and regular communications and updates help prepare people ahead of time and allow a gradual adjustment to the change.

Creating a communication plan

While communication planning is fairly straightforward in terms of the steps involved, the biggest challenge is often ensuring the plan can actually be delivered with the human and financial resources available to you.

The eight-step communication planning framework detailed here is designed for use by those who don't have a communications background. To devise a workable plan, you need to work through the following eight steps in sequence:

1. **Set communication objectives.**
2. **Establish key messages for your organisation.**
3. **Define and prioritise key stakeholders.**
4. **Establish additional key messages for each stakeholder group and their particular issues/concerns.**
5. **Develop effective communication tactics for each stakeholder group.**
6. **Allocate budgets and responsibilities.**
7. **Develop a quarterly communications calendar.**
8. **Assess results and adapt the plan.**

Pay particular attention to your audience and communicate in a way that will appeal to them. Naturally, early messages need to explain why the transformation is necessary, pointing out the consequences if nothing changes.

The communication plan should be agreed once the Lean Six Sigma business transformation programme has been defined, and then updated on a regular basis as the programme progresses.

Developing Employees' Skills

Making people feel that they're developing their skills is an important element in empowering them. Creating a learning culture within your organisation takes you one step beyond just acquiring the skills needed to deliver its products and services. It empowers your employees to achieve dramatically improved results compared to employees in more traditional organisations because they feel engaged. In turn, empowered employees more easily adapt to and anticipate change, which ultimately leads to an organisation that is more responsive to the marketplace and generates more energetic, loyal and goal-oriented employees.

Fostering a learning organisation

A learning organisation adheres to a set of attitudes, values and practices that support a process of continuous development. Training is a key element in the business strategy of an organisation dedicated to continuous learning. A true learning culture continuously challenges its own methods and ways of doing things. This ensures continuous improvement and the capacity to change.

A learning culture can be developed in an organisation only when top management is committed and deeply involved with it.

Aligning the learning culture to business needs is important. Management must make the employees feel that learning is aligned to business strategies.

Assessing learning needs

Providing new skills training for employees involved in the Lean Six Sigma transformation programme is a necessary element of the process. First you need to conduct a learning needs assessment and then you must develop a training and development plan. Appropriate training needs to be offered at each stage in the transformation process. The learning needs assessment identifies the required competencies and performance levels, assesses the gap between current knowledge/skill level, and plans training and education programmes. Figure 11-7 illustrates a typical approach to learning needs assessment.

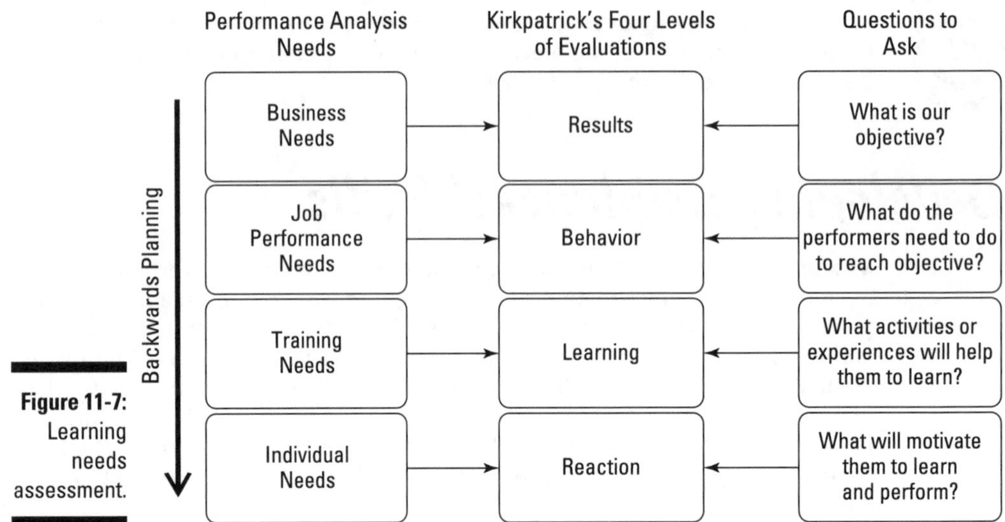

Figure 11-7: Learning needs assessment.

Role-specific training

Role-specific training plans need to be developed because different roles focus on different aspects of work, and will therefore require different types of training (see Figure 11-8). For example, the senior management team focuses on strategic issues and so will require training and coaching in strategy deployment methods and tools. Managers will usually be involved with operations and will need to have training in Lean Six Sigma techniques including problem solving, visual management and managing daily improvements. Team members will need problem-solving skills and to be able to use specific Lean tools and standard work processes.

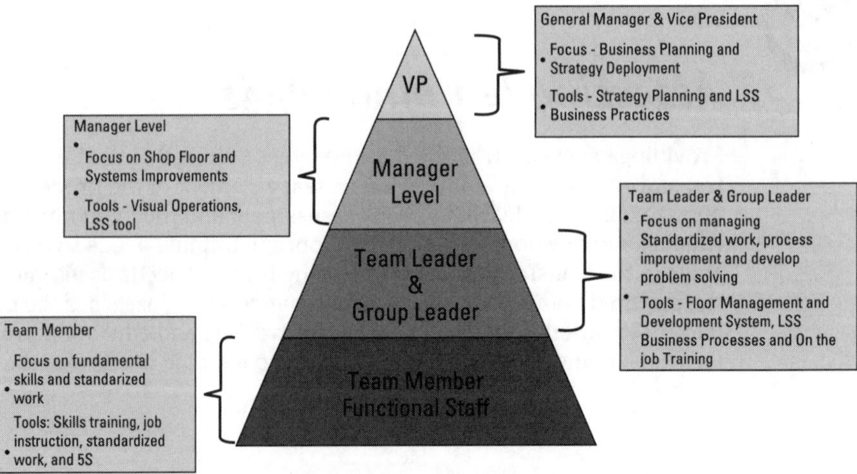

Figure 11-8: Role-based training.

To increase the overall capability of your organisation, staff training must be effective. Learning needs assessment must be aligned with organisational strategy, and training solutions must be deployed top-down to ensure leadership engagement.

Never under-estimate how much time is needed to change the culture of an organisation and to raise and maintain the skill level of staff.

Recognising that Change can be Rewarding

Everyone has a need to feel good about the work they do. Regularly rewarding and recognising your team members when they exhibit positive behaviours, rather than only noticing and commenting when they do something wrong, motivates them to keep up the good work and internalise the behaviour. You can let your staff know that they've done a good job in two ways:

- **Offering informal recognition:** This is the spontaneous pat on the back, warm word or sincere thank you that lets your employees know that you appreciate the job they're doing. Such recognition takes no time, money or planning to execute.
- **Setting up a formal reward programme:** This is a pre-planned, firm-wide approach for rewarding individuals, departments and teams who achieve outstanding results. In general, implementing a formal reward programme involves time, money and a good deal of planning.

Various studies have shown that people thrive when they receive personal recognition for the work they do. While money is important, it will never replace the need for genuine appreciation for the efforts people put in. While everyone is expected to do their job well, recognition encourages and motivates staff to exceed those expectations.

Knowing when to reward

Studies have shown that regularly offering informal recognition to employees is a stronger motivator than providing formal rewards. Simple praise, perhaps a hand-written note, is remembered long after the event because it tells your employees that you noticed their efforts and took the time and trouble to personally thank them.

Although they don't have the same everyday impact as informal recognition, formal rewards can become an important part of your strategy for service improvement. Quarterly and yearly award presentations should be highly publicised as part of your communications plan and send a clear message about the client service values and behaviours you hold in high esteem.

You may need to consider rewarding team performance as well as that of individuals.

Initiating a reward and recognition plan

You need to include a reward and recognition plan that provides appropriate rewards at each stage of the change process. The backwards visioning exercise we discussed earlier in this chapter (in the section 'Developing the Vision for Change') may help you identify the behaviours you want to see either more or less of.

Before the cultural transformation begins, you need to identify the behaviours that should be rewarded and agree appropriate formal and informal rewards. As the journey then unfolds, stop rewarding those undesirable behaviours that you need to see less of.

Depending on the scale of the changes needed, the new behaviours may have to be implemented in steps. The achievement of each individual step must then also be recognised.

Giving Power to the People

Employees must feel a sense of ownership for their work and the processes that they're involved in. Managers must create an environment that encourages employees to contribute to the Lean Six Sigma transformation.

Facing up to the management challenge

Good leaders show that they enjoy working with their staff and respect them; they recognise that everyone has something to contribute. They're excellent communicators and outstanding listeners, simplifying themes and messages and bringing clarity to the goals and actions needed. Effective leaders keep track of progress and are aware of the emotional climate of the team.

If the leaders in your organisation don't already possess these skills and attributes, they need to receive training. They need to be able to genuinely communicate with and understand key stakeholders – lip service won't work.

Following the Lean Six Sigma approach

Leaders also need training on using Lean Six Sigma techniques and methods. In particular, they need to understand that their role is to work on the processes with the people in the processes to ensure they're fully engaged and active participants in the transition to a culture of continuous improvement. They must walk the talk and live the key principles of Lean Six Sigma described in Chapter 1.

Giving power to teams

As part of the cultural transformation process management needs to introduce a new set of values and behaviours to remove existing barriers to employee empowerment.

If they're to be involved and empowered, people need to feel a sense of:

- Competence – they're learning from their experience and are gaining new skills and abilities.
- Significance – they're contributing to and influencing the team's performance.
- Community – they realise that they're an integral part of a larger effort.
- Enjoyment – they have fun and enjoy their work.

Their active involvement in the daily team briefing is an essential element in securing their engagement.

Give ownership of different activities to individual members of the team to increase their sense of participation.

Staying focused on the transformation process

The cultural transformation plan must be reviewed regularly and the culture of the organisation reassessed to ensure that it's aligned with the ongoing transformation programme.

Continue to communicate progress to all stakeholders and don't be afraid to make adjustments to the course of the transformation journey to deal with issues as they arise.

Cultural transformation is an ongoing journey and the organisation needs time to be effective in the new ways of working.

Chapter 12

Achieving Everyday Operational Excellence

In This Chapter

- Recognising the importance of training
- Identifying areas for improvement
- Staying the course and keeping focused

For everyday operational excellence to become a reality, managers and team leaders need to run their processes and activities effectively and efficiently. As Chapter 3 explains, these managers and leaders need to understand that their role is to work on their processes with the people in the processes to find ways of continuously improving performance. This chapter covers ensuring that people receive appropriate training, spotting improvement opportunities that benefit the organisation and give employees the chance to develop and master new skills, and keeping everyone on track for the long haul.

Deploying Lean Six Sigma Training

The people in the process need to feel that they're able to challenge and improve the process and the way they work. To do so, they need to be engaged and empowered.

If people are to feel empowered, they need to feel that they're being developed, and for that to happen the organisation must develop training plans. The primary focus in this chapter is on training people to develop Lean Six Sigma skills.

Hand in glove with the training and the training plan is the need to identify relevant projects. Such projects should be bite-sized and link to improvements to achieve strategy deployment. The projects need to tackle the right work and do the work in the right way. Not all improvement actions supporting strategy deployment will be DMAIC or DMADV projects (see Chapter 1). The operational areas, in particular, will need to adopt the Lean Six Sigma tools, techniques and principles in their day-to-day work too.

In many ways the key to creating a culture of continuous improvement hinges on how well managers understand the need to manage their processes and achieve everyday operational excellence. We look at the implications and requirements of that in the 'Establishing How You Do Things' section later in this chapter. For the moment, the focus is on training the belts.

Training the belts

The different levels of training in Lean Six Sigma are often referred to in terms of the coloured belts acquired in martial arts. Think about the qualities of martial arts Black Belts – highly trained, experienced, disciplined, decisive, controlled and responsive – and you can see how well this metaphor translates into the world of making change happen in organisations. Thankfully, you won't be required to break bricks in half with your bare hands!

Yellow Belts

Some organisations develop a pool of *Yellow Belts*, who typically receive two days of practical training to a basic level on the most commonly used tools in Lean Six Sigma projects. The content is usually a sub-set of the Green Belt programme referred to below.

Yellow Belts work either as project team members or carry out mini-projects themselves in their local work environment, usually under the guidance of a Black Belt.

Green Belts

Green Belts are trained on the basic tools and lead fairly straightforward projects. The extent of training varies somewhat. In the US, for example, training typically takes from between five to ten days. In the UK some organisations break the training along the following lines: Foundation Green Belt level (four to six days' training) covers Lean tools, process mapping techniques and measurement, as well as a firm grounding in the DMAIC methodology and the basic set of statistical tools. Advanced Green Belts (an additional six days' training) receive further instruction on more analytical statistical tools and start to use statistical software. This approach ensures the training is delivered 'just in time' since early projects can be relatively simple, often involving an assessment of how the work gets done and enabling the identification and elimination of non-value-added steps, without the need for detailed statistical analysis.

Green Belts typically devote the equivalent of about a day a week (20 per cent of their time) to Lean Six Sigma projects, usually mentored by a Black Belt. Given that Green Belts already have 100 per cent of their time taken up with current work activities, organisations need to look closely at where the day a week is going to come from: there are only so many hours in a day! The long-term success of Lean Six Sigma initiatives can be compromised if people aren't given the time and space to work on their improvement projects.

Black Belts

An expert Lean Six Sigma practitioner is trained to *Black Belt* level, which means attending several modules of training over a period of months. Most Black Belt courses involve around 20 days of full-time training as well as working on projects in practice, under the guidance of a Master Black Belt. The role of the Black Belt is to lead complex projects and provide expert guidance on using the Lean Six Sigma tools and techniques to the project teams. Black Belts are often from different operational functions across the company, coming into the Black Belt role from customer service, finance, marketing or HR, for example. The Black Belt role is usually full time, often for a term of two to three years, after which the individuals return to operations. In effect, Black Belts become internal consultants working on improving how the organisation works by changing its systems and processes for the better.

Master Black Belts

The *Master Black Belt*, another full-time role, receives the highest level of training and becomes a full-time professional Lean Six Sigma expert. The Master Black Belt will have extensive project management experience and should be fully familiar with the importance of the soft skills needed to manage change. An experienced Master Black Belt is likely to want to take on this role as a long-term career path, becoming a trainer, coach or deployment advisor, and working with senior executives to ensure the overall Lean Six Sigma programme is aligned to the strategic direction of the business. Master Black Belts tend to move around from one major business to another after typically three or four years in one organisation. They're likely to have been a Black Belt for at least two years before moving into this role.

Assessing the skills

Selecting the right candidates for training is clearly essential. In fact, some organisations undertake assessment centres to identify suitable people. But in many ways, assessing the skills of the newly-trained belts is more important. Certification (see the 'Setting up certification' section later in this chapter) is obviously one way of establishing an individual's skill level. To some extent, you can also do so by using the framework created by Donald Kirkpatrick, a professor at the University of Wisconsin, and in particular, by reference to his levels two and three. Kirkpatrick's approach to evaluating the effectiveness of training has become the benchmark within the training industry. He identified four levels:

1. **Reaction:** The immediate response to the training event.
2. **Learning:** The increase in knowledge as a result of the event.
3. **Behaviour:** Changes in behaviour in the normal daily work environment as a result of the newly acquired knowledge.
4. **Results:** The benefit to the business as a result of the reaction, learning and behaviour.

Examples of how these levels are applied are shown below:

- **Level 1:** The trainers ask delegates to assess the course, perhaps using net promoter score (NPS) forms (Chapter 13 explains NPS in full) at the end of each training programme or workshop. NPS is a world-class best practice method of obtaining customer feedback. The results can form part of an organisation's balanced scorecard.
- **Level 2:** Delegates routinely sit (certification) exams after completing their training; in-company clients also often ask for the inclusion of specific tests and exams when delegates don't proceed towards external certification.
- **Level 3:** Here, clients target specific changes in behaviour resulting from the training – some very formally, some informally. Observed changes in behaviour can be as simple as trained managers using the new Lean Six Sigma tools more routinely, avoiding jumping to solutions, undertaking post-project reviews, and so on. In cases where learning and development specialists look for and assess very specific behavioural changes, some organisations use psychometric profiling as a way of measuring them.
- **Level 4:** At this level, organisations explicitly measure the outcome of their improvement projects (and in aggregate at programme level).

Setting up certification

Many organisations utilise certification processes to ensure that a set standard is reached through exams and project assessments. Certification processes are established in many countries by bodies such as the British Quality Foundation (BQF) and the American Society of Quality (ASQ).

Many large corporate businesses set up their own internal certification processes, with recognition given at high-profile company events to newly graduated belts.

Essentially, certification tends to be a three-part process. Complete the training, pass an exam (usually multi-choice for Yellow and Green Belt), and provide evidence of applying the tools in some way. This is often through the presentation of a project storyboard that walks through and explains the project from start to finish. The ASQ doesn't offer Yellow Belt certification.

You can find full details of both the certification and body of knowledge requirements of the BQF and ASQ on their respective websites: `www.bqf.org.uk` and `asq.org`.

A new term has recently been used to describe people who have merely received an introduction to the topic – White Belt. No certification process is involved and these programmes vary in length from an hour or two through to a full day.

Prioritising and Selecting Improvement Opportunities

Lean Six Sigma For Dummies (Wiley) covers the selection of Lean Six Sigma projects and introduces a number of selection and prioritisation tools for practitioners to use. These include:

- The XY grid
- N/3
- Paired comparisons
- Criteria- or priority-based matrix
- Pugh matrix

You can find descriptions of each of these selection tools in *Lean Six Sigma For Dummies* (Wiley), but the following diagrams provide at least an indication of how they can be used.

Figure 12-1 shows the XY grid, which is a simple format for making an initial assessment of priorities.

The N/3, shown in Figure 12-2, is a simple technique for making selections. We recommend using it to help reduce a lot of options to a more manageable number and then using paired comparisons to make a more objective selection.

- In the first example, prioritise based on the effort required and probability of success. So, how much time, resources, expenses etc. are likely to be required to complete the project? What are the potential risks? How big an impact will the results have on the process and the business ?

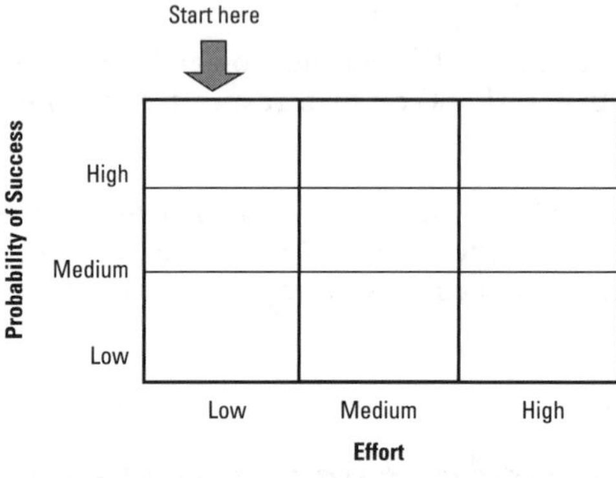

In Lean Six Sigma for Dummies, figure 14.6 on page 236 illustrates the technique comparing effort to benefit

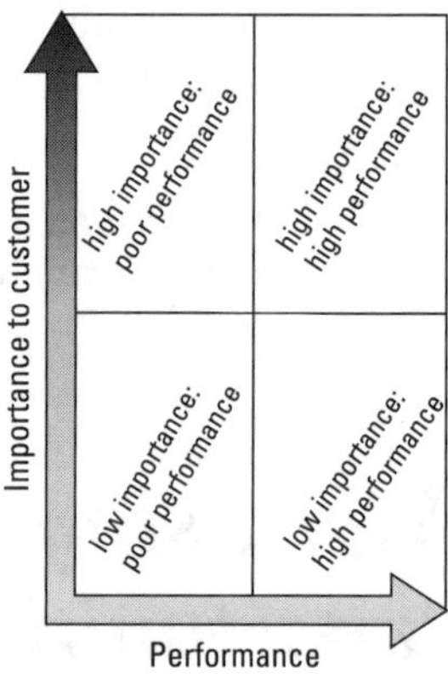

Here, we're looking to base our priorities on our performance and its importance to the customer

Figure 12-1: Assessing priorities with the XY grid.

In this example, N = 12
So, N/3 = 4
Each person has 4 votes

Figure 12-2: Voting using the N/3 process.

The paired comparisons technique (Figure 12-3) is often used to provide weightings to selection criteria and links neatly to the criteria- or priority-based matrix (Figure 12-4).

The criteria- or priority-based matrix can be used for a wide variety of selection issues, including suppliers following an invitation to tender, staff recruitment, or promotion, and even the next school you'd like to send your children to!

- Look at each pair of options
  - A & B; A & C; A & D
  - B & C; B & D
  - C & D; C & E
  - D & E
- Make your choice according to the criteria
- Total the votes, and the winner is...

Figure 12-3: Forcing selection through paired comparisons.

Item	Description				
A		A/B	A/C	A/D	A/E
B			B/C	B/D	B/E
C				C/D	C/E
D					D/E
E					

Figure 12-4: Weighing things up with the criteria- or priority-based matrix.

Criteria	A	B	C	Score (weighted)	Rank	%
Options / Weights	1	3	5			
Idea one	6 / 6	5 / 15	7 / 35	56	3	62
Idea two	3 / 3	7 / 21	6 / 30	54	4	60
Idea three	1 / 1	8 / 24	8 / 40	65	1	72
Idea four	8 / 8	6 / 18	5 / 25	51	5	57
Idea five	7 / 7	7 / 21	6 / 30	58	2	64

You and your team score each 'idea' out of ten depending on how well the item meets each of the criteria. That score is multiplied by the criterion weighting to provide a weighted score. In this example, the top scoring 'idea' is idea three, though it could have scored a maximum of 90 if it had met each of the criteria with a perfect score of 10 - the percentage column helps you see whether the top scoring item is really good enough (65/90 x 100 = 72%)

The Pugh matrix, shown in Figure 12-5, is often used to compare competing concept designs. One design is chosen as the 'datum concept' that will provide a standard reference point. The other concepts are then compared with it to determine whether they're better/easier, worse/harder or the same.

One additional selection tool that can be especially helpful in Kaizen rapid improvement workshops is the nominal group technique (NGT), which involves silent brainstorming and decision-making. NGT is a structured variation of small group discussion methods, and is ideal in rapid improvement events.

The process prevents the domination of discussion by a single person, encourages the more passive group members to participate, and results in a set of prioritised solutions or recommendations. NGT can thus be seen as an opportunity to secure buy-in and engagement.

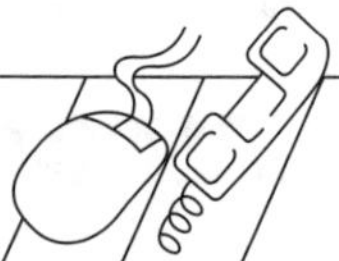

Key Criteria	Concept 1 the datum	Concept 2 E-Loan	Concept 3 Phone loan	Concept 4	Concept 5	Concept 6	Concept 7	Importance rating
Loan term	S	S	–					3
Interest rate	S	S	–					2
Complexity of information	S	S	S					5
Availability of help desk	S	+	+					1
Time to complete form	S	+	–					4
Staff training time	S	+	–					3
Activity time	S	–	–					5
Unit cost per transaction	S	+	–					3
Opportunity for error	S	S	–					3
Development costs	S	–	+					5
Sum of positives	0	4	2					
Sum of negatives	0	2	7					
Sum of sames	10	4	1					
Weighted sum of positives	0	11	6					
Weighted sum of negatives	0	10	23					

Concept selection legend
Better +
Same S
Worse –

Figure 12-5: Making a datum with the Pugh matrix.

NGT involves the following steps:

1. **Divide the people present into small groups of five or six, preferably seated around a table.**
2. **Ask an open-ended question, for example: 'What could we do to help reduce the set-up time for this process?' or 'How could we improve the on-time delivery of customer orders?'**
3. **Instruct each member of the team to spend several minutes in silence individually brainstorming possible ideas.**
4. **Ask each group to write their ideas on sticky notes and to put them on a flipchart.**
5. **Work through the ideas, without judgement or criticism.** Do encourage clarification in response to questions.
6. **Ask members to individually rank the solutions as first, second, third, fourth and so on.** Add up the rankings each solution receives: the solution with the best total ranking is selected as the final decision.

In a way, some similarity exists between NGT and the simpler N/3 technique (refer to Figure 12-2) in that voting is involved in the process, but this time individuals are sequencing options in terms of their perceived priority.

Whichever selection techniques you use, the process *must* support strategy deployment. Clearly prioritised criteria always help to maintain appropriate focus.

Sometimes the improvement solution really is clear. Having described a problem in the Define phase of DMAIC, it may well be that by clarifying how the work gets done – perhaps by using process stapling – one or more non-value-adding steps can be seen. Making sure that no unintended consequences may result, these steps could then simply be removed. Process stapling is described in *Lean Six Sigma For Dummies* (Wiley). It's one way to really understand a process and its related chain of events. Very simply, *process stapling* means taking a customer order, for example, and literally walking it through the entire process, step-by-step, as though you were the order.

No matter where the order goes, you go too. By following the order you start to see what really happens, who does what and why, and how, where and when they do it. Process stapling is an ideal first step in mapping out a process.

Rapid improvement events

Kaizen (pronounced Kai Zen) means change for the better. It's often associated with short, rapid, incremental improvement and forms a natural part of an organisation's approach to continuous improvement.

Kai Sigma is developed from the Kaizen approach and adapts the framework of the DMAIC phases in a series of facilitated workshops. The facilitator doesn't need to use the language of Lean or Six Sigma. Kai Sigma aims to involve the people in the process in making improvements to that process, and the approach makes use of team knowledge rather than detailed analysis. The solution may be known by the team, but historically they've not been listened to! *Lean Six Sigma For Dummies* (Wiley) provides more detail about Kai Sigma workshops and the importance of pre-event preparation.

DMAIC projects

Typically, Green Belt DMAIC projects are likely to run for three to four months, assuming the Green Belts are generally spending only 20 per cent of their time working on the problem. Black Belt projects may well take longer, even though the Black Belts are usually working full time in this role.

Yellow Belts tend to be members of improvement teams, but are perfectly able to pick up their own, albeit very focused, projects. These are typically tackling local operational issues, for example helping their team establish more effective visual management or taking part in process stapling, described earlier in this chapter.

DMAIC projects always start with a problem statement. In the context of business transformation, the project should be related to progressing strategy deployment.

Check out Chapter 1 for more on DMAIC projects.

Applying manufacturing process improvements to services

One of the most interesting observations we've made in comparatively recent years is the realisation on the part of manufacturing organisations that Lean Six Sigma can be applied to their back office and transactional processes.

On the shop floor, many manufacturers have already seen the success that can result from the deployment of Lean Six Sigma. But they've never considered whether the process could work outside of manufacturing. It's probably fair to say that many of our clients are service and public sector organisations.

Recognising that the tools of Lean Six Sigma have as much relevance in service as in manufacturing has always seemed harder for organisations to accept. The difficulty, perhaps, is that service products and office applications may not appear either so physical or so visual. Because manufacturing always involves tangible products, waste/scrap is so much easier to spot, especially when it's in a skip in the back yard.

In terms of training, there tends to be more awareness of the need for statistical analysis in a manufacturing environment, especially where precise engineering specifications are involved. That said, techniques such as statistical process control (SPC), are hugely relevant in the service arena, where measurement systems are generally not as refined as in manufacturing. Raising awareness of the need for more statistical analysis in the service sector is likely to take some considerable time. *Lean Six Sigma For Dummies* (Wiley) provides more detail about statistical control and *SPC in the Office* by Mal Owen and John Morgan (Greenfield Publishing) contains a wide range of service applications using control charts.

When we work with manufacturing clients, Yellow Belt training typically takes three days rather than the two needed in a service company. Also, the manufacturing organisation is more likely to train its Black Belts in DMADV, though, again, this may be down to historical misunderstandings about the potential of the design and innovation method in service organisations. Arguably, since errors in many service processes occur in front of the customer, a greater need for the analysis and prevention of defects exists in the service/government/healthcare sectors, and with it the need for better-designed processes.

The example below highlights how Lean Six Sigma works in a service process. It describes an insurance company's new business team as it processes new policy applications. The measurable customer requirements, the CTQs (critical to quality requirements), indicated that policies must be issued within five working days and the documentation must be error free.

The organisation's executive team realised that the company needed to differentiate itself in the eyes of its customers, the Independent Financial Advisers (IFAs) who sell and, to some degree, service policies for the end customer. The company wanted to establish itself as the natural choice for IFAs or, at least, a targeted segment of them. Superior service and the ability to demonstrate value were key elements of the strategy. Current performance indicated that it was some way from this ideal situation, with considerable variation in the processing of new business applications, especially those requiring medical evidence from a GP or specialist.

The time taken to issue policies ranged from between a couple of days to a couple of months, and approximately 10 per cent of all policy applications had to be reworked, either due to errors or missing information. Without significant improvement, little prospect existed of their strategy being achieved.

The leadership team believed that its business could benefit from Lean Six Sigma. It needed to show how, with each step in the new business process, value is added to the work in progress, just as a car on the production line gets doors or parts added to it as it flows down the assembly line.

A number of Lean Six Sigma tools were applied to enable the work to flow – none involved rocket science, simply a little time and the involvement of people:

- The current state picture for the end-to end-process was developed starting with a high level view of the process and followed by process stapling and process mapping. The exercise involved a mix of people from the process together with a Green Belt, and the outcomes were discussed by the team with management. The exercise highlighted many improvement opportunities.
- Linked processes in the end-to-end process were placed near to one another. Work had been organised by function in separate departments and teams, which created a silo effect and delays in transferring applications to other areas that performed different functions. Delays were compounded as the work was also processed in batches. The functional silos were eliminated, helping facilitate a move from batches to single piece flow.
- Processes and procedures were standardised, and techniques such as visual management and daily team meetings were used to support the overall aims. As a simple example, prior to the application of Lean concepts, people had been allowed to choose their own system for storing files. This meant that new or temporary staff had difficulty finding files that had been stored in various different ways, such as by policy number, by date received, or alphabetically. The new system required files to be stored alphabetically and in the same clearly labeled cabinet at each work area.
- Some processes involved returning work to a previous step for further processing. This system caused confusion, disrupted flow and resulted in waiting time in some steps. The process was changed to avoid the need for such to-ing and fro-ing.
- The work flow was further smoothed by applying the concept of takt time. Takt time tells you how quickly you need to action things in relation to customer demand, given the number of available hours in the working day or shift. Takt time is explained in more detail in *Lean Six Sigma For Dummies* (Wiley). The business established a takt time of five minutes per application or 12 applications per hour, encouraging and empowering employees to make process improvements to reduce the cycle time needed in order to meet the takt time required. Continuous improvement meant the 'one best way' was updated regularly.
- Workloads were balanced where possible, ensuring the work was evenly and sequentially distributed. The previous approach, whereby new applications were allocated alphabetically, was replaced by a 'date received' allocation so that every team received the same number of applications. This approach reduced unnecessary delays in the system and meant customers were being dealt with in an appropriate time sequence.

- Tasks were separated into categories based on their level of difficulty and the processing skills needed. For example, two categories were developed for applications, whereby one handled cases needing medical evidence and the other handled less time-consuming cases that didn't require GP reports.
- Visual management came into play in the form of performance data displayed on white boards for everyone to see. Where practical, the information was updated by the team members. The boards became the locations for the daily team meetings where work levels and improvement ideas were discussed.

These actions led to enhanced performance and increased employee and customer satisfaction. Turnaround times for policies issued were reduced by 65 per cent for medical cases and 80 per cent for non-medical applications. Rework fell from 10 per cent to just over 1 per cent.

Ongoing, the organisation made further changes by segmenting its IFA customers into different categories and creating customer-facing teams dealing with new business through to claims. This 'cradle to grave' set-up helped to make further improvements in both employee and customer satisfaction, leading to increased market share, and though its creation involved a significant investment in training time, process costs were similarly reduced.

Establishing How You Do Things

Everyday operational excellence is all about doing things well each and every day and creating a culture of continuous improvement. And it begins by understanding how the work gets done and how well – just like in the example in the previous section. Essentially, the tools and techniques used in the Measure phase of a DMAIC project can help you understand the current situation.

Understanding the value stream

Lean Six Sigma For Dummies (Wiley) looks at developing either a deployment flowchart or value stream map. Both provide effective pictures of how the work gets done.

The value stream and the process are one and the same. The only difference is how they're presented. As a reminder, Figure 12-6 provides an example of each.

The deployment flowchart

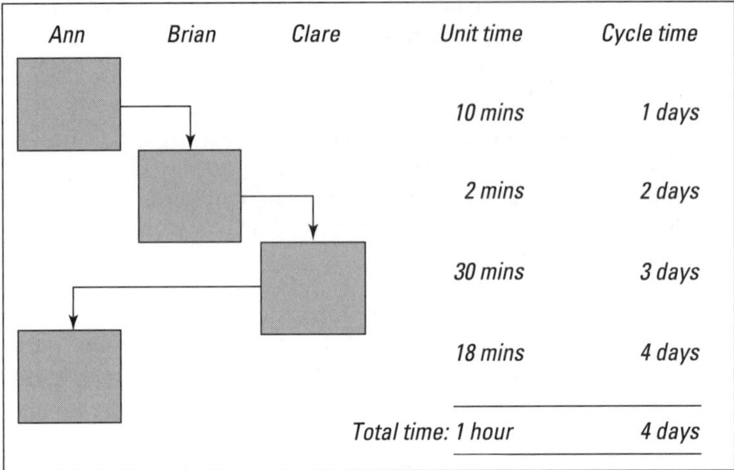

The value stream map

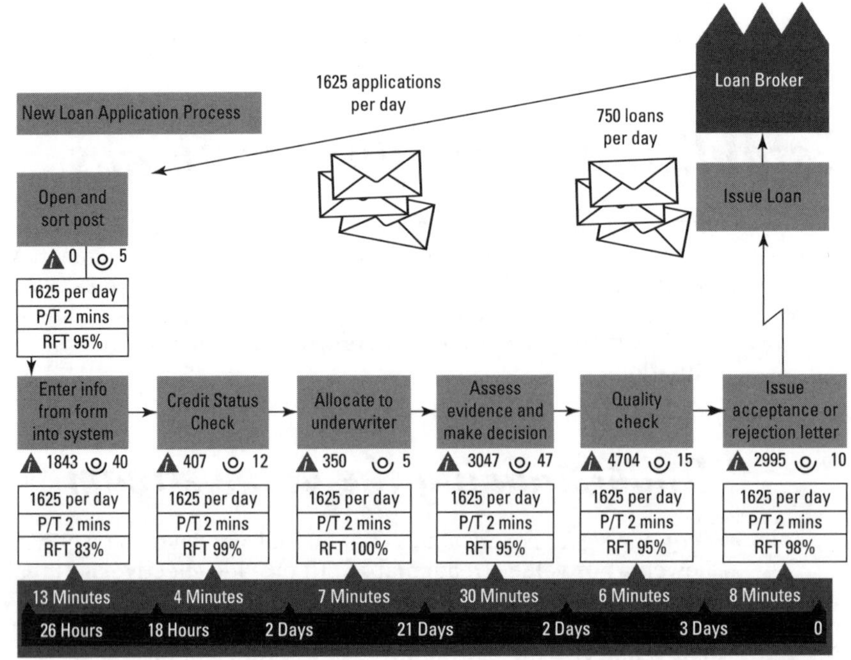

Figure 12-6: Developing a picture of how the work gets done.

In both these examples, you can see how the addition of data has highlighted opportunities for improvement. So, not only do the pictures show *how* the work gets done, they also provide a framework for measures to help understand *how well* it gets done.

As you come to understand the current situation and spot the opportunities for improvement, you need to decide whether these are 'just do it' activities, Kaizen/Kai Sigma rapid improvement workshops, or more formal DMAIC or DMADV projects. Often these are decisions that can be made at the daily team meeting, or referred from there through the organisation's governance system.

Using Kaizen effectively

A typical outline Kaizen event plan is presented in Figure 12-7.

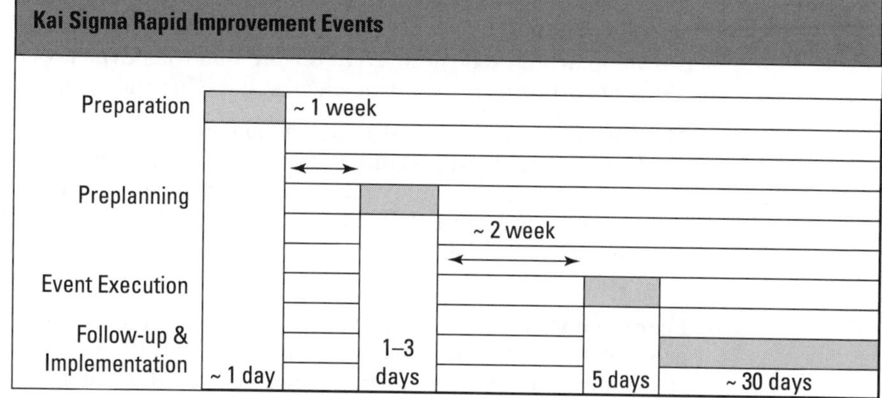

These events are known by a variety of names, including 'rapid improvement' and 'kaizen blitz'. Our 'Kai Sigma' title looks to highlight the use of DMAIC in achieving a systematic approach to improvement.

Figure 12-7: Preparation and planning are essential ingredients for successful events.

Essentially, you need to identify what it is you're going to tackle, for example the key wastes in the current state that need to be removed in order to achieve the future state of how you would like the process to operate. These might already have been highlighted on a process or value stream map. For example, the wastes may relate to:

- Steps with high correction rates
- Steps with long processing times
- Excessive delays between steps
- Excessive checking
- Steps with high inventory or work in progress

To ensure that the event is a success, some planning and pre-work is needed. Where appropriate, look to see if data is available or whether you need to collect some in advance of the event. You may well find yourself being asked to facilitate workshop sessions or specific activities, so it's worth considering the need for facilitation skills.

The role of the facilitator is to ensure that Kaizen/Kai Sigma rapid improvement events, meetings, and interactions between people are effective and productive. Making best use of the skills and contributions from everyone involved is vital. The facilitator needs to make sure that all aspects of the event are orchestrated to ensure success and to consider it in three phases: preparation, the event process itself, and the event and meeting follow up.

Preparation

Some of the key things that need to be considered in preparation for the event include:

- **Purpose and agenda:** Does the event have a clear purpose? Is everyone who is attending the event clear about that purpose? Has an agenda been drawn up, which is structured to ensure that the purpose is achieved? In terms of authority, is everyone clear about what they can and cannot do?
- **Attendees:** Based on the purpose and agenda, are you clear about who needs to attend? If critical inputs need to be made, who is going to make them? Do you need people at the event because they may have relevant background knowledge that will add to the quality of the discussion? Everyone attending should be there for a reason, and they should be clear about expectations for their contribution.
- **Event dynamics:** Knowing the purpose, agenda and attendees, you can probably predict in advance potential areas of difficulty. Are people attending who have very strong views and may be in conflict? Must difficult issues be discussed? Are people attending the event who just don't get along? Either way, stakeholder analysis can be very useful here (see *Lean Six Sigma For Dummies* (Wiley) for details). It may well lead you to identify key influencers that need some pre-positioning beforehand to make sure that they come to the session in the right frame of mind. If you can identify these potential difficulties up front you can structure the agenda and the event process to help address these issues and minimise any negative impact on the proceedings.
- **Event structure:** With an outline agenda, knowledge of how much time you have available and awareness of the likely event dynamics, you need to consider how to allocate time across the different agenda items; where to place emphasis; and how much time to allocate to inputs, discussion, and decision-making. In setting the event structure you also need to take account of the need for breaks at various points (coffee, lunch, tea), and to be aware of how these breaks will impact the flow of the discussion. For long events, you also need to think about how to keep people engaged throughout the day, for example structuring the event so that people have something interesting to do after lunch.

- **Event roles:** Typically, the event will have a champion or sponsor who helps establish the purpose of and objective for the event. They'll also clarify the authority the team has been given.

  The role of the facilitator is clearly different. As part of the preparation, the champion/sponsor and facilitator need to agree their different roles and the overall purpose and plan for the event. Someone within the team should be appointed timekeeper during the event to keep an eye on the clock and the progress being made. Another team member should be given responsibility for taking notes, capturing information and the decisions made.

- **Event venue:** A key part of a successful event is the venue. Consider what sort of environment you want to create for the outcome you want to achieve. People's behaviour during the event is likely to reflect the surroundings and environment they're in, so you might want to make sure everything is clean and tidy beforehand. Decide whether the event will be on- or off-site. If the former, think about how you can avoid attendees being distracted by operational demands that might cause them to leave the event.

  Consider room layout in terms of its size and formality (or otherwise). You may need break-out rooms to work on specific issues. Equipment is another important issue. You'll need a number of things in the room. The toolkit is likely to include a flipchart and stand, paper and spare flipchart pads, pens, brown paper, sticky putty and sticky notes. You might also need tape measures, stop watches, a digital camera and possibly a video camera, batteries (just in case), a laptop and a projector. Much will depend on the purpose of the event and whether during the day you intend to be monitoring and measuring the process activity as it happens.

The event process

The role of the facilitator is to ensure that the overall process is orchestrated and runs to time. With good preparation you'll be clear about the outline process you want to take people through. Of course, you'll need to be flexible and respond appropriately as the dynamics dictate, but your pre-work gives you a good framework.

Event and meeting follow up

At the end of the event, or shortly afterwards, the facilitator and the champion review the event to note what went well, what could have been improved, whether objectives were met, and the follow up required. This review will help in preparing for the next session. Where appropriate, the facilitator needs to make sure that actions and next steps from the event are circulated as quickly as possible.

Once the improvement solution has been implemented, an effective handover must take place and a control plan agreed.

Achieving results

Improvements naturally flow from the use of the Lean Six Sigma tools and approach, and the evolving culture of continuous improvement. Holding the gains is often the more difficult task.

The control plan is an essential ingredient of everyday operational excellence, and is described in *Lean Six Sigma For Dummies* (Wiley). As part of the control plan, you need to deploy a 'one best way' of doing things, a 'standard work' approach, but you also have to recognise that, in an evolving culture of continuous improvement, the one best way will change with further improvement activity. All of this standardisation should be coupled with effective visual management to help ensure not only that everyone knows what's happening, but also to create a safer working environment and make it easier to find things.

Where a standard process isn't in place, the first thing to do is to create one! If something then goes wrong, you need to understand whether or not the standard process has been followed. If it has, it clearly needs some enhancement and a new standard process has to emerge – a new one best way.

Keeping the focus

No matter how good the initial improvement results are, it's crucial that everyone recognises that Lean Six Sigma thinking isn't simply a case of applying some tools and techniques to solving a problem. You need to adopt the concepts, and the thinking and behaviours that accompany them, to hold the gains and create new ones in an environment that really is pursuing perfection en route to your True North.

Organisations tend to get what they measure, so it's vital to ensure that the right things are being measured and the right behaviours encouraged and recognised.

If you want to reach True North, personal objectives must reflect that. If the executives' bonus structure rewards travelling south, the strategy will clearly fail!

Jack Welsh, former CEO of General Electric, sent a very clear message to his managers when he told them no one would be promoted until they'd led or championed an improvement project. Guess what happened?

Giving Power to the People

Everyone involved in a transformation process will find it challenging at some point. You need to ensure that people receive appropriate training, are able to express doubts and concerns and, most importantly, feel that everyone's in it together and knows where they're going. They also need the proper resources and infrastructure to support the change process.

Recognising the challenge management faces

Chapter 3 identifies the need for managers to work on their processes with the people in the processes to find ways of continuously improving the performance of those processes. For many managers, that in itself is a significant challenge.

The majority of managers will probably need training in everyday operational excellence. Our three-day everyday operational excellence training programme covers a sub-set of the Lean Six Sigma tools taught at Yellow and Foundation Green Belt levels. But these are the tools that need to be applied to daily activities and not just improvement projects. Used in this way, these tools enable processes to be owned as well as effectively and efficiently managed, leading to stable processes, whereby:

- **A clear customer-focused objective exists, together with prioritised customer requirements.** In other words, measureable CTQs have been identified.
- **Appropriate process maps are in place.** These will involve at least a SIPOC (Suppliers, Inputs, Process, Outputs, Customers) diagram and a deployment flowchart or value stream map; perhaps both.
- **A balance of input, in-process and output measures exists.** That is, an effective data collection process is in place. The vital few Xs and Ys are being measured and the correlation between these variables is understood and managed.
- **The process is stable and in statistical control.** Control charts are part of visual management, helping to ensure that variation is understood. Where special causes are present, improvement activity is underway and is picked up at the daily team meeting, if not before.
- **The process meets the CTQs.** Performance in meeting CTQs is monitored and understood and improvement activity is underway where the CTQs are not being met. Progress is picked up as part of the daily team meeting.

- **The process has been error-proofed.** Failure Modes and Effects Analysis (FMEA) has been carried out, prevention has been built in where possible and the identification of new error-proofing opportunities forms part of the daily team meeting.

  Refer to Chapter 2, or see *Lean Six Sigma For Dummies* (Wiley), for more on FMEA.
- **A control plan is in place that clearly identifies what to do if things go wrong.** An example is a situation in which ongoing data indicates a warning in some way.

The training and ongoing application of the learning also serves to begin the process of introducing a common language of Lean Six Sigma tools, techniques and principles. In turn, this supports the ongoing identification of improvement opportunities that can be actioned either by managers and their teams or through more formal DMAIC or DMADV projects. Each DMAIC or DMADV project should have a champion.

Managers and leaders have their own set of challenges to deal with. In fact, generating a list of the challenges facing champions and their teams is easy. The 'top ten' list below reflects many of the common problems experienced in organisations:

- Ineffective improvement charters that are too vague or too large.
- Team members not sharing a unified direction or vision.
- Teams with the wrong mix of skills or functional representation.
- Champions, team members or leaders not spending enough time on the projects.
- Pressure for immediate financial impact leading to inappropriate shortcuts that frustrate team members and discredit the systematic approach being promoted.
- Other key stakeholders not being fully supportive of the project or the team's approach.
- Inadequate budget to complete the project or implement recommended solutions.
- Competing or conflicting project objectives among different improvement teams, leading to confusion.
- The project scope keeps getting bigger.
- Poorly managed handovers fail to integrate the improvements throughout the organisation.

Generate your own list of challenges using negative brainstorming. This technique turns brainstorming on its head. So, for example, rather than brainstorming 'What reasons may account for project failure?' you can instead brainstorm 'How can we ensure projects fail?' This activity is good fun, albeit somewhat disturbing when you consider the output and then realise you're actually doing some of these things.

What's important is being aware of these issues and actively seeking to anticipate and thus prevent them.

Empowering teams

In owning and working on the process, you need to ensure it's 'managed' – that you really are working on the process with the people in the process. You need to involve the relevant employees so that they feel able to challenge and help improve how the work gets done. They must feel engaged and their active involvement in the daily team brief is an essential element in securing that engagement. Agreeing ownership of different activities is one way to help increase people's sense of participation.

You also need to make absolutely sure that the training and accreditation skills charts are up to date and that the scheduling of training and coaching is at an appropriate pace (see the skills and accreditation matrix for assessing employees' skills in Figure 3-10 and the training plan in Figure 3-11 in Chapter 3).

Konosuke Matsushita, the founder of Panasonic, contrasted his organisation's approach with that of typical Western organisations:

> *'For us, the core of management is the art of mobilising and putting together the intellectual resources of all the employees in the service of the firm. Only by drawing on the combined brainpower of its employees can a firm face up to the turbulence and constraints of today's environment.'*

Overall, balance is the key to successful empowerment. Transformation needs to be a whole-brain concept. Using a left-brain only approach, one that's all rules and structure, means everything grinds to a halt, ossifies and crumbles. But in a right-brain only approach, where there's total creative and emotional freedom and no rules or structure, things break down and anarchy rules. A whole-brain approach is needed: appropriate rules and structure together with creativity and freedom.

The following leadership and management practices must be established:

- Developing people
  - Coach and train people during new assignments
  - Help people develop their skills
- Building trust
  - Promote an atmosphere of co-operation
  - Trust people to do an effective job

- Promoting autonomy
  - Encourage people to take the initiative
  - Provide appropriate coaching and support when needed
- Encouraging openness
  - Forgive mistakes made by others
  - Admit to mistakes
- Recognising accomplishments
  - Celebrate successes
  - Reward people for innovations
- Shaping direction
  - Provide a vision of the future
  - Take on controversial activities
- Demonstrating objectivity
  - Use facts in decision-making
  - Respond to facts rather than unsubstantiated data

Autonomy isn't all it seems. Granting people autonomy with no support is like giving them a rope with which to hang themselves. People want challenging work but need development and coaching by their managers to feel assured of some success.

Maintaining focus on the overall transformation

The main thing must always be the main thing if the transformation journey is to stay on track. From time to time you need to take stock and review just where your time is being spent – you should be crystal clear on what and what isn't important.

Becoming sidetracked and tempted down some interesting improvement diversions is all too easy. Before darting off, ask yourself whether these opportunities will be helping you progress to True North. Take special care to avoid scope creep, whereby the project keeps growing. Spend time up front to get the scope right and avoid wasting time later on.

Naturally, a vision of the future that captures the energy and commitment of the people in the organisation is essential. But where the journey is likely to take some time, do remember to take the occasional pit stop to recharge everyone's batteries and recognise the progress made so far.

Part V

Sustaining the Transformation

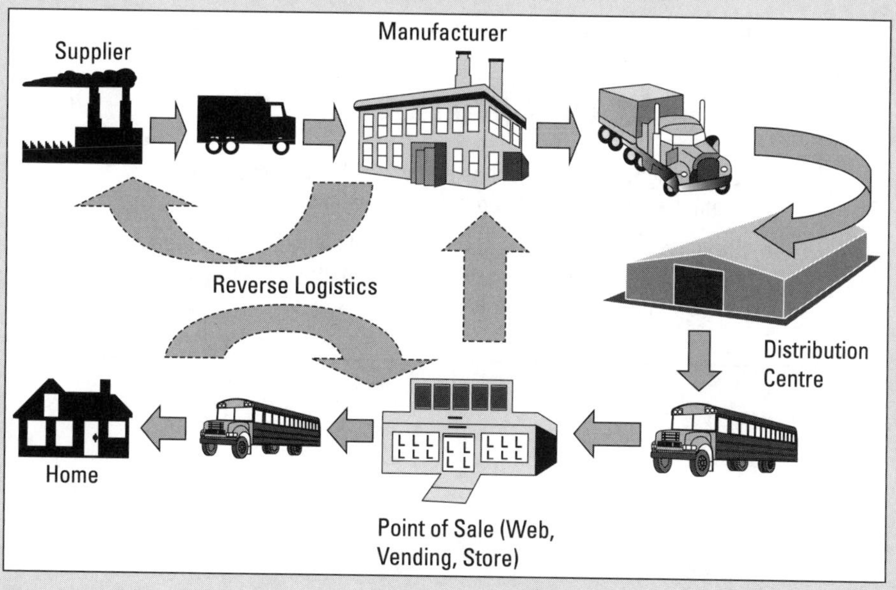

For a great free article about lean six sigma business transformation, go online and visit `www.dummies.com/extras/lssbusinesstransformation`.

In this part . . .

- Gain insight into approaches that will help business transformation extend across the organisation and beyond.
- Develop a pragmatic approach to establishing Lean Six Sigma Capability Maturity during an on-going multi-year Business Transformation programme.

Chapter 13

Widening the Scope of the Transformation

In this Chapter

- Differentiating between types of organisational structure
- Focusing on the customer
- Scrutinising the supply chain

This chapter provides insights into approaches to extend the transformation approach across the organisation and beyond. We discuss how Lean Six Sigma can be deployed within different organisational structures; how to maintain and improve your focus on your customers; and how you can involve your suppliers in the transformation journey.

Looking at Different Organisational Structures

Organisational structures evolve over time and often become very complex, involving both divisional and functional hierarchies. A divisional structure often occurs when companies operate in multiple geographic regions and also when quite different products or services are provided to customers. Functional structures have separate reporting lines for each function, such as operations or finance. In planning and deploying the Lean Six Sigma transformation, you need to consider the existing organisational structure and how it will need to adapt to accommodate the needs of the transformation.

Ideally, a Lean Six Sigma organisational structure will be designed to allow the flow of products or services through the relevant value streams that provide products or services to customers. For instance, some companies incorporating Lean Six Sigma set up integrated product and process teams as self-organised work teams. A dedicated team for each value could include expertise from different functional areas such as marketing, purchasing, manufacturing, quality assurance and customer relations. Work teams in Lean Six Sigma organisational structures should focus on a connected set of processes within a value stream, rather than being set up to report through many layers in a hierarchy.

Unless you're deploying the Lean Six Sigma transformation from scratch, it's unlikely that you'll be able to start the transformation journey with the ideal structure. Many small and medium-sized organisations operating in a single region have a functional-based structure and may be able to adapt readily to a value stream-based approach. In contrast, for a large global organisation with multiple product divisions in many geographic regions, you'll need to consider how the roll-out of the transformation is to be phased.

Differentiating between divisional and functional structures

Consider what's meant by divisional and functional structures so that you can understand how they're likely to impact the transformation programme. Figure 13-1 provides a visual overview of these different types of organisational structure.

Divisional organisational structure

In a business that's structurally organised according to geographical areas, markets, or products and services, each division operates as an autonomous business. For example, a company might have European, Asian and American divisions, or exploration and production divisions. Using this structure, division heads have decision-making powers which they rely on to quickly respond to changes in their particular markets or areas of responsibility. A potential disadvantage of this form of organisational structure is that creating production, finance and marketing departments for each division inevitably duplicates some efforts and increases costs. In addition, divisions may compete for resources and market standing, just as one company competes with another. This structure presents a challenge for the transformation because the autonomy of individual divisions may cause strategy deployment to be overly complex as a result of differing market and product needs and the need to manage improvement programme standards and consistency.

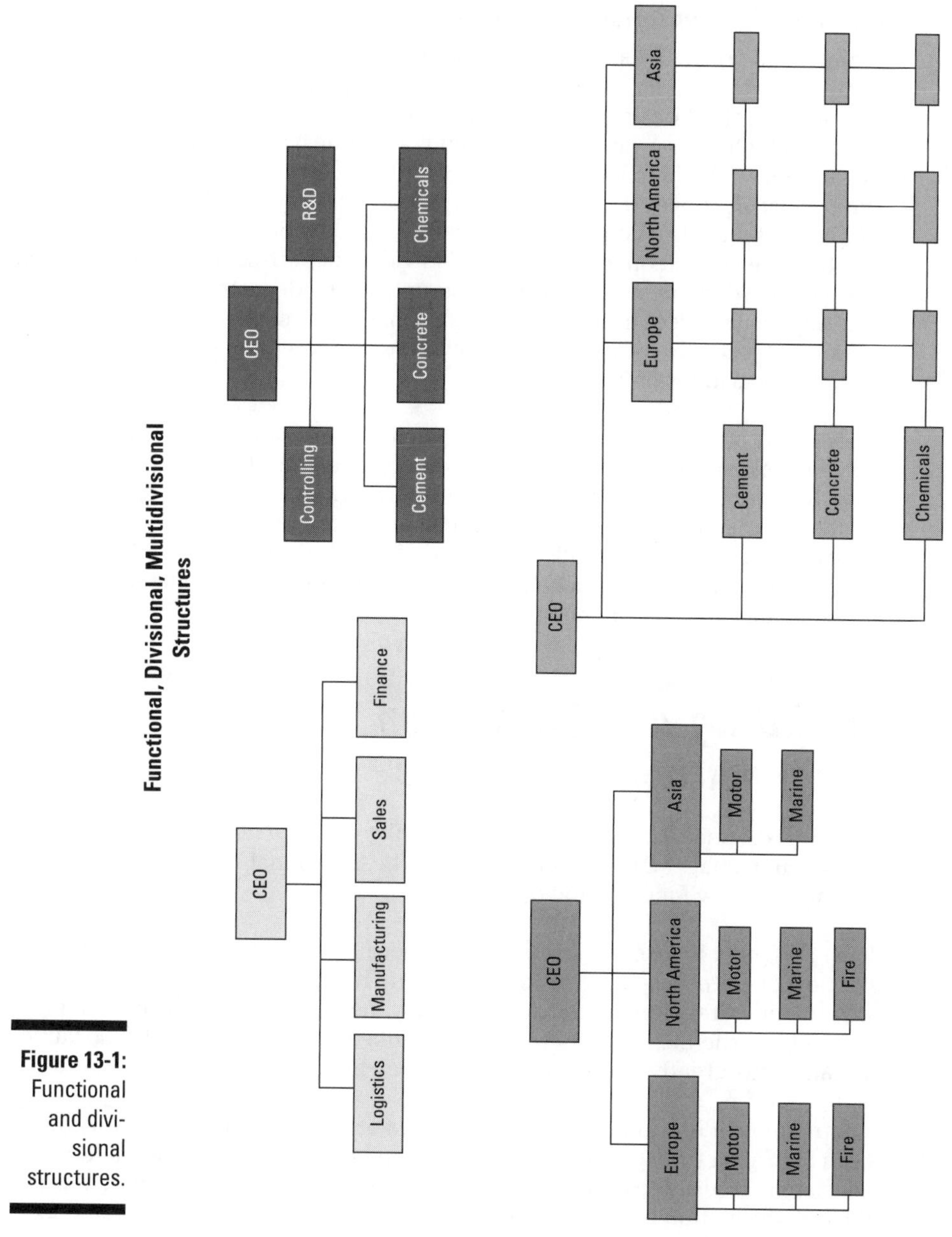

Figure 13-1: Functional and divisional structures.

Functional organisational structure

A functional organisational structure forms when a business organises according to the activities performed by individual groups within the business. Small and medium-sized businesses frequently implement this organisational structure, which often includes production and operations, finance, and marketing departments. The functional structure enforces a clear chain of command, with the company's top-level executive acting as the primary decision-maker. In this organisational structure, departments commonly develop specialists who greatly influence the operation of their individual departments. Communication flows freely within departments, but less so between departments, which can increase the time required to accomplish some business objectives. This organisational structure may also complicate strategic decision-making as a result of the functional focus of individual employees.

Prior to the introduction of Lean Six Sigma techniques in manufacturing, most companies were organised by production departments. These departments were designed to be highly efficient at performing one particular operation in the process; however, identifying the flow of products and processes in an organisation structured in this way can be difficult. As you move into a system of value streams, the flow becomes much clearer and you can manage and improve the value stream and its associated processes.

Initiating a value stream organisational structure

A Lean Six Sigma organisation needs to manage value streams. Doing so entails a different management focus from that of the traditional company organised and managed by function and division.

Lean Six Sigma focuses on value streams because they're the best way to see the flow of materials, information and cash. They also provide an excellent way to understand and increase the value you're creating for the customer, and to grow the business, increase sales and generate more profit. The value stream focus greatly simplifies the management of the company.

Another consideration that will impact organisational structure is how the Lean Six Sigma transformation approach can be standardised and made consistent across the organisation. A large global organisation may require the transformation programme to be rolled out in phases. The programme management office function, which we cover in Chapter 10, must be able to support the roll-out of the transformation programme. A need clearly exists for the programme management office function to operate at the corporate level to provide consistent governance and standardised approaches to the deployment of Lean Six Sigma across the organisation. In a large decentralised organisation, doing so is obviously more challenging, and a small corporate team with small regional programme management office teams may need to be created to support many product divisions in different regions.

Considering the role of Lean Six Sigma programme leadership

The role of the corporate continuous improvement programme manager is often established to ensure adherence to the transformation standards at both the divisional and site levels (see Chapter 10 for more on this role). The person in this role supports operational Lean Six Sigma project leaders via required and special team meetings and provides technical and operational recommendations for meeting productivity, material control, product quality, and customer service goals. In addition, this person is responsible for ensuring that the organisational structure has been reviewed and that resources are aligned for the Lean Six Sigma implementation. In multi-site divisions, the corporate continuous improvement programme manager helps develop operational Lean Six Sigma project leaders and champions to develop the division's goals, objectives and implementation plans relative to division strategy deployment and future-state site plans.

Ultimately each company is different and it will be necessary to plan any required organisational changes as part of the development of the capability maturity roadmap, which we discuss in detail in Chapter 14. In reality, organisational structures change and evolve as the transformation programme is deployed over several years.

Establishing value streams

As the Lean Six Sigma implementation is deployed and the organisation matures, it becomes increasingly necessary to manage the value streams. Managers with profit and loss responsibility for the value stream need to be assigned. Growth and improvement strategies for the company will revolve around specific value streams.

A useful way to look at this situation is to imagine the company made up of several small companies, each aligned to the overall company strategy. Each one is responsible for achieving the necessary improvements to their respective value streams in line with the process improvements defined during the strategy deployment process. We discuss strategy deployment in detail in Chapters 8 and 9. This form of organisation is ideal because it simplifies management and provides the visibility necessary for managing continuous improvement.

It's common for the departmental structure to remain in place while the organisation is restructured into value streams. In this case, team members still report to their functional leaders, but are assigned to work in particular value stream teams. This matrix management structure is often the most convenient way to make the changes without disrupting the organisation of the company. The matrix organisation is most often employed by companies with large and complex operations, where they find that their size and complexity make it more convenient to retain the departmental structure.

Small and medium-sized organisations often have the agility to take the leap and redraw the organisational chart to reflect value stream management and simply abandon the functional structure. Figure 13-2 illustrates a range of value stream structures.

For the business transformation to be successful, it will require continuous improvement, which will be achieved through improving processes related to the value streams. Lean Six Sigma organisations often have continuous improvement teams assigned to each value stream. These are made up of people working in the value stream but may be supported by Lean Six Sigma Master Black Belts (Chapters 10 and 12 cover the Lean Six Sigma belts). The purpose of the continuous improvement team is to review the value stream performance measurements each week and initiate projects to make these measurements improve every week.

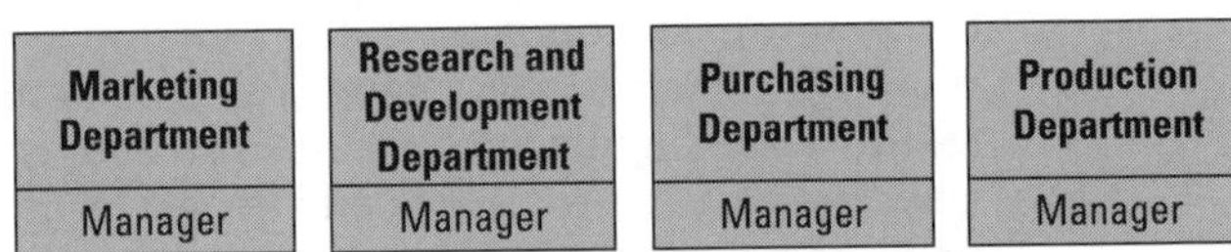

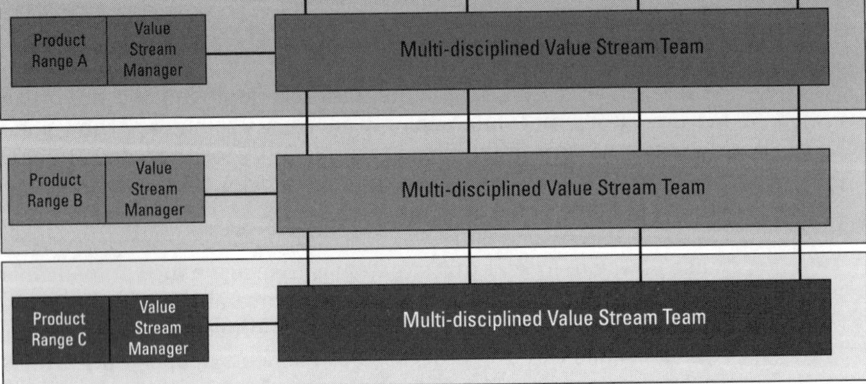

Figure 13-2: Value stream organisational structures.

Managing value streams

Companies organised by value stream usually allocate the responsibility for specific value streams to individual value stream managers. These are key roles in an organisation and are often staffed by senior executives who've previously managed functional areas within an organisation. In organisations with poor collaboration between functions, this situation can often be remedied by giving heads of functions the responsibility for value streams as well as their own function. Product managers from marketing functions make excellent value stream managers because they're used to a long-term focus on the product and the customer.

Typically, the value stream manager is responsible for that value stream's productivity, including cost analysis and opportunities, equipment set-up time, strategy deployment process improvements, quality improvements and manufacturing productivity, together with implementation of long-term manufacturing strategies. This role is operational and involves leading the value stream in daily operations and continuous improvements, which include, but aren't limited to, supply chain production control, establishment of manufacturing priorities, co-ordination of activities, and order shipments. The value stream manager also meets regularly with the team, reflecting on problems, countermeasures, solutions and challenges, and is responsible for creating a culture of continuous improvement.

Getting Closer to the Customer

Maintaining customer focus during a Lean Six Sigma implementation is both challenging and essential to the success of the business transformation. Typically, when organisations start out on the business transformation journey, they initially tend to focus on deploying basic Lean Six Sigma tools, which often results in the organisation being focused on functionally-based improvements. This approach can become a problem if customers feel that the organisation is no longer interested in them and can ultimately impact on customer loyalty.

Ensure that external customer requirements remain in focus as you deploy the Lean Six Sigma transformation, but don't forget your internal customers!

As the Lean Six Sigma transformation becomes more imbedded in the organisation, improvements are directed towards end-to-end value streams and are externally focused, requiring the company to become customer driven to improve service levels and profitability.

Over a period of time, the organisation becomes more mature and will operate in the higher gears of the DRIVE model (see Chapter 3 for more on these). At this stage of maturity the organisation becomes strategically focused, with enterprise-wide adoption of the continuous improvement approach and integration of the supply chain, which will provide the most effective way to delight customers.

A customer experience focus must be strategically applied throughout the Lean Six Sigma transformation journey to drive a continued customer focus and to enable customer-driven prioritisation of improvement initiatives and the introduction of new products and services. This focus will lead to sustained growth, and dramatic improvements in customer satisfaction and loyalty.

Identifying your customers

When you think about your customers, who do you consider? The customer is often thought of as the person (or company) who buys the goods and services produced by your organisation. Clearly, providing the product or service at the required price, quality and time desired by that customer is crucial. However, you must not forget the consumer of the end product and service, because your products and services may be part of a larger or more complex offering. The consumer is the individual who buys the products or services for personal use and not for manufacture or resale.

You must also consider the needs of internal customers. These are the people who are involved in the creation of value in the end-to-end value streams or are the providers to these processes. These internal customers may be either upstream or downstream of your function within the value stream processes. Internal stakeholders may also exist who are affected by, or can influence, the value stream but who are not directly involved with creating the end product or service. Examples include managers, process owners, internal departments that support the process, customers, suppliers and the financial department.

You can establish who your various customers are by creating a SIPOC and mapping your end-to-end value streams. These mapping techniques are discussed in detail in *Lean Six Sigma For Dummies* (Wiley). Clearly, all customers are not equal and understanding end customer requirements in terms of their CTQs (critical to quality requirements) is essential. To differentiate your product or service from those of your competitors, you need to understand and improve the customer experience.

When you're defining Lean Six Sigma projects and identifying customer CTQs, ask lots of questions so that you really understand who the customer is and how you can delight them.

Improving the customer experience

According to customer relations consultants Peppers and Rogers, 'The customer experience has emerged as the single most important aspect in achieving success for companies across all industries.' However, a Bain & Co. survey (2005) reveals just how commonly companies misread the market. Surveying 362 firms, the company found that 80 per cent believed they delivered a 'superior experience' to their customers. However, when we asked customers about their own perceptions, we found that they rated only 8 per cent of companies as truly delivering a superior experience. In today's highly competitive marketplace, differentiating your company's products and services from those of competitors can be challenging. A focus on improving the customer experience is likely to be a large item on the strategic agenda and is likely to result in the need for customer experience-related process improvements.

Considering customer experience management

Customer experience management comprises both processes and tools that capture specific customer feedback (the voice of the customer) at critical customer 'touch points'. This information provides real-time feedback to the organisation, and can be acted upon to result in:

- Identification of customers that are delighted with your product, service or support solutions and will actively promote your offerings, thus providing significant growth opportunities.
- Opportunities to delight customers with the introduction of innovative product, service or support solutions that will provide significant value to the customer and will lead to business growth.
- Opportunities to reduce or remove existing products, services and support activities that are no longer valued by the customer, providing significant cost reductions.
- Identification of issues related to products, services and support that are negatively impacting customer satisfaction and need immediate resolution.

Recognising the critical voice of the customer

Most feedback is received via the 'voice of the process'; that is, from internal stakeholders who are likely to see the world from an inward-looking perspective and may thus misinterpret the voice of the customer.

Tapping directly into the *voice of the customer*, in contrast, provides an unbiased view, enabling you to resolve immediate problems, drill down using data from your processes to root causes, and improve processes and products to achieve a higher level of customer satisfaction and loyalty. Figure 13-3 illustrates the concept of the voice of the customer.

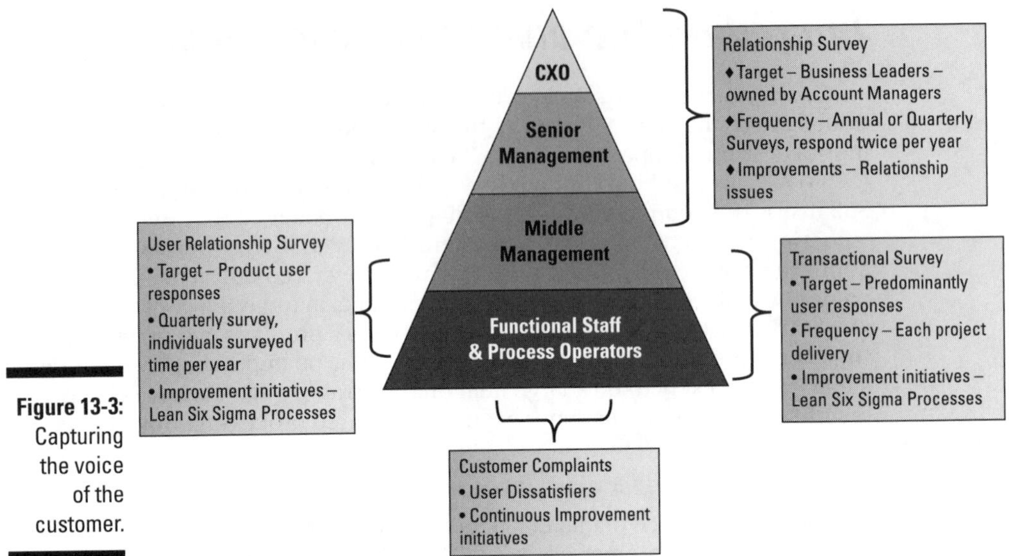

Figure 13-3: Capturing the voice of the customer.

By capturing the voice of the customer you can:

- Understand what customers care about and so define requirements
- Set priorities and goals consistent with customer needs (CTQs)
- Identify the customer needs you can profitably meet
- Measure levels of customer service and customer satisfaction

You can capture the voice of the customer in several ways:

- *Interviews* to develop a thorough understanding of customer needs.
- *Point-of-use observation* to observe the point of contact between customer and product/service and gain greater insight or confirm interview results.
- *Focus groups* to gain feedback on existing products, services or proposed ideas from the point of view of a group of customers.
- *Questionnaires and surveys* to gain quantitative data across an entire segment or group of segments on customer reactions to a particular product, service or segment. Relationship surveys can be very useful for understanding the needs of key customers and transaction surveys can be used to obtain real-time feedback on products or services to enable timely corrective actions to be implemented.

- *Kano analysis* to better understand the value the customer places on the features of your product or service. It can reduce the risk of providing products or services with an over-emphasis on unimportant features or ones that miss CTQ requirements. For detailed information on Kano analysis, refer to *Lean Six Sigma For Dummies* (Wiley).
- *Customer complaints* to gain a direct insight into elements of the product or service with which customers are dissatisfied.
- *Quality Function Deployment* to capture customer requirements in order to create new products, services or processes. This is a key component of the DMADV process that we discuss in Chapter 1.

Using the net promoter score

Many companies are now including customer experience metrics in business key performance indicators (KPIs; see Chapter 7 for the lowdown on these). The net promoter is a customer survey process by which companies can identify how to profitably grow by focusing on its customers. The questionnaire is based on asking a key question – 'Would you recommend us?' – followed up by the supplementary question, 'Why?' A successful net promoter programme includes five elements:

- Metrics proven to link to growth
- Leadership practices that result in customer focus, passion and core values
- Organisational strategies to ensure adoption
- Integration with core business processes
- Operational systems to support the initiative

The net promoter questionnaire places customers into three groups:

- **Promoters:** Customers who are highly likely to recommend a company (a rating of 9 or 10) and exhibit the highest purchase rates and referral behaviour.
- **Passive:** Customers who are somewhat likely to recommend a company (average ratings) and exhibit moderate purchase rates and referral behaviour.
- **Detractors:** Customers who are less likely to recommend a company (poor ratings) and exhibit the lowest purchase rates and referral behaviours.

The overall net promoter score is created by dividing the number of promoters by the number of detractors to create a percentage ratio. Many leading companies struggle to achieve ratios of more than 50 per cent! Figure 13-4 provides an example of net promoter scores for particular types of technology.

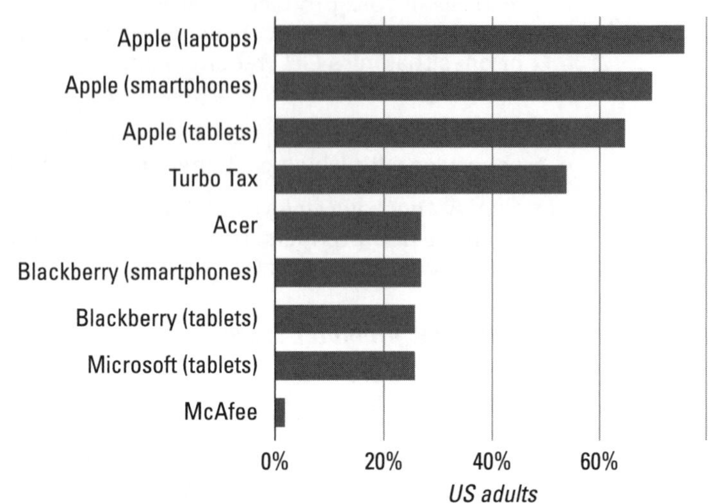

Figure 13-4: Net promoter technology sector scores, 2013.

Understanding the customer journey

For many businesses whose products aren't differentiated from those of competitors, creating and managing a positive and memorable customer experience is their single greatest source of potential differentiation. The challenge is to identify genuine customer frustrations and to deliver a differentiated experience that addresses them. In doing so, you also need to continually assess improvement options and track outcomes.

Customer journey mapping can help your organisation to identify how it treats its customers during each contact with them. Such journey mapping is carried out from the perspective of how the customer 'feels' towards the organisation during a particular end-to-end experience. This information helps management to decide what improvements, if any, are required.

Each different type of customer interaction needs to be mapped separately as they differ slightly depending upon, for example, whether the initial interaction is prompted by the customer or the supplying organisation, or if it's an existing or a potential customer.

Mapping the customer journey

Customer journey mapping is a process designed to encourage the supplying organisation to think as its customers do about what it's like to interact and do business with them. It's a structured way to understand your customers' wants, needs and expectations at every stage of the supplier to consumer cycle.

Each point of interaction with your organisation can be referred to as a *moment of truth*, a concept first introduced by Jan Carlzon, the former president of SAS group, the Scandinavian airline. According to Carlzon, 'Anytime a customer comes into contact with any aspect of a business, however remote, is an opportunity to form an impression.' Customer journey mapping builds on this concept by providing a strategic tool to start the process of ensuring that every interaction with your organisation is a positive one.

Customer journey mapping is a tool for visualising how customers interact with organisations across multiple channels and touch-points. It provides a map of the interactions that take place and of the emotions created at each touch-point. And it provides a platform of factual data from which customer-facing executives can drive change.

You can approach the mapping of a customer journey in a number of ways, but typically the process is started by thinking about when your customers or potential customers interact with the organisation. These interactions are typically grouped as follows:

- **Marketing communication:** For example, via advertisements, websites, company literature or human contact.
- **Telephone:** For example, to your staff, call centres, telesales/telemarketing personnel, administration staff and so on.
- **In person:** For example, via reception, business development, sales people, delivery and assessment team, and so on.
- **Physical interaction:** For example, visiting your premises, using your facilities – even parking in your car park!

The customer journey mapping process involves first, mapping the current state (the current customer experience); second, identifying how you can improve the customer experience; third, creating a future state map (the desired customer experience); and fourth, providing input to the strategy deployment and Lean Six Sigma transformation plans to ensure that you maintain a focus on improving the customer experience.

Customer journey mapping helps your organisation to:

- Deal with its customers more effectively
- Improve customer retention
- Increase organisational efficiency
- Reduce the number of dissatisfied customers (who potentially tell up to ten others about their negative experience)
- Put you in control of managing and defining your customers' experience across the whole of your organisation

Figure 13-5 provides an example customer journey map.

Figure 13-5: Customer journey map.

Product Delivery Process

Key Touch Points		●	●	●		●
Stakeholder	Planning	Q/C; Planning	Courier Service	Warehouse	Customs	Test
Journey Steps	Notification of delivery	Pre-alert documentation sent	Product arrives	Receipted into Warehouse	Cleared by FDA	Sampled
Customer Experience at each Step	• E-kanban meeting • Word document sent to state what batches will be delivered (Thurs)	• Includes PDF copies of AWB, Packing list, Customs Invoice, Declaration letters/Vet certificates • Sent by freight forwarder by e-mail (Wed) • Despatch report sent (Thurs) • Excursion report sent (Thurs/Fri)	• Clears USDA and US Customs (wheels up clearance) • Arrives into San Juan (Fri pm) • Picked up by transportation arranged by iPR and delivered to site • Original paperwork (AWB, Packing list, Customs invoice) arrives with the delivery • Originals of Declaration letters/Vet certificates sent to customs broker by courier (should arrive by Wed before delivery arrives)	• Product in LD3s delivered to cold store by non warehouse staff (Fri pm) • Documentation /security seal check and receipt onto SAP • Remove temp-tracers from drums and download data • Record excursion time remaining	• Shipping documents (AWB, Invoice, Packing List) • IND / NDA # • NDC # / Drug Listing (not that frequently) • HTSUS / Tariff Code • Material Description • FDA Product Category (most of IPR products fall under FDA's category FD2, which means that material requires FDA approval) • FDA Product Code	• Each batch sampled by warehouse • Samples delivered to QC for testing
Priority Activities	• Check stock level • Check scenario information • Chair e-kanban meeting	• Apply for correct declaration letter/vet certificate • Make sure documents are sent in a timely manner	• Robust distribution process • Letting client know about any issues/delays • Accurate documentation	• Accurate documentation • Labelled correctly • Necessary security seals applied	• Accurate documentation • Labelled correctly	• Ensure enough liner available to take sample and re-seal

However good you think your existing customer-facing staff, communication procedures and processes are, if your customers' perception is that your systems don't deliver, that your staff appear not to deliver and don't care – even if only on rare occasions – or that your facilities aren't up to scratch, such moments of truth will mean that your organisation's relationship with its customers has suffered or will suffer. Customer journey mapping enables you to focus on removing the anomalies and beginning to deliver a consistent, predictable experience.

By understanding your customer's journey, you can ensure that strategy deployment is focused on optimising customer experience and will ultimately result in increased customer loyalty and business growth.

Deploying to the Supply Chain

As the Lean Six Sigma transformation is deployed and the organisation becomes capable of effectively managing end-to-end value streams, opportunities to involve your suppliers in the transformation and to deploy Lean Six Sigma to supply chain processes will arise.

A supply chain consists of all the stages involved, directly or indirectly, in fulfilling a customer request. The supply chain not only includes the products or services offered by your company and suppliers, but also your transporters' warehouses, retailers and your customers themselves. The supply chain process is illustrated in Figure 13-6.

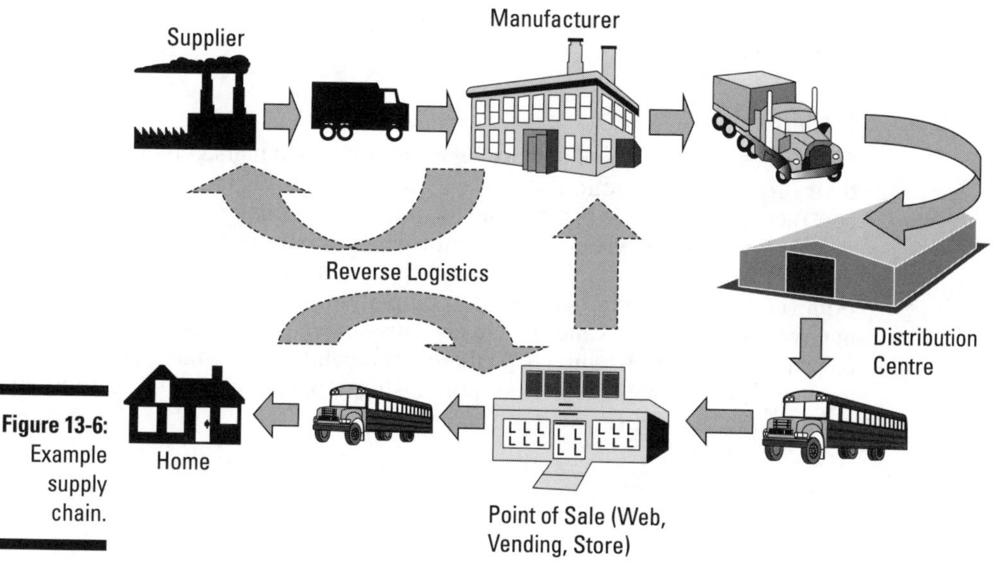

Figure 13-6: Example supply chain.

A Lean Six Sigma supply chain is one that produces or provides only what's needed, when it's needed and where it's needed. This type of supply chain typically has a number of key advantages over traditional supply chain management, including:

- Supply is more tightly linked with demand
- Lower inventory risk
- Processes that focus specifically on activities that add value for the customer
- A greater focus on mistake-proof processes

Lean Six Sigma is now an accepted methodology in managing inbound supply, internal processing and onward distribution.

Today, high volume manufacturing and retail sectors are the champions and beneficiaries of this approach. High-tech companies such as Apple, grocery retailers including Sainsbury's, and online distributors such as Amazon have emulated these achievements and become highly respected leaders in Lean supply.

A recent Aberdeen Group report on Lean strategies revealed that only two-thirds of manufacturers are using these techniques. More than 90 per cent are still using spreadsheet and paper-based solutions to perform high-value functions.

Understanding the supply chain

A number of opportunities exist to apply Lean Six Sigma in the supply chain, as described below.

Procurement

Companies that practise Lean Six Sigma supply chain management reduce their procurement function so that each vendor has one point of contact, one contract and offers one price for all locations. Such businesses are looking to new technologies to assist them in improving procurement processes. These include online purchasing, which allows procurement teams to purchase items from vendors' catalogues containing company-wide contract prices. Changes in payment options to vendors can also streamline processes. Companies that use a two-way match, which is payment on receipt rather than payment on invoice, reduce resources in their purchasing department as well as improve supplier relationships.

Manufacturing

Lean supply chain management gained popularity in the manufacturing area as this is where significant improvement can be achieved. Manufacturing processes can be improved to reduce waste and resources while maintaining operational performance. Companies that have adopted Lean Six Sigma supply chain practices have examined each of their routings, bill of materials and equipment to identify where improvements can be achieved.

Warehousing

Warehouse processes should be examined to identify areas where wasteful use of resources and non-value adding steps can be eliminated. One area that companies should always be working on is the reduction of unnecessary inventory. The accumulation of inventory requires resources to store and maintain it. By reducing unnecessary inventory, a company can minimise warehousing space and handling, in turn reducing overall costs.

Transportation

Businesses that want to implement Lean Six Sigma processes often look to their transportation procedures to see where they can be streamlined. In many instances, companies find that their efforts to improve customer satisfaction lead to poor shipping decisions. Orders are shipped without combining additional orders to minimise costs or expensive shipping options are selected in response to a customer request. Businesses often find that they're using a number of shippers unnecessarily when they could be reducing their shipping options and reducing overall costs.

Five guiding principles of Lean supply

Here are some key points to bear in mind:

1. **Involve people:** Engage colleagues in improving continuously through waste elimination and problem solving.
2. **Build in quality:** Engineer processes to make them mistake-proof, thus preventing errors before they happen.
3. **Reduce lead times:** Establish a continuous flow of materials, equipment and processes such that products are pulled through the supply chain at the right place, the right time, and in the right quantity.
4. **Standardise:** Document the best practices and make sure that they're followed.
5. **Improve continuously:** No matter how good a process seems, there's always room to improve it. Your competitors are working on it.

Involving suppliers in the transformation journey

End-to-end value streams can include more than just what occurs within the production plant. Organisations with finished goods warehouses usually include them in the value stream. The warehouse may be outside the immediate control of the plant team, but it contributes to both customer value and waste. Similarly, if the operation pulls materials from a supplier or another plant within the same organisation, these suppliers are often included as a part of the value stream. A company that sells through distributors may include the distributor as part of its value stream in order to 'see' the flow through to the end customer.

Chapter 14

Managing the Capability Maturity Journey

In This Chapter

- Getting to grips with the capability maturity road map
- Creating the capability maturity matrix
- Sticking to the route

This chapter looks at pragmatic approaches to establishing Lean Six Sigma capability maturity during an ongoing multi-year business transformation programme. As you start out on the LSS transformation journey, you need to be able to establish whether the organisation is developing the required capability to execute the organisational transformation. It is essential that the organisation has the necessary resources and skills to enable it to successfully implement the improvements necessary for achieving the business transformation.

Introducing the Capability Maturity Model

In Chapter 3 we introduce the capability maturity roadmap for the business transformation and we briefly introduce several approaches based on different models. In this chapter we take a look at a specific capability model approach based on the DRIVE model.

The DRIVE capability maturity model has two aspects. The first is the five 'gears' that represent an increasing level of capability over time. The gears are rated from first to fifth and an organisation is expected to go up a gear as it accelerates the rate of transformation over several years.

The second aspect of DRIVE is its eight elements, which are the key focus areas that drive the business transformation. These two aspects are illustrated in Figure 14-1.

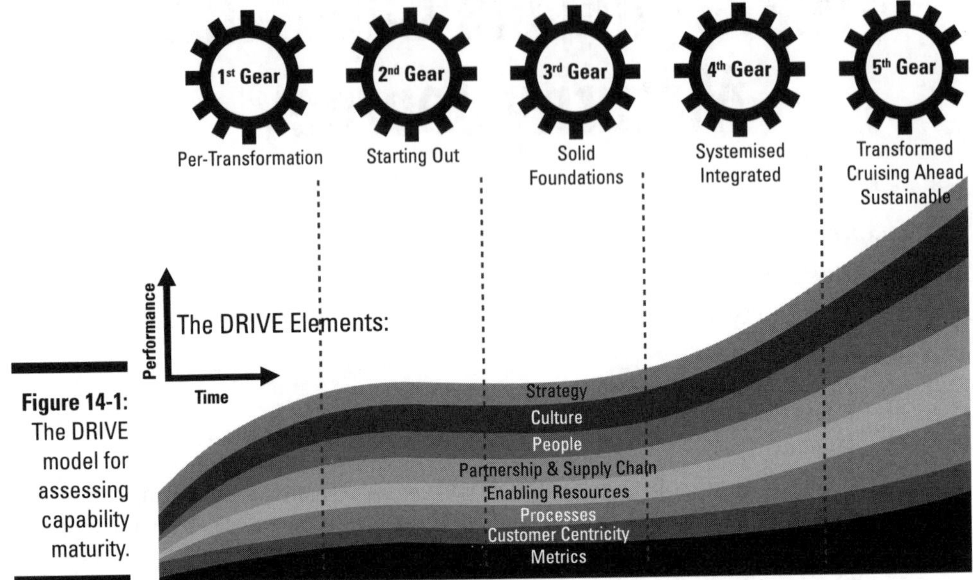

Figure 14-1: The DRIVE model for assessing capability maturity.

Working through the gears

The DRIVE model is based on the following five gears, which represent the organisation's evolving maturity:

- **1st gear – Pre-transformation:** Approaches to transformation unstructured and tactical; need is recognised.
- **2nd gear – Starting out:** Starting points defined and communicated, transformation infrastructure created, strategy deployment established, initial skills in place, short-term wins achieved.
- **3rd gear – Solid foundations:** Plans aligned to strategy, organisational capability assessed, gaps identified, first tranche improvements delivered, ability to launch and support transformation projects established, culture compatible with roll-out of continuous improvement.
- **4th gear – Systemised, integrated:** Approaches fully deployed across the organisation, regular monitoring of improvement activity performance, continuous improvement is fully integrated within normal business and end-to-end value streams.

- **5th gear – Transformed, cruising ahead, sustainable:** Continuous improvement programmes systematically used to gain market advantage, extended enterprise multiplier, innovation and breakthrough, thought leadership, outstanding results; continuous improvement culture spans extended enterprise.

Examining the elements

The DRIVE model involves the following eight elements:

- **Strategy:** Strategy is based on a business vision and is goal orientated; strategies and systems are aligned across the organisation; strategy deployment is in place, together with goal setting that's cascaded down to the point of impact.
- **Culture:** A culture of continuous improvement is developed over time. New leadership, behaviour and ethics become embedded in the organisation.
- **People:** A training system is established to develop employees; staff are empowered and involved; a reward and recognition policy is in place; staff are aware of health and safety protocols.
- **Partnership and supply chain:** Value streams are managed and leveraged end to end; the organisation collaborates with suppliers and partners for strategic gain.
- **Enabling resources:** The resources needed to deliver the strategic goals are identified and exploited, including finance, IT, asset management, buildings and equipment, security, and employee safety.
- **Processes:** Organisational processes and continuous improvement are related throughout the organisation; a value-stream approach is applied (rather than a functional approach); employees are able to discuss a process or problem, suggest improvement ideas, implement suggestions, evaluate impact and adjust as necessary; business processes are standardised from department to department.
- **Customer centricity:** Customer focus and relationship management are at the centre of the organisation; product/service development and delivery are based on customer CTQs.
- **Metrics:** The organisation measures itself on the customer experience of cost and productivity; it tracks significant trends; it compares its performance to that of competitors or specific industry performance levels; organisational behaviours are aligned with desired results.

Building the Capability Maturity Matrix

Most organisations planning to implement a business transformation are doing so to differentiate themselves from their competitors in specific market sectors, and their business strategies provide the direction and timescale for achieving their goals. This means that each business transformation is unique and specific to a particular organisation and, although generic capability maturity road maps can provide a useful starting point for the business transformation, a customised road map is necessary.

Each organisation will need to develop a capability maturity road map for their specific business transformation. The capability roadmap comprises the eight DRIVE elements on the vertical axis and the five gears (maturity levels) on the horizontal axis in an 8 × 5 matrix. This layout makes it very easy to assess the maturity of your process against the maturity descriptions in the matrix. Each maturity level will need to be described in enough detail to allow an assessment of performance to be carried out.

An example of a generic capability maturity description for the strategy component of the DRIVE capability maturity model is shown in Figure 14-2.

	1st Gear	2nd Gear	3rd Gear	4th Gear	5th Gear
Strategy	• No formal Strategy planning process • Strategy disconnected from CI • Proliferation of Initiatives	• Business case done • Customer thinking embedded • Vision communicated	• Strategy Deployment goals & KPIs established • Direction management process established	• Strategy Deployment goals & KPIs Institutionalised • Key value streams	• Excellence systematically used as a market advantage • Renew vision

Figure 14-2: Example of the strategy component in the capability maturity model.

Assessing capability maturity

Many organisations base their organisational assessments on well-known assessment methodologies such as the EFQM, Baldrige and Shingo Prize models. We discuss these assessment methods in Chapter 5. These methods provide an excellent set of assessment criteria and require experienced assessors to obtain evidence of conformance to them. The EFQM assessment process is illustrated in Figure 14-3 and the Shingo Prize Model™ is shown in Figure 14-4. The Baldrige assessment model is shown in Chapter 5.Typically, these assessment approaches use a numerical rating scale based on achievement of specific outcomes. You establish maturity levels based on the numerical scores as you design your specific capability road map.

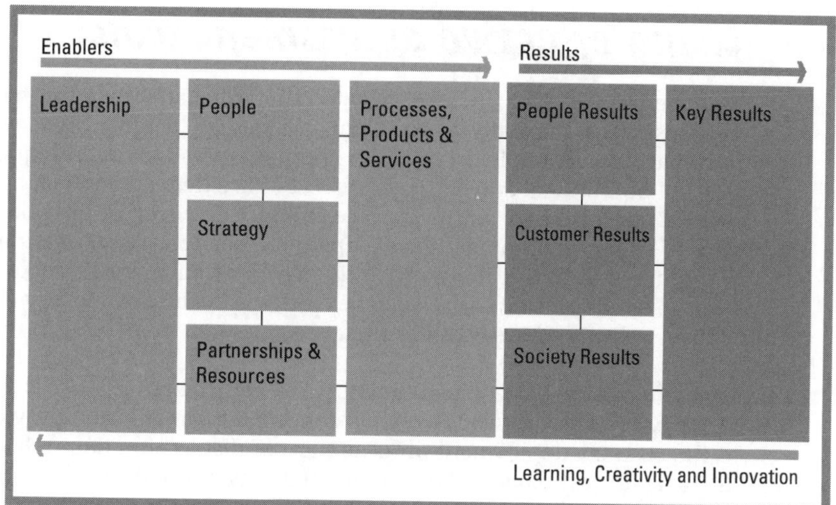

Figure 14-3: EFQM Excellence Model.

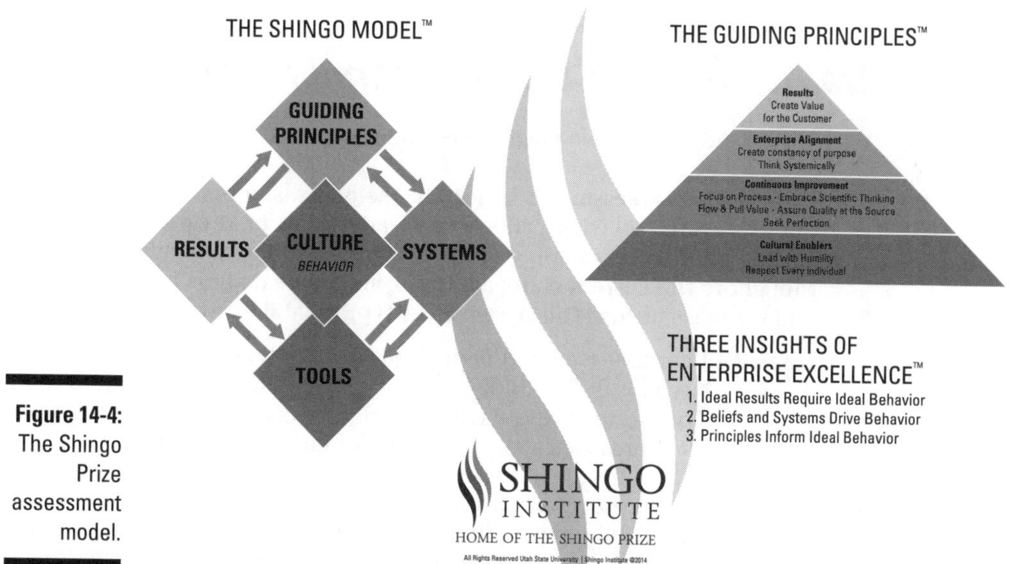

Figure 14-4: The Shingo Prize assessment model.

Whichever assessment tool you select, ensure that it provides assessment based on levels of capability maturity.

Using effective assessment tools

You need to consider the level of detail that you can obtain for the top-level of assessment. Typically, assessment criteria can be quite high level in the first place; for example, a typical assessment question might require evidence that 'all operational and support processes are defined and managed'. This level of question may not be specific enough, however, to provide a realistic view of specific component-level capability, particularly in relation to Lean Six Sigma tools and techniques. In that circumstance, for example, you may want to establish that 'daily management has been sustained by the plant manager within all areas of the site'.

We recommend that you implement two levels of maturity assessment. First, strategy-level assessment, which is conducted annually and provides input to the strategy deployment process that we discuss in Chapter 8, as well as top-level assessment of capability maturity. Second, DRIVE component assessments, which are conducted during the year to provide input at plant or functional level.

Going through the assessment process

We recommend using a two-stage assessment process:

- **Stage 1 – Self-assessment:** An internal self-assessment using a structured questionnaire tool which allows site leaders and/or key personnel to gain a better understanding of the required standards; to apply critical thought to the current state; and to formulate next steps based on gaps and business needs. This assessment typically takes two days.
- **Stage 2 – Peer assessment:** Carried out by external assessors, this is designed to calibrate the findings of the self-assessment. The same structured questionnaire is used, typically by assessors from other sites or locations. It provides an opportunity for knowledge transfer.

The peer assessment process typically takes two to three days, but may be significantly longer depending on the number of operations or divisions to be assessed and the size of the assessment team. On the first day all assessors meet with the management team to receive a brief overview and undertake a tour of the organisation. The team then disperses into smaller groups in order to observe as much of the organisation as possible and reconvenes at the end of the day to discuss their observations. The second day is a continuation of small-group observations, culminating with the team gathering and beginning formal development of the assessment summary. Figure 14-5 illustrates the assessment process.

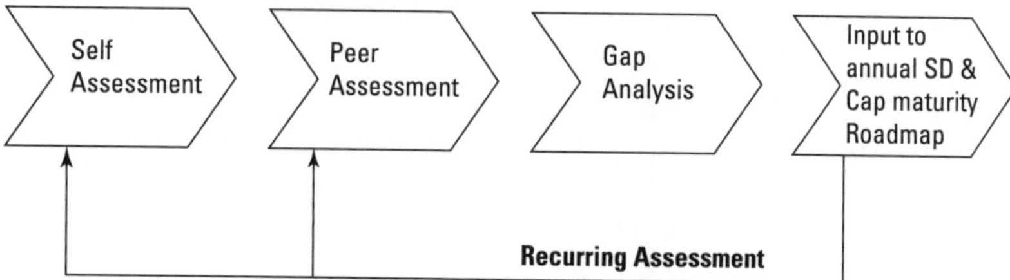

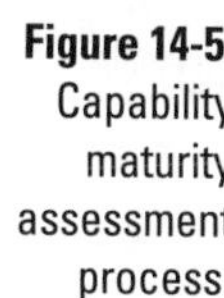

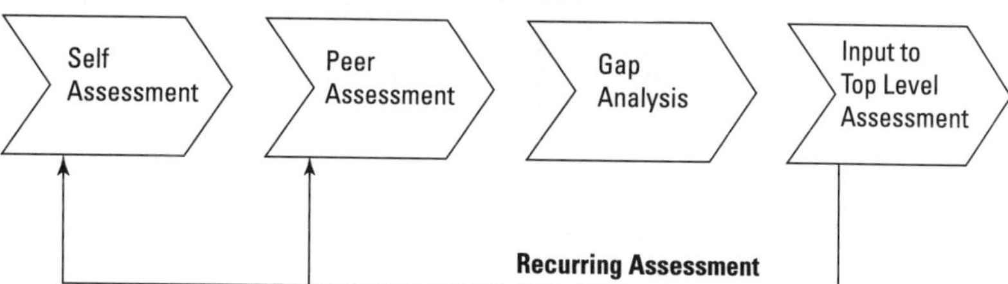

Figure 14-5: Capability maturity assessment process.

The assessment process establishes a baseline of strengths and weaknesses in relation to the DRIVE elements at both strategy and individual level. Self-assessments will ideally address the whole organisation or substantial units or locations within it. The two-stage assessment process also aims to improve cross-divisional participation and leadership engagement.

Developing customised questionnaires

Questionnaires need to be developed for the capability maturity assessments at the strategic level and for each of the DRIVE components (see Figure 14-6). The strategy-level assessment questionnaire must include questions that will assist the assessor in establishing the maturity level (gear) for each of the DRIVE elements described in the capability maturity road map. For the strategy-level assessment, it may also be possible to adapt existing assessment tools, such as EFQM, to provide appropriate questions to assess maturity levels (gears).

The element-level assessments will require more development because the questions will be more detailed and tool or process specific.

Figure 14-6: Example component-level questionnaire.

DRIVE ELEMENT PROCESSES	1st Gear	2nd Gear	3rd Gear	4th Gear	5th Gear	Strengths	Opportunities
Time-based or just-in-time manufacturing						Production model has significant Build-To-Order business so JIT is not a concept that should meet resistance	Inventory and focus on efficiency indicate there is an opportunity to improve the effectiveness of the schedule pattern
Systematic identification and elimination of all forms of waste	1						Learn the types and apply specific tools to combat the waste and drive for elimination
Value Stream Mapping		1				Started a VSM for both admin and manufacturing	Knowledge has not been transferred, Corporate lean leader has knowledge. Apply VSM as part of the COE
5S Standards and Disciplines	1						Initiate use of the tool to support increasing throughput of the facility
Standardized work (including takt time, sequence, and standard WIP)	1						Implement first std work after VSM is complete
Total productive, preventive, or predictive maintenance	1					Team has attempted the initial steps of TPM by trying o install a maintenance program for the Plasma Welder	build on experience and implement as the critical machines get introduced to the concepts and then initiate TPM (the process) to the organization.
Quick changeover or setup reductions (SMED)	1					Team realizes how significant changeover is to capacity	
Source inspection and poka-yoke		1				Many quality checks are part of the make up of the organization. Therefore, enhanced quality system tools sholud be a welcome addition to the	Determine the correct poke-yoke through the data collection and root cause problem solving

Choosing assessors

The corporate or regional Lean Six Sigma programme management office (refer to Chapter 10 for more on this) typically provides an assessment service for the organisation. Key members of the programme management office need to be trained in the assessment methodology. The role of this team is to provide support during the peer assessment process, and its members will typically have specialised consulting skills and more advanced transformation experience.

In cases where the organisation is already using an assessment methodology, such as EFQM, at the strategy level, trained assessors may be available to support the customised capability maturity assessments. Alternatively, external consultants can be used to support the assessment process.

Peer assessments are usually carried out by representatives from other sites or plants and will typically include members of the operational leadership team as well as programme management office members. Use of operational leaders for the assessments enables the sharing of knowledge and best practice between locations, which also assists in the creation of standards across the organisation. An additional benefit of peer assessment is that it enables operational teams to prioritise the order in which improvements are undertaken to maintain alignment with objectives, which prevents them from overloading the system with projects and change initiatives.

Checking out assessors' skills

Assessors need to be trained by the transformation programme management office team (refer to Chapter 10) in the assessment process and have experience in conducting structured assessment interviews. They require good analytical skills, and should preferably be experienced Lean Six Sigma Black Belts. Assessors should also have a good working knowledge of the business and ideally be familiar with the following functions:

- Human resources management
- Supply chain management
- Finance
- Marketing and sales
- Operations management

Interpreting the outcome

On completion of the assessment observations, the assessment team need to analyse the results and conduct a gap analysis, comparing actual results with the planned maturity level (gear) to establish gaps in capability. Every assessment should include a gap analysis. A gap analysis involves the assessment team comparing each of the planned DRIVE capabilities defined in the capability road map with the actual capability observed. We recommend that, for each of the gaps in capability, you define countermeasures to establish their root cause and identify corrective actions to address them.

Monitoring the Capability Maturity Journey

You need to be able to assess your organisation's capability maturity so that you can keep track of the business transformation programme's progress and identify components that are lagging behind and require additional focus. In addition, capability maturity assessment provides valuable input to the annual strategy scan and strategy deployment processes to ensure that the organisation is capable of deploying annual process improvement plans. In the light of assessment results, critical objectives and focus areas can be reviewed in relation to actual capability, thus permitting realistic annual process improvements to be identified. For example, if during strategy deployment a need for a new process is identified, people with DMADV expertise will be required. If this capability is not currently available, action must be taken to address the situation.

Dealing with changes of direction

Although a possibility always exists that unexpected events, such as a hostile takeover, may cause a dramatic change of direction, generally changes in strategy are driven through the annual strategy planning process.

If a major change in business strategy is necessary, it's likely to result in changes to the strategy deployment planning process (which we discuss in Chapter 8). Longer-term critical objectives may change, resulting in a change of both focus areas and the short-term process improvements with which they're aligned. The capability maturity road map needs to be reviewed and updated to maintain alignment with the new strategic direction, and current levels of capability need to be reviewed to ensure that the organisation is able to effectively implement the process improvements.

Constantly updating the route

The business transformation is an ongoing process that needs to be assessed on an annual basis and, from time to time, realigned with the organisation's evolving long-term strategic vision. Strategy deployment supported by constantly developing capability and a transformational culture will provide the necessary foundations for a successful business transformation.

Part VI
The Part of Tens

Enjoy an additional Part of Tens chapter online at www.dummies.com/extras/lssbusinesstransformation.

In this part . . .

- Don't let perfect get in the way of better – and take note of other things you need to do.
- Don't focus too much on short term objectives – and watch out for other pitfalls.
- Remember to ask your colleagues – and discover other places to go for help.

Chapter 15

Ten Tips for Smoothing the Transformation Process

In This Chapter

- Keeping lines of communication open
- Acknowledging each success
- Learning from your mistakes

This chapter summarises ten best practices to help you achieve a successful transformation. If you adopt these you are more likely to stay focused on the right things and carry the people you need along with you. There's no panacea and your transformation journey may be long and challenging but you'll make it seem shorter and straighter with these tips.

Obtain Leadership Ownership

Business transformation starts at the top. Success can only be achieved through having a clear overall vision and related business strategy. Obviously, it's in implementing that strategy that things most often go wrong. Strategy is the responsibility of the leadership team of the organisation; so is its deployment. Hence obtaining leadership ownership is fundamental and critical to success.

Leadership ownership is both individual and collective. While individual leaders may be responsible for some particular aspect of strategy and transformation, success only comes about if all members of the leadership team fully buy into and support the transformation. Any doubters or leaders who are 'off-message' will likely derail the whole effort. The analogy of the chain being as strong as its weakest link applies here. Without the wholehearted commitment of the entire leadership team those people in the organisation who are reluctant to change will exploit the conflicting messages to block or hinder progress.

Ultimately the senior team may have to replace members not wholly committed to the agreed course of transformation.

Communicate, Communicate, Communicate

Successful transformation requires that the actions of all those involved be tightly aligned to the critical transformation objective. Unless people at all levels – from the leadership team through to frontline managers and staff – are kept informed and engaged, this alignment won't be achieved. And it's not just top-down communication that's important; people also need to be able to challenge what's being demanded of them so that the eventual plans and actions are realistic – albeit stretching. The 'catchball' process through which the different levels or groups of managers align their objectives (described in Chapter 8) is the main vehicle for much of the communication during the planning phases, but the other normal internal communications media will need to support and inform people as the plan unfolds.

The RACI (responsible, accountable, consulted, informed) model is appropriate here. Distinguish those who are directly *responsible* at the sharp end for the actions from those who are *accountable* and ultimately responsible, those who are in the loop and need to be *consulted,* and finally those who need to be *informed* so that they can take appropriate action as a result. Communications with those to be consulted must be two-way; in contrast, those with people who need to be informed must essentially be one-way. The key point is to structure an overarching communications plan that identifies the audience at different levels and locations and the role that each member plays. The plan should include the media specific to transformation, such as the catchball process, as well as normal internal communications such as team briefs, emails, intranet messages, and others.

You can never over-communicate during the transformation process, although timing is of the essence.

Use Strategy Deployment to Drive Improvement Programmes

Strategy deployment in its Hoshin Kanri form is the best-in-class mechanism available to you for decomposing and aligning the actions and plans in the transformation process. Improvement programmes only deliver to their full potential if fully aligned to the strategy and core objectives of the organisation. So it's natural that strategy deployment should be the vehicle used to drive your improvement programmes.

Remember that strategy deployment focuses on a very limited number of breakthrough objectives and includes a separate stream for business fundamentals – or everyday operational excellence. Likewise, you must tightly limit the scope of specific improvement projects to avoid loss of focus and ensure timely delivery. In both senses 'less is more' here – not everything needs to be changed to effect a transformation. Addressing the critical few objectives and undertaking the vital projects can enable a quantum leap.

Don't Let Perfect Get in the Way of Better

Business transformation, strategy deployment and Lean Six Sigma aren't difficult concepts but they require effort and commitment to implement effectively. So it's not surprising if you make mistakes along the way, or at the very least don't get it perfectly right the first time you try.

As the old adage tells us, 'practice makes perfect' and this is as true of business transformation as it is of any sporting or other activity in life. When one of the authors first implemented strategy deployment in his operation at Hewlett-Packard, it took two rounds of annual planning before the approach became fully effective. The company made the mistake of trying to apply strategy deployment to too many business objectives rather than just the absolute critical few. However, it persisted with the approach and eventually it transformed the way the company undertook business planning. There's no more effective method of aligning critical objectives across an organisation – and even if imperfect the first time around, the degree of alignment will be better than without attempting this approach.

Lean Six Sigma is about continuous improvement. Obviously, you don't seek to do things imperfectly to give you the headroom for continuous improvement, but the reality is that, no matter how well you do things, room for improvement always exists. Toyota has been seeking to eliminate waste for more than 40 years and continues to do so. Its ongoing business transformation, strategy deployment and Lean Six Sigma efforts mean that it is constantly dealing with this issue. Your aspiration is perfection – but getting there is a never-ending journey.

Recognise and Celebrate Successes

There's no better predictor of success than success itself. So, success needs to be encouraged, celebrated, and recognised. A successful outcome will act as a 'proof of concept', encouraging participants to continue and others to replicate and extend the transformation process. Evidence suggests that fun is itself a strong motivating factor – so no better combination exists than success and its celebration and recognition.

Recognition doesn't need to be expensive. A simple handwritten note from the CEO or the opportunity to present a successful project to the leadership team or more widely across the organisation can have more impact than a prize or monetary award. Simply being valued and being seen to be valued may be reward enough!

Create a Capability Maturity Roadmap and Regularly Review it

We all need a map from time to time to help us reach our destination. Business transformation is a journey and the capability maturity matrix (see Chapter 5) helps you to better understand where you are and where you're headed. It acts as your compass and guide, and the information contained includes the experience of others who have journeyed there before us on their particular transformations. Better you learn from the mistakes of others than have to learn from your own – and you can learn from their successes as well.

Transformation often comes in stages and usually takes time. During the journey the environment can change; competitors don't stand still and also respond to changes in the market place, whether or not in direct response to the specific transformation you're undertaking. It's not just a question of reviewing where you are on the roadmap; the roadmap itself needs to be periodically and regularly reviewed and amendments made in line with circumstances. Maintaining an up-to-date roadmap is an integral part of the overall strategy deployment process and is covered in Chapter 14.

Provide Appropriate Training as it is Needed

Training is essential for all levels in the organisation to effectively implement transformation through Lean Six Sigma. At the very least, the leadership team and their reports will need to learn how to undertake strategy deployment, and those at the operational level will need to learn how to lead and undertake Lean Six Sigma projects.

Training is most effective when delivered 'just ahead of time': too early and it will be forgotten if not built on through practice (remember that learning isn't just in the classroom but is also on the job); too late and it will clearly be of little use. Plan training sessions well in advance of when they're actually needed and bear in mind that not everyone learns and absorbs new techniques and ways of working at the same pace.

To avoid learning overload, offer training as it's needed.

Encourage Leaders and Managers to Manage Daily Improvements

Although transformational change is exciting and important, attending to the daily operational issues is also vital. Simply 'fixing' the problems that occur is insufficient. Yes, you need to fix them, but you need to go further and improve the activities and processes that caused them in the first place so that the same problems don't recur in the future.

To this end, you must encourage leaders and managers to manage daily improvements. Everyone in the organisation must be encouraged to identify problems, defects and waste and to make these visible so that they can be addressed. In many instances, the individuals and teams that discover them may be able to lead the improvement actions themselves; in other cases, they may not have the skills, competencies, or resources to do so, in which case leaders and managers need to identify and enable others to do so as part of the overall continuous improvement effort.

Visual management is a key approach to helping identify and manage work backlogs and other problems and issues. Simple methods of presenting real-time information and demonstrating whether processes and systems are operating in a normal manner underpin this. Co-ordinating actions locally through daily team meetings at the start or end of shifts, particularly when located around visual information displays, can transform daily performance and highlight issues to be addressed through structured improvement activity.

Listen to the Voice of Your Customers and Other Stakeholders

The first principle of Lean Six Sigma is to listen to the 'voice of the customer' and focus on their requirements. Remember that any instance where you fail to meet the needs of a customer – or other key stakeholder – is a 'defect' and one of the key goals of Lean Six Sigma is to minimise the level and rate of defects. Customer satisfaction and profit are inextricably intertwined. However, customer requirements aren't static; things that delight the customer and create market leadership today may rapidly become obsolete.

So listening to the voice of your customers isn't something to be done just once – for example, before starting out on a business transformation. You need to do so continuously to ensure that you promptly pick up on changes in customer needs and market trends.

Don't Be Afraid to Make Mistakes, but Do Learn from Them

Making a mistake isn't a sin – but not learning from it arguably is. One story goes that a senior manager at IBM made an error of judgement that cost the company $2 billion; when he was summoned by his boss he fully expected to be fired. But his boss simply commented that he'd just spent $2 billion on training his manager and that the real mistake would be if he wasted that training investment by firing him. Clearly, people don't seek to make mistakes; indeed, most aspire to getting things 'right first time, every time'. However, if you're too afraid of making mistakes, then you'll never get anything done.

You need to plan and train well to maximise the likelihood of getting things right, but be prepared sometimes to get them wrong and then to learn from the experience. Where possible, learn from the mistakes of others rather than repeating them personally. Where doing so isn't possible or practical, then don't be so afraid of making mistakes that nothing gets done. What's vital overall is optimising the level of risk; there comes a point where the risk to the business of inaction overtakes the risk of making mistakes by acting. Over time you reduce the overall risk to the organisation by preparing well, learning from others and taking action. If mistakes do happen, you then learn from them.

Remember to learn from your successes as well. Learning what and how to do something right is an easier lesson than learning how not to do something.

Chapter 16

Ten Pitfalls to Avoid

In This Chapter

- Avoiding too much focus on the short term
- Making sure the 'soft stuff' is on the agenda
- Ensuring appropriate up-front planning and preparation

The journey to True North is unlikely to be entirely straightforward. En route you'll encounter all sorts of potential diversions, barriers and pitfalls. This chapter describes some of the things that can so easily go wrong if you take your eye off the road and try to cut corners. So here we share our experience of observing many diverse organisations to help you avoid a bumpy ride.

Too Much Focus on Short-Term Objectives

Transformation is about fundamental and significant change in, and to, an organisation. It's not something to be done lightly nor will it happen immediately. Transforming an organisation takes significant time and effort, and needs to be seen in that context.

The bigger the scale of change, the longer it takes. As benchmark examples, a rapid improvement or Kaizen event (refer to Chapter 12) may last a week, a Lean Six Sigma Green Belt project (also covered in Chapter 12) may take three months or more, and a product, service or process design/redesign may involve generational phases spanning more than a year. Of course, along with other actions, the transformation programme comprises elements such as shorter-term Lean Six Sigma projects, and their execution will be directly driven by short-term objectives. However, just as these may be elements of the larger-scale transformation programme, their corresponding short-term objectives are part of something bigger, collectively contributing to the longer term-strategic objectives and, again, need to be seen in that context.

While all longer-term strategic objectives need to be broken down into shorter-term tactical ones (refer to Chapter 8), not all short-term objectives necessarily relate to one of the vital few critical breakthrough objectives. Those that do should have been identified and aligned to them through the strategy deployment process.

Creating the right balance between longer-term strategic objectives and day-to-day operational objectives is crucial. Too much focus on the short term and the organisation will twist and turn with no regard for the longer-term direction, but without translating longer-term objectives into bite-sized shorter objectives and executing those, the company won't move forward in a timely manner.

You have to continually deliver results within the context of the organisation evolving and changing over the longer term.

Strategies that aren't Clearly Defined

Until you have to explain something to someone else, you don't really know if you actually understand it. You can apply this truism to strategies, which must be clearly defined and communicable. Of course, a strategy also has to be appropriate and well-judged, but it's unlikely to be either unless it's completely understood by those who have developed it.

Defining a strategy particularly clearly will force you to review and reconsider it, check whether it's complete and thought through, whether it links appropriately to other strategies and plans, and if you've forgotten to take anything into account.

You can ensure you describe a particular strategy in SMART terms (specific, measurable, achievable, realistic and time-bound) or you can use a strategy map to trace out (with quantified targets) how the strategy will link with other strategies to deliver key performance results. If gaps exist in the strategy linkage, the strategy has not yet been fully thought through and defined.

Unless a strategy is clearly defined it will be impossible to properly deploy it and the intended transformation will be impossible from the outset.

Not Enough Programme Planning

Figure 16-1 illustrates the difference between the traditional Western approach to projects and programmes (the dotted line) and the Japanese approach (the solid line). As can be seen, the Japanese put greater initial effort into programme planning.

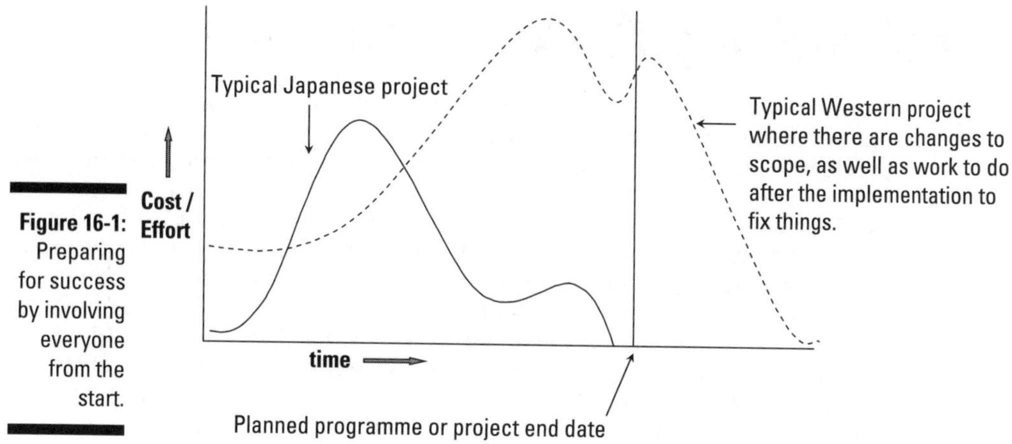

Figure 16-1: Preparing for success by involving everyone from the start.

Although the Japanese approach (including strategy deployment) requires more effort at the beginning, it pays off over the lifetime of the programme or project. Without this intensive prior planning and preparation, progress initially seems to be faster and requires fewer resources. However, the deficiencies inherent in this approach catch up later and you're likely to need significant rework and potential changes to the scope of the project. As a result, a disproportionate amount of resources is required to address and rectify problems and costs thus increase.

What you invest in planning right from the beginning pays off in spades throughout the transformation process.

Making Assumptions about the Needs of Customers and Other Stakeholders

Listening to the 'voice of the customer' is one of the core principles of Lean Six Sigma. It becomes even more essential when you're considering a programme of transformational change. Assuming that you know what customers (external or internal) want is all too easy, but unless you ask them you can never be sure.

Even a not-for-profit organisation has customers – stakeholders whose requirements are ultimately the reason for the organisation's existence. A business organisation's long-term survival and prosperity depend on the profits generated from the value it delivers to its customers. And a necessary condition for doing that is really understanding customers' needs. Doing so consistently requires an effective dialogue with your customers.

Not Obtaining Process Ownership

A process owner takes responsibility for a particular process. They champion Lean Six Sigma projects to design or improve that process; commission, review and steer those projects; and then monitor performance and take corrective action as necessary to maintain that improvement. Collectively, the various process owners enable the projects comprising the transformation to be effectively identified and executed, and the overall change to be nurtured and subsequently sustained. Without obtaining process ownership, the transformation programme wouldn't be supported effectively at the constituent project level and at least some of the projects would likely flounder. Given the tight alignment required for effective strategy deployment, the transformation programme may collapse if key constituent improvements no longer provide the basis on which to build the breakthrough change.

Ignoring the Soft Stuff

Many traditional Lean Six Sigma training courses and strategy deployment publications cover the 'hard stuff' such as the statistical techniques, the DMAIC methodology (refer to Chapter 1), the X Matrix (covered in Chapter 8) and the catchball process (also Chapter 8), not to mention an extensive array of other tools and techniques. However, they often don't deal with the softer tools; the people issues that you need to gain buy-in and overcome resistance. Consequently, those new to strategy deployment (just as with those new to Lean Six Sigma) may try to run programmes and projects focusing on the tools and techniques rather than the people who need to enact them. Doing so can lead to a lack of buy-in from managers or operational staff, who either don't understand or cannot accept the approach.

Don't forget the $E = Q \times A$ formula (covered in detail in Chapter 2). The *quality* (Q) of the solution that results from the hard tools and the *acceptance* (A) of the solution that results from the soft tools are equally important. You need both quality and acceptance to win support and achieve an *effective* (E) outcome.

Leading and carrying people along with you are vital to the success of your transformation programme. Our years of business experience tell us that the really hard stuff is the soft stuff!

Assuming that No Response Means No Resistance to Change

Research suggests that for every customer who complains about something, perhaps ten or more others are silently dissatisfied. We have every reason to believe that a similar picture applies to the transformation process – for every person who actively challenges the proposed change many more still are silently resistant.

The biggest resistance to change is apathy rather than open rebellion, and for the transformation programme to succeed it needs to actively engage most people. Hopefully, some degree of simply passive acceptance shouldn't derail it. Attitudes to change need to be actively managed, which requires management by fact not assumption in keeping with the principles of Lean Six Sigma. The bigger the scale of change, the more important actively engaging people becomes.

You can assess people's attitude to change using simple tools such as stakeholder analysis and then seek to verify this picture through appropriate discussions with the groups involved. You need to establish whether silence means they're simply 'neutral' on the issue or silent in expressing their disagreement.

For more on stakeholder analysis, see *Lean Six Sigma For Dummies* (Wiley).

Not everyone needs to be supportive; neutrality may be acceptable in some situations. However, don't assume people's positions; assess the information and then adopt an appropriate approach to expose and address unspoken objections to steer your stakeholders' position to where you require it to be.

Strategic Breakthroughs that aren't Really Breakthroughs

Undertaking the strategy deployment of breakthrough objectives is challenging and time-consuming, especially if Lean Six Sigma is a new approach for your organisation. Deploying more than a very limited number of strategic breakthrough objectives at any one time thus isn't practical, and to be effective and successful you need to focus on the vital few objectives. Don't waste time and effort on those that aren't really breakthrough objectives.

Ultimately success is all about focus. You need to concentrate on the really vital breakthrough objectives and getting those successfully deployed, executed and delivered. Achievement of these objectives is essential to the sustained future health of the organisation, and failure is not an option. Although the other objectives also need to be managed, they require less effort and attention.

Avoid chaos and overload – prioritise, focus and ruthlessly pursue the truly vital few!

Not Organising Monthly Strategy Deployment Reviews

Just because something has been planned doesn't mean it will happen to plan. Lean Six Sigma stresses the importance of understanding and managing variation. In a similar way, variances from plan will occur for a variety of reasons, including:

- Imperfect, incomplete or delayed actions
- Off-track Lean Six Sigma projects
- Incorrect assumptions in planning
- Absence of key people
- Changes in the business environment, market or economy
- Competitor developments

Regular monitoring and review of progress is essential to identify such variances and promptly initiate corrective action if and as appropriate. Monthly review is a key component of the PDCA cycle (described in Chapter 8) inherent in the strategy deployment process. Strategy deployment isn't just about planning; it's also about review and corrective action. The tight alignment of objectives and actions secured initially through the planning element of strategy deployment needs to be retained, sustained and maintained, and the mechanisms for doing so are the monthly and annual reviews and resulting corrective actions. Without the discipline to regularly and routinely undertake the monthly strategy deployment reviews, you can't expect to sustain the hard-won alignment.

Lack of Trained Lean Six Sigma Practitioners

The transformation programme will include many different elements tightly aligned through strategy deployment. Among these will be many Lean Six Sigma projects to design or improve individual processes to secure the required change or enhancement in performance. Other elements also benefit from the application of appropriate individual Lean Six Sigma tools and techniques. For all of these to succeed and deliver the planned improvements in a timely manner, the organisation needs a sufficient number of project leaders and team members with the appropriate skills and knowledge; that is, trained Lean Six Sigma practitioners. While you can engage consultants, the most cost-effective long-term solution is to develop a cadre of trained and experienced practitioners from within your own organisation.

Our experience tells us that many, if not most, organisations undertaking transformation experience a shortfall of trained and experienced staff. Surprisingly, we've also seen many organisations exacerbate this situation by letting go of key Lean Six Sigma practitioners when they scale up from an initial Lean Six Sigma programme to full-scale transformation and hiring external consultants to focus on the 'new' approach.

Don't throw out the baby with the bath water! The very skills you need to lead and support many of the projects may already exist within your organisation – so use them. If you discover you need more practitioners, first establish whether you have sufficient time and resources to train and develop your own staff before deciding to buy in skills and expertise from outside.

Chapter 17

Ten Places to Go for Help

In This Chapter

- Tapping into a wealth of knowledge and experience
- Using the power of the Web
- Considering software applications
- Joining a community of interest and developing a network

Sometimes Lean Six Sigma seems a bit daunting. But don't worry, plenty of help and good experience exists if you know where to look. In this chapter we show you where to find all the advice and resources you need.

Your Colleagues

A well-managed transformation supported by Lean Six Sigma relies on excellent leadership, teamwork and support being available for everyone involved across the organisation through an internal network.

The senior team need to really show their support through their active involvement in the journey, perhaps taking on the role of Champion or ensuring resources are provided and supported for the transformation projects.

Every project deserves a good sponsor, or 'champion'. When things get tough, as most projects do from time to time, your project champion is a good source of help. Your champion supports your project team, helps unblock project barriers and assists you when you need buy-in at a more senior level in your organisation. And, of course, they are there to help ensure things stay on track.

Support can also be offered through a spectrum of different coloured 'belts'; for example, Black Belts supporting Green Belts. Ideally, Black Belts will be able to call on support from Master Black Belts who are professional experts in Lean Six Sigma, but in smaller organisations this support may be outsourced to a specialist Lean Six Sigma practitioner.

The 'belt' terminology isn't mandatory, by the way. Many organisations just use terms such as 'practitioner' and 'expert' instead of Green Belt and Black Belt.

It's also essential that everyone does what they say they will do and commits to what's been signed up to on the transformation charter.

Being able to access this kind of support network is important. You probably already know that a big difference exists between using a tool in a training environment and operating in the real world, where your first port of call for help is usually your own colleagues.

Other Organisations

Every year, the number of organisations deploying Lean Six Sigma increases. Over time, the combination of tools and techniques may have changed, but the essentials of using a systematic method, focusing on understanding customer requirements and improving processes are well tried and tested. Visiting some other organisations and learning from their experiences is well worthwhile. You may not be able to look deep inside your competitors' businesses, but you can discover lots by visiting similar-sized companies in different sectors. Industry and government special-interest groups are a good source of help and often arrange visits for groups to observe companies at work. If you have the chance to visit a Toyota plant, for example, in just a few hours you'll learn a lot about the cultural approach that forms the basis for continuous improvement and Lean thinking in general.

The American Productivity and Quality Center is a useful source for considering the process architecture you might need, and their generic level 1, 2 and 3 process models also provide a helpful framework for benchmarking with other organisations.

At least some of your projects are likely to be using the framework of Quality Function Deployment, where benchmarking data will be essential in your unfolding product or process design.

The Internet

Following are some of our favourite websites devoted to Lean Six Sigma and associated improvement approaches, but there are lots more to delve into by using your search engine:

- www.asq.org: The site for the American Society for Quality, offering very comprehensive online resources and publications.
- www.catalystconsulting.co.uk and www.enablingresults.com: The authors' own websites, regularly updated with new articles.
- www.efqm.org: Full of useful material and a link into the knowledge library of the European Foundation for Quality Management – essential for anyone serious about developing quality and excellence across an entire organisation.
- www.isssp.com: Dedicated to Six Sigma, with plenty of articles.
- www.isixsigma.com: The number one (US-focused) Six Sigma website, with bulletin boards, job ads and links – for addicts only.
- www.qualitydigest.com: A useful online magazine on quality.
- www.qfdi.org: The site for the Quality Function Deployment (QFD) Institute. QFD is an approach to really understanding customer requirements and linking these to processes, products and services; it's often used when Lean Six Sigma companies want to design new products and services. QFD is an additional tool used in Design for Six Sigma (DfSS).
- www.goldratt.com: This website focuses on the Theory of Constraints, an approach to help manage and reduce process bottlenecks.
- www.shingoprize.org: This website provides information about the Shingo Prize Model™ and award.
- www.nist.gov/baldrige: This website provides information about the Baldrige model and award.

A note about search engines

The Internet's awash with useful information, articles and guides – if only you could find what you want!

Search engines can speed up your research or investigation – you may even find details of a Lean Six Sigma project similar to one you're working on somewhere on the Web.

Google is a very useful resource for searching on specifics and is the most popular search engine by far.

Social Media

Here's a resource that continues to grow and provide a wealth of information. Put your key words into a search engine, for example 'policy deployment', and you'll find all sorts of sites to look at. You can also view a host of videos on sites such as YouTube.

Maybe you can find someone to follow on Twitter, too, or perhaps you can start something yourself.

LinkedIn is an excellent source of information related to Lean Six Sigma transformations. Several Lean Six Sigma groups enable you to network with practitioners and champions.

Networks and Associations

You can find all sorts of networks and associations relating to Lean Six Sigma. Some networks offer online and offline services to encourage collaboration and knowledge exchange between members, and often hold regular members' meetings.

For example, i&i is a European community of practice for business improvement and innovation. To avoid any 'selling' connotations, this network doesn't permit consultancy organisations to become members.

National and regional quality associations such as the American Society for Quality (ASQ), the European Foundation for Quality Management (EFQM) and the British Quality Foundation (BQF) provide opportunities to share good, and not so good, practice through meetings, visits to businesses, conferences, workshops and online resources, although these aren't dedicated purely to Lean Six Sigma. The EFQM provides an extensive knowledge library to members offering insights into the approaches used in different organisations.

Conferences

Lean Six Sigma conferences are a regular feature of the conference calendar these days. Conference organisers hold Lean Six Sigma 'summits' every year at different locations around the world. These summits provide a range of mainstream speakers, smaller workshops and networking, and informal discussions regarding every aspect of Lean Six Sigma. Whether you're just starting out or want to keep up with the latest thinking and new developments, these summits are a great source of information.

Books and Publications

A wide range of books covers strategy and its deployment; you can even find books focusing solely on the X Matrix, for example. We don't feel able to recommend any one book in particular, other than *Lean Six Sigma For Dummies* (Wiley), of course, which provides the additional information you're likely to need to fully utilise this book.

Rather, we suggest you take a look at what's available, perhaps taking advantage of Amazon's 'look inside' feature so that you can get a better sense of the content. That said, *The Team Handbook* (Third Edition), by Peter R. Scholtes, Brian L. Joiner and Barbara J. Streibel (Oriel Inc.), focuses on both soft skills and managing a team and is thus worth a look.

Periodicals

Several journals are devoted to Lean and Six Sigma, including:

- *International Journal of Six Sigma and Competitive Advantage* – keeps at the forefront of Six Sigma developments
- *Quality World* – the magazine of the Chartered Quality Institute in the UK, with regular features on Lean Six Sigma
- *Six Sigma Forum* – a specialist magazine of the American Society for Quality (ASQ)
- *UK Excellence* – the magazine of the British Quality Foundation, with regular features on Lean Six Sigma

Software

You can certainly start down the Lean Six Sigma road without having to invest in specialist software, but as your journey proceeds you may want to enhance your toolkit with statistical and other software. In this section, we mention a few of our essentials.

One area of Lean Six Sigma where we recommend *not* using software, especially when starting out, is value stream mapping and process deployment flowcharting. For this, we suggest that you map the process using sticky notes, a pencil and a large piece of paper pinned to the wall.

That said, if you do decide to use software for process or value stream mapping, consider Visio from Microsoft, iGraphix (`www.igrafx.com`), SmartDraw (`www.smartdraw.com`) or FlowMap (`www.flowmap.com`). Lots of other software options are also available, so just see what suits you.

Statistical analysis

Most everyday mortals use only a fraction of the full capability of their spreadsheet program such as Excel. These programs are good at statistical analysis – but because they weren't designed specifically for this purpose, producing even the most basic Pareto chart without help from a kind soul who's produced a template for this purpose is surprisingly challenging.

Fortunately you can find several plug-ins for your spreadsheet program to help you perform Pareto analysis, and slice and dice your data quickly and easily without having to design your own template.

Microsoft provides a useful data analysis 'Toolpak' for Excel, which has been extended with the latest versions. For more complex statistical analysis, try the Excel plug-in SigmaXL, which lets you produce a variety of displays including SIPOCs, cause and effect diagrams, Failure Mode and Effects Analysis (FMEA) and several types of control chart, as well as a comprehensive range of statistical tools.

Most Black Belts and Master Black Belts favour Minitab ® Statistical Software. This package has been around for many years and is a favourite of universities and colleges teaching statistics. Minitab is a very comprehensive statistical analysis package designed for serious statistical analysis. Don't try it at home without some serious training as part of an advanced Green Belt or full Black Belt course.

JMP ® Statistical Discovery Software is another package gaining in popularity for use in the world of Lean Six Sigma. It links statistics to a highly visual graphic representation, allowing you to visually explore the relationships between process inputs and outputs, and then to identify the key process variables.

For more advanced statistical and predictive modelling, take a look at Crystal Ball from Oracle. This popular bit of software is good for forecasting, simulation, and evaluating optimisation options.

Deployment management

For large-scale deployments, consider forming a project library and use tracking software to help you and your colleagues across the organisation manage and report on projects. Similarly, the strategy deployment process, when deployed across multi-division/cross-functional organisations, can benefit from enabling software systems. Software packages such as those from i-Nexus and Instantis are designed specifically for this purpose, and are well worth investigating as your deployment grows across the organisation.

Training and Consultancy Companies

A wide range of specialist training and consulting companies provide services for clients in the Lean Six Sigma arena. In your quest for training, you'll find a few global players and lots of smaller specialists and one-person bands.

When you choose a training and consulting partner, try to use the 'quality × acceptance' equation. You want your trainer to have excellent technical skills, but also consider how well they would work with your organisation. Will your organisation's culture accept the trainer/consultant? Will the trainer/consultant instil confidence and provide all the services you require?

In our experience, few organisations bother to check suppliers' references. But unlike choosing a partner or spouse, in business asking previous clients how well the partnership worked is fine! Working over a long period with a training and consulting company is a bit like a marriage – shared values are a good foundation for belief, integrity, respect, trust and honesty.

Index

• D •

• E •

• F •

• G •

• M •

• N •

• O •

• P •

• Q •

• R •

• S •

• T •

• U •

• V •

• W •

About the Authors

Roger Burghall has more than twenty years of experience in continuous improvement and is an expert in Lean Six Sigma Transformation and Operational Excellence. He has a track record of achieving rapid business and operational process improvement within a diverse range of domestic and international market sectors and cultures. Roger originally qualified as an electronics engineer and he gained his MBA from Cardiff Business School. In addition, Roger is a certified MBTI practitioner and is a frequent speaker on operational excellence at European manufacturing strategies and shared services conferences.

In his spare time Roger enjoys hiking in the Cotswold countryside and taking part in endurance cycling events, which keep him fit! He also loves collecting and playing acoustic and electric guitars. He has played in folk and rock bands in the past and now enjoys playing his instruments in his home studio.

Vince Grant is an expert on Lean Six Sigma and Business Transformation and continues to assist many leading organisations with their business improvement journeys. He has been a senior (lead) assessor for the European and UK National Quality Awards on several occasions and passionately supports the principles, values and practices associated with the EFQM Excellence Model. Vince was selected by General Electric to train many of their people in Europe on Six Sigma to Master Black Belt level when GE first implemented this in their Financial Services businesses.

Vince is a Director of the Lean Six Sigma specialists Catalyst Consulting having jointly founded that company almost 20 years ago. He is a Fellow of the Chartered Institute of Management Accountants, and holds a Physics PhD from Manchester University and an MA from Selwyn College Cambridge.

Before founding Catalyst Vince held senior management positions in the IT, Telecommunications and Financial Services industries in the UK and various other European countries. He continues to use his financial expertise as Finance Director of Catalyst, although this is just a small part of his overall role. His interest in the physical sciences continues – but on an amateur basis these days.

His experience of Strategy Deployment stems from the mid 1980's when his operation in Hewlett-Packard was one of the first in Europe to import from Japan and apply Hoshin Kanri as its preferred method for deploying and tightly aligning its business strategy. He had the good fortune to spend time in Japan at a later date, learning first hand from their leading experts and companies how to apply this and other leading management practices. Hopefully some useful best practice from this is also reflected in this book.

Vince's other active interests include gardening, playing the organ for local church services, and walking – particularly overseas in warmer climates during the English winter months.

John Morgan is the author of several books, including *The Lean Six Sigma Improvement Journey* and *Go Lean,* and is co-author of Lean Six Sigma for Dummies, now in its second edition, and *SPC in the Office*. His experience has led to him being interviewed on BBC Radio 4 about the potential of Lean Six Sigma in the UK, especially in the public sector and National Health Service.

John has been a Director of the Lean Six Sigma specialists Catalyst Consulting for almost 20 years, and much of their highly acclaimed material has been created by him, including tailored work for companies such as General Electric, BAA, Saint-Gobain Glass, Barclays and British Telecom. In addition to training delivery and coaching, John's primary responsibilities are in the areas of product design and development.

John also jointly heads the British Quality Foundation's Lean Six Sigma Academy. A Chartered Insurer and Fellow of the Chartered Insurance Institute, John's early career background was in Aviation Insurance and Reinsurance. He first started to apply Lean Six Sigma techniques in his role as Customer Service Director in a North American Financial Services company before helping to set up Catalyst.

A keen song writer, he is also working, albeit very slowly on his first novel, Black Widow Blues, which he hopes to publish next year. It's fair to say that writing a Dummies book is probably easier and there are agreed deadlines to meet, of course!

Authors' Acknowledgements

I have found writing this book to be both enjoyable and challenging and I would like to thank my wife, Anna-Liisa and my friends and colleagues for all their support.

I would like to thank David Cowburn and Bob Lyons for their immense contribution and collaboration in the development of the Rapid SD methodology and also Barbara Bird for her contribution to the capability maturity and assessment process.

RB

My thanks to my wife Pat and my family, and friends and business colleagues for being so understanding on those occasions when writing my contributions to this book took priority over other things more important to them at those times. I hope that one day my various grandchildren now in their early years will also find some interest and value from this book.

A particular thanks to my colleague John Morgan – co-author of this book – who has coordinated our efforts and brought his experience from previous books (including another one in the 'Dummies' genre) to keep us from straying too far from the proper path (dare I say 'True North'). Also to my other colleague and co-author Roger Burghall whose particular interest in Strategy Deployment and Hoshin provided that final push to encourage me to sign up to this task.

My thanks also to the many business people and academics I have worked with over the years from whom I have learnt so much. I have been fortunate to have worked at the leading/learning edge of applying best practices with organisations and individuals in the UK, elsewhere in Europe, and in the US and Japan.

Finally I would like to thank all our other colleagues and partners at Catalyst for all their professional and personal support. This is not only for the time we've been writing this book but also over the years and the contributions they have all made and continue to make to the success of our business and our clients. Their knowledge and skills have helped to inform and support mine and are inevitably reflected in the content and views expressed in this book.

VG

Writing any book tends to take a fair bit of concentration, time and effort, so there's a general thank you to my wife Margaret, and my family, and friends for putting up with that.

In pulling this second Dummies title together, it was a question of trying to get the balance right in terms of how much material to incorporate specifically about Lean Six Sigma. The authors felt that anyone buying this book should already have at least a reasonable understanding of the topic, so there was quite some debate with Wiley, and indeed ourselves, about how best to deal with that. We hope you'll understand and appreciate the approach we have taken, which is somewhat different from other Dummies titles.

As ever, there's a general thank you to everyone at Catalyst who has helped in some way, and to the team at Wiley who have provided great support, too, especially Iona Everson, Jo Jones and Claire Ruston who has since left them to explore a new venture.

JM

Publisher's Acknowledgements

We're proud of this book; please send us your comments at `http://dummies.custhelp.com`. For other comments, please contact our Customer Care Department within the U.S. at 877-762-2974, outside the U.S. at (001) 317-572-3993, or fax 317-572-4002.

Some of the people who helped bring this book to market include the following:

Acquisitions, Editorial and Vertical Websites

Project Editors: Iona Everson, Jo Jones

Development Editor: Kate O'Leary

Commissioning Editor: Claire Ruston

Copy Editor: Martin Key

Technical Reviewer: Jim Alloway

Proofreader: Kerry Laundon

Publisher: Miles Kendall

Cover Photo: © iStock.com/Kalawin

Project Coordinator: Sheree Montgomery

FOR DUMMIES®
A Wiley Brand

BUSINESS

978-1-118-73077-5

978-1-118-44349-1

978-1-119-97527-4

MUSIC

978-1-119-94276-4

978-0-470-97799-6

978-0-470-49644-2

DIGITAL PHOTOGRAPHY

978-1-118-09203-3

978-0-470-76878-5

978-1-118-00472-2

Algebra I For Dummies
978-0-470-55964-2

Anatomy & Physiology For Dummies, 2nd Edition
978-0-470-92326-9

Asperger's Syndrome For Dummies
978-0-470-66087-4

Basic Maths For Dummies
978-1-119-97452-9

Body Language For Dummies, 2nd Edition
978-1-119-95351-7

Bookkeeping For Dummies, 3rd Edition
978-1-118-34689-1

British Sign Language For Dummies
978-0-470-69477-0

Cricket for Dummies, 2nd Edition
978-1-118-48032-8

Currency Trading For Dummies, 2nd Edition
978-1-118-01851-4

Cycling For Dummies
978-1-118-36435-2

Diabetes For Dummies, 3rd Edition
978-0-470-97711-8

eBay For Dummies, 3rd Edition
978-1-119-94122-4

Electronics For Dummies All-in-One For Dummies
978-1-118-58973-1

English Grammar For Dummies
978-0-470-05752-0

French For Dummies, 2nd Edition
978-1-118-00464-7

Guitar For Dummies, 3rd Edition
978-1-118-11554-1

IBS For Dummies
978-0-470-51737-6

Keeping Chickens For Dummies
978-1-119-99417-6

Knitting For Dummies, 3rd Edition
978-1-118-66151-2